Springer Series in Transitional Justice

Volume 10

Series Editor

Olivera Simic

For further volumes:
http://www.springer.com/series/11233

Jill Stockwell

Reframing the Transitional Justice Paradigm

Women's Affective Memories in Post-Dictatorial Argentina

Springer

Jill Stockwell
The Swinburne Institute for Social Research
Swinburne University
Hill End
Australia

ISBN 978-3-319-03852-0 ISBN 978-3-319-03853-7 (eBook)
DOI 10.1007/978-3-319-03853-7
Springer Cham Heidelberg New York Dordrecht London

Library of Congress Control Number: 2013958313

Printed on acid-free paper

Springer is part of Springer Science+Business Media (www.springer.com)

Preface

This book explores some of the consequences of political and state violence in Argentina during the 1970s and 1980s. Over the last few decades, moral and political claims about how this past should collectively be remembered by the nation have caused deep political and societal divisions. This book's findings are based on interviews I conducted with women from two ideologically-opposed groups, each of which is connected to antithetical versions of the recent Argentinian past. These interviews elicited memories of trauma and narratives which do not sit comfortably with the forgetful objectives of transitional justice. The research herein contributes to our understanding of the power and significance of the deep emotions and affects that shape memories in post-transitional contexts.

I went to Argentina with my husband and my 3-year-old daughter Bonnie in 2008, seeking to interview women who were living with traumatic memories of violence and loss. More than three decades since the completion of a transitional process of truth and justice was declared in Argentina, I wished to analyse women's memories of violence in light of their subsequent experiences and, with temporal distance, to understand any reinterpretations or new meanings they may have made to their lived experiences. I was therefore drawn to exploring the process of Argentine women recalling their individual past memories and the various internal layers and levels at which this takes place. I was deeply interested in gaining insight into the myriad issues that impact on the women's assimilation of their traumatic pasts.

Women play a key role in transmitting memories to the next generation in Argentina, and as such are an important source in understanding this historical period of political and state violence. As the majority of those who were disappeared during the military dictatorship were men, many women became the main providers for their single-parent households. In fact, 70% of those who were disappeared were male (Crenzel 2008). Left to bear the burden of mourning, to endure their own loss and grief and sometimes that of their children, the women I interviewed had faced enormous emotional torment over many years. However, many of them made new 'homes' and forged new 'families' on the basis of political ties. These families were paramount in the creation of many of the human rights organisations that emerged out of the dictatorship, driven by a moral and cultural imperative to remember the past in order to prevent it from happening again. In publicly and privately remembering the past, they have played, and continue to play, an important role in the creation and shaping of collective identities.

While it is clear that women have done, and continue to do, the lion's share of work in terms of remembering the political and state violence of the 1970s and 1980s, this was not the sole reason why I became interested in exploring women's traumatic memories of loss and violence in Argentina. My other reasons were more personal. Over a number of years in my work as a Protection Delegate with the International Committee of the Red Cross (ICRC), I engaged primarily with women to record human rights abuses in the aftermath of conflict, given that the majority of men had been imprisoned or killed in the communities in which I worked. As the women—often surrounded by their children—told me their painful stories, the powerful role they played in the intergenerational transmission of their memories of violence in a post-conflict environment became very clear. Studies have shown collective memory to be the cross-generational oral transmission of events deemed socially important for a society (Leydesdorff et al. 2005). Despite women playing a central role in the transmission of memory to the next generation, in many transitional contexts the role women play is marginalised; their memories of violence are pushed out to the margins of the public sphere.

In Argentina, however, there is a direct connection between women remembering experiences of violence at a grassroots level and their attempt to gain a place in the public sphere. Important works by Elizabeth Jelin (1990) and Temma Kaplan (1997, 2004) have made a direct appeal for the reinvention of democratic values and human rights based on oral histories (Leydesdorff et al. 2005). I suggest that we can learn a great deal from looking at how Argentine women have mediated and assimilated their traumatic pasts, both publicly and privately, as well as the ways in which their practices of remembrance impact and shape social relations, and apply these learnings to better understanding women's experiences of violence in other transitional contexts.

I had the opportunity to talk to two different groups of Argentine women who represent two very different versions of the recent Argentinian past: those affected by military repression *and* those affected by armed guerrilla violence. The women's memories of loss and violence have been shaped by the fissure of decades-old, deep-seated social and political animosity. The memories of enduring personal trauma that both groups of women carry are commonly perceived as incompatible and unable to coexist in a shared mnemonic space—as if remembering one history of violence is immediately seen as an attempt to forget or violate the other history of violence and trauma.

This book explores the evolving and complex historical, political, social, legal and cultural factors that have shaped the cultures of remembrance in the post-dictatorial Argentina. However, in the story of remembering and forgetting, these factors—though essential—are not sufficient to account for the animosity pervading Argentine memorial cultures. I contend that we need to look beyond political and ideological contestations to a deeper level of how memorial cultures are formed and sustained. I argue that we cannot account for the politics of memory in modern-day Argentina without acknowledging and exploring the role played by individual emotions and affects in generating and shaping collective emotions and affects. Affect may be a pre-political and pre-social force, but I argue that it has major consequences for the perpetuation of fault-lines running across particular memorial cultures.

I avoid cleansing oral testimony of its emotional and affective dimensions. Instead, I explore how the women's affective memories of trauma offer a type of indispensable truth about the political and state violence of the 1970s and 1980s. Patricia Yaeger (2006, p. 413) tells us that 'if recent scholarship on trauma teaches us anything, it is that testimony demands more in the way of nearness, proximity, entanglement: not less'. Thus, I turn my attention to the affective residues held within the women's personal memories of violence and loss. I apply oral testimony as a methodological tool differently from the ways in which it has been traditionally used in Argentina. I drill down underneath the women's more formalised accounts of historical events and engage with the inaccessible, unconscious and inexpressible layers of the women's affective memories of trauma. I uncover those memories so that can remain vulnerable to revival and reveal themselves in affectively powerful ways. This approach is designed to help understand how these memories may be a different source of insight into the deep animosities within and between Argentine memorial cultures.

This study does not attempt to establish a hierarchy of suffering or make judgements about the equivalence or non-equivalence of the violence that was inflicted by the state and the armed political groups. To take a revisionist path to this research would only contribute to an already extremely polarised debate. I have consistently faced criticism from others within the academy for having engaged individuals affected by the violence of the armed guerrilla movement. I have often been called upon to defend the reasons why I chose to give space to these individuals to talk about their traumatic experiences. It is as if the topic of those affected by armed guerrilla violence is a taboo subject, and in raising it I have threatened a fragile sense of balance. I would argue that these sorts of reactions are a symptom of the antagonisms that I am attempting to describe. Debates about the equivalence or non-equivalence of the violence suffered by these two groups of women do not justify dismissing the value of a study of both groups' testimonies. Argentina is a very divided society in which there are different groups of victims resulting from the period of violence between 1973 and 1983. I consider it valuable to produce new lines of sight into the lived experiences of the different social groups affected by the violence. This book considers a different approach to the way this decades-old conflict is remembered, and therefore goes beyond these old, ideological ways of thinking about the past.

The first part of the book explores the myriad issues that impact on the women's assimilation of their traumatic pasts, particularly when the political and social legitimation of their memories has been radically different. I consider the historical, political, legal and social factors that shape the politics of remembering in Argentina. The book opens with an Introduction, which explores the complexities inherent in remembering the past for the two groups of women I interviewed. It also discusses the way I worked in Argentina to gather and present testimony from the women I interviewed.

In Chap. 2 (Argentina 1969–2003), I synthesise the existing body of literature to trace the historical events of a very complex period for Argentina. I develop an account of the traumatising politics that produced the divided memories of the two groups of women I interviewed. I cover four key periods relevant to this study: the period of guerrilla violence (1969–1976); the military dictatorship (1976–1983); the creation and function of the National Commission on the Disappearance of Persons (CONADEP) and the trials of the military juntas (1983–1985); and the legacy of both the military dictatorship and guerrilla violence (1983–2003).

In Chap. 3 (Politics of Remembering the Military Dictatorship and Its Aftermath) and Chap. 4 (Politics of Remembering Armed Guerrilla Violence), I consider how decisions about the ways in which memorial culture was created following the return to democratic rule have had crucial implications for the politics of remembering and oblivion. The various ways in which the Argentine public sphere has become an arena of struggle over how to remember the political and state violence of the 1970s and 1980s are analysed, as will the two groups' subsequent struggles for the political, social, legal and moral recognition of their traumatic memories.

In the second half of the book, I extend the conversation by looking at both groups' struggle through an affective lens—one that foregrounds the many varied legacies and traces of individual and collective trauma. What sort of account of memory cultures in the post-authoritarian Argentina could be created if trauma became our starting point? I engage in depth with three concepts I consider crucial: 'deep memory', the transmission of emotions and affects, and the social phenomenon of haunting. In Chap. 5 (Deep Memory), I consider how individual memory may be structurally transformed by trauma. I draw on Charlotte Delbo's notion of 'deep memory', and consider how those mnemonic layers that are unconscious, inexpressible and uncontainable in language—lodged deeply within a survivor's body—can be prone to involuntary eruptions. Delbo's concept provides a powerful way of understanding the vital role deep memory plays in producing real-time somatic experiences for the women I interviewed.

In Chap. 6 (Social Forces Shaping Memory Transmission), I consider the interpersonal pathways of traumatic histories and memories. I focus on the transmission of emotions and affect as structuring of individual and group identities as well as of the continuously refashioned public sphere itself. I explore the role of the transmission of emotions and affects with regard to how and why they can stir individuals and collectives to such an extent that the past continues to operate as a source of social and political division.

In Chap. 7 (Haunting), I map the traumatic legacies of Argentina's recent history on a societal level by turning my attention to the notion of haunting. I consider what happens to the psychic life of a society when it endures impossible, irresolvable and protracted mourning and loss in the wake of mass violence. I contemplate how the stasis of haunting at both an individual and societal level can be such that transformative and discursive possibilities between competing memorial cultures are prevented from emerging.

In the final chapter (Chap. 8), I consider how the exploration of these women's affective memories produces a different kind of narrative about how remembrance has worked in Argentina over the past decades. In direct contrast to the nominally objective and universalist sensibility that traditionally has driven transitional justice endeavours, I look at how affective memories of trauma are a potentially disruptive power within the 'reconciliation paradigm', and thus need to be taken into account. I think about what it means to reimagine memorial culture and key notions around transitional justice if we are to extend the current framework to include affect. I also consider how my research findings in relation to Argentina may prove illuminating for other transitioning contexts and may benefit women survivors in other contexts dealing with the aftermath of trauma.

I have received an inordinate amount of support since beginning this journey. First of all, my deepest debt is to the extraordinary Argentine women who trusted me with their memories and their stories. It is their insights and experiences that grant this book whatever power and authenticity it may possess. I would like to highlight my gratitude to a number of organisations in Argentina, including Las Abuelas de la Plaza de Mayo, Las Familiares de Desaparecidos y Detenidos por Razones Politicas, El Centro de Estudios Legales sobre el Terrorismo y sus Víctimas and Memoria Abierta, all of which contributed generously of their time, records and sensibilities. Thanks to the Swinburne Institute for Social Research of Swinburne University, for its support, both moral and financial, particularly during my 12-month stay in Argentina. My thanks to Dr Chris Healy and my deepest gratitude to Dr Maria Tumarkin, who stuck with me the entire way. Maria, thank you for your faith, guidance, friendship, never-ending support, generosity and the sharing of your wisdom and intelligence. I am also grateful for the personal support of my friends and family. You all believed in me more than I did myself, and for this I am deeply grateful. To my Davy darling, there are no words. Thank you Billy Sundance, my turbo- booster near the end. And thanks to my BonBon, who sat on Irma's knee and demonstrated that I was not dreaming after all.

Brisbane, Australia Jill Stockwell
September 2013

Contents

Chapter 1
Introduction

1.1 The Starting Point

> It angers me that justice in this country is not used in a way that finishes with this business, because the longer this goes on, the sicker Argentina becomes as a society. It's 33 years ago! Can you believe it? A country that doesn't want to heal itself; that doesn't want to begin anew. (Alonso 2009)

When I interviewed Maria in 2009, she had just given her oral testimony at the Tribunal Oral Federal 6, a court located in the Argentine capital of Buenos Aires. Her testimony described the torture she suffered at Campo de Mayo, a clandestine detention centre in Buenos Aires during the 1976–1983 military dictatorship. An eyewitness to the military's human rights abuses, Maria told me about the risks she takes and the fear she has for the safety of her children by speaking publicly about her experiences. Pinned to Maria's shirt is a badge showing a photo of her partner, Guillermo Oscar Sigalli, who was a fourth-year architecture student before he was disappeared in 1978.[1]

Maria, a human rights campaigner, was 4 months pregnant at the time. Though they initially were illegally incarcerated together following their abduction by the military's security forces, Maria now has no idea what happened to Guillermo, and nobody has ever been held accountable for his disappearance. She told me just how unsafe she feels living in a society such as Argentina, where those responsible for gross human rights violations during the years of military rule continue to live with impunity. Maria confided that she had lost her unborn baby as a result of the torture she endured at the hands of one of the dictatorship's worst known offenders of kidnap and torture. She again encountered this man many years later in a downtown Buenos Aires café. After the offender made an off-hand, flirtatious remark to her, Maria screamed at him, "Don't you know me? You don't have the right to

[1] Coined by the military as a way of denying the kidnap, torture and murder of its citizens, the word *desaparecer,* "to disappear", began to be used as a transitive verb in the Argentine language from the time of the military coup, 24 March 1976 (Feitlowitz 1998). Those who were disappeared by the military are referred to in Argentina as *los desaparecidos*. The majority of these individuals were abducted by the security forces and taken to clandestine detention centres, where they were tortured and later murdered (CONADEP 1986).

J. Stockwell, *Reframing the Transitional Justice Paradigm,*
Springer Series in Transitional Justice 10, DOI 10.1007/978-3-319-03853-7_1,

say anything to me." The offender replied, "Be grateful. You were one of the lucky ones" (del Socorro Alonso 2009). Maria continued:

> I feel bad because of the cynicism of these assassins. Because I see they live among people, they walk [freely], they live among ... Argentine civilians ... a lot of whom they have [tortured and killed]. An infinity [of disappeared individuals] ... dozens, thousands of dead and this can't be that a person [is allowed] to live [within society] like this. They could be a neighbour, they could be anyone ... a custodian [of our children], a teacher, because ... those we have been able to recognise, that's all well and good, but those we haven't [recognised] are mixed in with the rest of us [society]. (del Socorro Alonso 2009)

Argentina is a society where an estimated 30,000 individuals were disappeared between 1976 and 1983—in many cases, the bodies have never been recovered[2]—where up to 500 children who were taken from their kidnapped and illegally incarcerated mothers and given to families with close military ties are still unaware of their real identities,[3] and where victims continue to run into their torturers. The relatives of the *desaparecidos* are concerned that the violence that pervaded Argentine society in the 1970s and 1980s is not finished; they fear a future in which their children will experience the same terror. A Lexicon of Terror author Marguerite Feitlowitz (1998, p. xi) conveys this fear, which runs so deeply throughout Argentine society: "There is constant vigilance, the certainty of disaster, carnal knowledge of fear, a sense that history never moves on, but circles, raven-like, round and round." You only have to visit the Plaza de Mayo in central Buenos Aires any Thursday afternoon to witness Feitlowitz's powerful observation played out time and again. Though more than three decades have passed since the end of military rule, the *Madres de los desaparecidos* (Mothers of the disappeared) continue circling around the plaza in their weekly vigil, demanding to be told the truth about what happened to every single one of their missing children, demanding the legal redress of human rights violations committed under the ruling military junta between 1976 and 1983.

For nearly 40 years, the motto, "remember so as not to repeat!" (*recordar para no repetir!*), has been central in the lives of the families of the *desaparecidos*. These families, and the women in particular, have continued to play a highly visible and active role in Argentine memorial culture as they regularly give oral testimony in the public sphere in a bid to prevent history repeating itself. The telling and retelling of their traumatic stories has become one way for the women to educate the next generation of Argentines about the horrors they lived through, and to warn them

---

[2] The total number of disappeared is contested (see Brysk 1994). While the official Comisión Nacional sobre la Desaparición de Personas (CONADEP) (National Commission on the Disappearance of Persons) report documented 8,960 cases of disappeared individuals, the figure is likely to be greater due to forces that prevented individuals from testifying to the CONADEP taskforce, including aggravated threats made to witnesses and fear of reprisals for offering information (CONADEP 1986). Argentina's Under Secretariat for Human Rights has confirmed about 3,000 new cases, bringing the official number up to 12,000 (Barahona de Brito 2001). Thirty thousand is considered an emblematic figure used by the majority of Argentine human rights organisations. The vast majority of disappearances occurred from 1976 to 1977 (CONADEP 1986).

[3] As of August 2013, 109 of an estimated 500 children taken from their mothers after birth while held in one of the military's clandestine detention centres have been recovered with the assistance of Las Abuelas de la Plaza de Mayo (Grandmothers of the Plaza de Mayo) (www.abuelas.org).

that the perpetrators of physical and psychic abuse during the 1976–1983 military dictatorship have managed to keep their identities concealed, and continue to walk freely among them.

In the process of speaking to the women—mothers, wives, partners, sisters—and gathering as much research as I could, I began to think there was a lot more to Maria's observation that Argentine society did not want to heal itself, that it did not want to begin anew. It became clear just how unreal the concept of "national reconciliation" was in present-day Argentina, where victims of human rights abuses still anticipate meaningful justice. Eliana, whose sister Evangelina was disappeared in 1976, was adamant that her future held no possibility for reconciliation:

> Forgive? The criminals? Forgiveness isn't possible. They have to seek forgiveness from god. There is no forgiveness. It is this way. There is no forgiveness. There is a very fashionable word; that is about finding within the individual "reconciliation". Reconcile what? We will never reconcile. Reconciliation is not possible. (Carreira 2009)

I began to wonder how to make sense of this striking and haunting realisation of the place at which contemporary Argentina had arrived, despite it being a transitional justice pioneer. After all, was not this Argentina, which had struggled for legal, political and social accountability of those who had committed gross human rights abuses during the military dictatorship 1976–1983 and became an indisputable exemplar of transitional justice for other democracies emerging out of violent pasts? Was not this Argentina, which had seen the formation of a truth commission in 1983 and numerous judicial reforms and procedures since 2004?

Near the end of my year-long stay in Argentina, I discovered that there was another group of women giving oral testimony in the public sphere in memory of their loved ones—of those who were kidnapped and murdered by the armed guerrilla movement, predominantly in the democratic period leading up to the start of the 1976 military dictatorship. This group also fears a return to past violence and demands legal redress for those individuals within the armed guerrilla groups suspected of human rights abuses. Since 2010, while legal trials have ensued for those in the military ranks no member from the armed guerrilla movement has been prosecuted.[4] As a result, this group of women also feels compelled to live in a society that has failed to prosecute perpetrators of past violence. They too feel as though those responsible for human rights abuses circle overhead like ravens.

While I had initially thought to focus exclusively on women, whose lives were directly affected by the military dictatorship, I ended up feeling that it was crucial to widen my focus and to explore the personal memories of the two different groups of Argentine women—those affected by military repression *and* those affected by armed guerrilla violence. Both of these groups are engaged in the inexhaustible labours of mourning and remembering, yet they are understood to occupy radically different positions in Argentina's memorial culture and to belong to the oppos-

[4] By August 2013, a total of 381 sets of criminal proceedings in relation to state terrorism were in process, in which 2071 armed forces personnel, security officials and civilians are facing faced charges linked with state terrorism during the military dictatorship 1976–1983. Of these, 405 have been sentenced, 370 have been condemned, 35 have received pardons (www.cels.org.ar).

ing ends of the political and ideological spectrum. In Argentina, the two different groups fall into two political/ideological camps. More broadly, and in a complicated and not entirely satisfying way, individuals affected by military repression are commonly referred to as the political "Left", and individuals affected by armed guerrilla violence are referred to as the political "Right".

The women's memories of loss and violence have been shaped by the fissure of decades-old, deep-seated social and political animosity. The memories of enduring personal trauma that both groups of women carry are commonly perceived as incompatible and unable to coexist in a shared mnemonic space. It is as if remembering one history of violence is immediately seen as an attempt to forget or violate the other history of violence and trauma. In some respects, these two groups of women are commonly viewed as representing antithetical versions of the recent Argentinian past—two versions that have actively sought recognition and legitimacy amidst intense ideological battles in the political, social and cultural arenas over "who has what rights to determine what should be remembered and how", and over the "ownership of historical memory" (Jelin 1998, p. 25).

In this book, I seek to grapple with the cultural condition of "stuckness" that Maria has articulated in her interview with me. I attempt to gain a deeper understanding of what is preventing Argentina from, in her words, "healing itself". I wish to understand how, despite the passage of time, the divisions between the two groups of women are self-perpetuating and growing only deeper; and why, despite pioneering those mechanisms designed, in the transitional justice speak, to "deal with", "work through" or "come to terms with" the past in transitioning democracies, Argentine memorial cultures appear beholden to the entrenched political and ideological divisions of old.[5]

Since the return to democratic rule in 1983, competing claims about how the period of political violence and state terrorism of the 1970s and 1980s should be collectively remembered by the nation have caused deep political and societal divisions. Argentine scholar Elizabeth Jelin (2003) suggests that, at any time Argentina has experienced political change, debates have surfaced over what and how to remember—or forget—the period of repression and political violence in the 1970s and 1980s. Various actors who have taken part in these debates have linked their political programs and orientations towards the future with the memories of a violent past (Jelin 2003). As a result, the two different groups of victims have come to view the public sphere in which they articulate their memories of trauma as a "scarce resource" (Rothberg 2009). It is as if different memories vie for pre-eminence in a constant struggle for political, social and legal recognition in which (again) there are only winners and losers (Rothberg 2009). As Barbara, whose father, José Miguel, was killed by the armed guerrilla movement in 1976, told me:

[5] A number of such terms have emerged within the field of transitional justice to describe strategies and initiatives used to achieve justice and to build trust among adversarial communities. Discourse around national reconciliation has more recently relied upon a therapeutic model, which seeks to heal wounds in connection with past violence and focuses on recognition of the victims of violence to recover sovereignty (Humphrey 2005).

> I'm tired of it all. If they think they're the "goodies" and I'm not, how am I ever going to be able to talk with them [human rights organisations, the government]? I don't understand. What kind of communication could there ever be because we're never going to understand each other? ... There is no such thing as "goodies" and "baddies". There is no Left and Right. There are all sorts of people and we all, both Left and Right, make up a society. There's us and then there are the politicians. They're meant to represent us but they don't represent me ... I am discriminated against and segregated [within society] ... Argentina is like a jigsaw puzzle and my story has to be a part of this puzzle. (Tarquini 2009)

As political actors have advocated that certain groups of victims be publicly remembered, and others sidelined within the creation of Argentina's collective memorial culture, contentious debates about past violence within society have intensified. These debates have resulted in the polarisation of groups that struggle to overcome the additional sense of injustice generated by the contest for public recognition over whose history and political culture should ultimately be recognised. According to Nancy Fraser (2009, p. 15):

> Whether the issue is distribution or recognition, disputes that used to focus exclusively on the question of what is owed as a matter of justice to community members now turn quickly into disputes about who should count as a member and which is the relevant community. Not just the "what" but also the "who" is up for grabs.

This dynamic has created a sense of enmity between two groups of victims struggling for justice, and for the memory of their loved ones to be recognised and legitimated in the public domain. These competitive ideological battles have had major consequences for the make-up of the public sphere in which individual memories enter and circulate in the present day; they have also had crucial implications for the shaping of Argentine collective memorial culture and identity. With an increasing need for collective identity amidst social and political conflicts over how to remember and account for violations experienced during this traumatic past, Argentina has developed into a society of "memory groups" (Misztal 2004), with each claiming recognition and the legitimacy of its voices and demands. As those who personally experienced suffering have talked of their experiences with others, memory has become a common language through which individuals have been able to articulate and share their traumatic experiences. As a result, memory has become a dominant form of belonging in Argentina. Members of particular political and ideological groups have created a shared fabric of a lifeworld in which remembering their loved ones who were affected by political and state violence is central. The spread of these community-based groups, whereby being a group member means assuming a shared identity and subscribing to a shared group past, has resulted in the "pluralisation and problematisation of memory" (Misztal 2004, p. 68). As the boundaries of memory parallel the boundaries of group identity, there is a sense of competitive victimhood as groups compete for the recognition and legitimisation of their memories of victimhood at the exclusion of others within collective forms of remembrance (Rothberg 2009).

Argentine writer Graciela Scheines likens Argentine history to being a "living burden" that produces "sorrow and anguish" (cited in Roniger and Sznajder 1999, p. 189). Widespread abuses by the state and armed political groups have left behind a powerful legacy of deep pain in Argentina. This was abundantly clear as the women told me of their traumatic experiences with what seemed to me to be the same emotional charge as that of nearly 30 years ago when some of them gave their first public testimonies. Both groups were as committed as ever to the daily task of bearing witness to those experiences that had irrevocably changed the course of their lives. Attesting to their losses in the form of oral testimony in the public sphere was something most of the women had done for decades, in the fulfilment of a debt of fidelity to the disappeared and the deceased. It was also an approach they increasingly seemed to be pursuing as a response to the ever-changing political, social, legal and cultural treatment of their memories of violence and loss in the public sphere.

Truth-telling and reparation mechanisms, such as truth commissions, have been adopted since the end of the Cold War as a way of achieving acknowledgement of human rights violations and national reconciliation, as well as a way of healing psychosocial trauma in post-conflict societies at both an individual and collective level. It is still commonly accepted within the current truth commission literature and conflict resolution theory that psychological issues—whether individual or collective—can be healed through mnemonic performances of oral testimony or storytelling (Millar 2010). Little evidence is available to prove this assumption, however, and over time it has become clear that the psychological benefits from participating in these mechanisms of "reparative remembering" (Dawson 2007, p. 84) may be overstated (Hayner 2011). Indeed, as Rigney (2012) acknowledges, reconciliation efforts in post-conflict contexts have more often than not yielded a "'thin' form of mere co-existence" rather than the "'thicker' form of social integration and solidarity invoked by redemptive narratives of 'national reconciliation'". This is certainly true for Argentina, where the public performance of witnesses', victims' and perpetrators' stories of political and state violence has not been the catalyst for the collective psychological or socio-emotional reconciliation that has been sought in other transitional contexts. For most of the women I interviewed, talking about their traumatic memories in the form of oral testimony has not played any such role in helping them deal with their painful memories. Silvia, whose father, Roberto, was kidnapped in 1974 and later killed by the armed guerrilla movement, told me:

> I haven't felt any sense of relief [from talking about her father's memory] ... no ... I haven't felt any sense of relief ... It [talking about her traumatic experience] hasn't relieved me internally in any way. It's not like I go around talking about it and a weight is lifted off me, no, no. (Ibarzábal 2009)

In thinking about how to approach the sense of irreconcilability of memories and experiences, I was initially inspired by the argument of *Multidirectional Memory*'s author Michael Rothberg (2009), who recommends exploring the kinds of ideas and conditions that could enable a shift away from a politics of antagonism and competition towards one of mutual recognition. Rothberg (2009, p. 18) writes: "The greatest hope for a new comparatism lies in opening up the separate containers of memory and identity that buttress competitive thinking and becoming aware of the mutual constitution and ongoing transformation of the objects of comparison."

In my research, I at first sought to bring the two groups of women together conceptually in the hope of finding redemptive narratives that could provide fertile ground for the mutual recognition of the deep pain they had both experienced. As Rothberg (2009, p. 313) suggests, I wanted to work towards a more nuanced understanding of the interlacing of the disparate narratives within the "force field" of public space. "The only way forward is through their entanglement", he writes (2009, p. 313). However, after months of grappling with the hundreds of pages of oral testimonies before me, I came to realise that the more deeply I delved into the two groups' suffering and pain, the less confident I felt of ever being able to bring them together in a meaningful and truthful way. By trying to identify commonalities between the two groups of women, I had only reinforced just how separate they really were. Slowly, I began to accept that perhaps what Maria was telling me was true: no amount of engaging in public mnemonic practices—which form the basis of transitional justice—could bring about a social transformation in present-day Argentina.

It is within this context that I propose we take a deeper look at the condition of "stuckness" that is so profoundly entrenched within Argentine memorial culture. I contend that we need to look beyond political and ideological contestations and engage in a deeper analysis of how memorial cultures are formed and sustained. I am not attempting to depoliticise the conversation about memory and trauma in contemporary Argentina, nor am I seeking to deny that the two groups exist in a heavily politicised arena. Even when the women talk privately of their pain, their narratives are inevitably mediated by a very politicised memorial culture that influences and shapes, both overtly and obliquely, every word the women utter. While I am by no means suggesting that we could—or, for that matter, should—completely disregard the political and ideological content and entanglements of the women's narratives, I am proposing that we shift our attention away from the exclusive focus on the political and ideological nature of their stories of violence and incorporate an affective reading of the women's traumatic memories.

I argue that we cannot account for the politics of memory in modern-day Argentina without acknowledging and exploring the role played by individual emotions and affects in generating and shaping collective emotions and affects (Hutchison and Bleiker 2008).[6] Affect may be a pre-political and pre-social force (Healy and Tumarkin 2011), but it has major consequences for the perpetuation of fault lines running across particular memorial cultures. Thus, rather than simply rendering a factual narrative of the past, the second part of this book engages emotions and affects as a way of exploring how these may become the source of a different kind of understanding of existing societal antagonisms.

[6] Affect can be used as a broad term to refer to emotions, feelings, and affects in the narrower sense (Forgas 2000). Though they are often used interchangeably, it is important to define the difference between the three. Feelings are personal and biographical, emotions are social and affects are pre-personal. Displays of emotion can be genuine or feigned; when we relay our emotions publicly, they may be an expression of our internal state or they may be contrived in order to fulfil social expectations. Meanwhile, affects are more abstract than emotions because they cannot always be fully realised in language. They are non-conscious and unformed, and refer to the body's way of preparing itself for action in a given circumstance with an added dimension of intensity (Shouse 2005). Affects are linked to autonomic responses, which can expand or diminish the body's capacity to act or engage with others (Clough 2007).

1.2 Politics of Memory in Argentina: Through an Affective Lens

On arrival in Buenos Aires, Argentina, I spent some months at local archive organisation Memoria Abierta, watching audiovisual recordings of individuals testifying to their abduction, disappearance and torture during the 1976–1983 period of military rule.[7] Time and again, I was struck by the way in which interviewees would keep control of their emotions during their testimonial accounts. I was particularly intrigued by the fact that participants often showed no hint of emotion while talking about extremely traumatic experiences. Testimonial standards that are adopted in official juridical or historical contexts concerning accuracy and reliability are more stringent than those applied in the case of, for example, video testimonies (Assmann 2006a). In a courtroom setting, the witness's main role is to provide factual information that will assist in discovering the truth (Assmann 2006a). The witness, as a person, is of less importance than his/her testimony (Assmann 2006a).

Since so many records held by the military were destroyed during the transition to democratic rule, oral testimony has played a vital role in constructing both the historical legacy of the dictatorship and evidential proof in the case of prosecution (Jelin and Kaufman 2002). However, a series of calibrations around testimony led to a distinctive system of value. For example, while, in a bid for juridical recognition of witnesses' voices, bodily injury was deemed acceptable as "legal proof", emotional expression was not legitimated (Jelin and Kaufman 2002). The mode of the testimonials taken by the Comisión Nacional sobre la Desaparición de Personas (CONADEP) (National Commission on the Disappearance of Persons) immediately following Argentina's return to democratic rule tended to be affectless, in the sense that the elaboration of "useable evidence" was the rationale of the Commission: "When emotion overtook the witnesses, the judges halted testimony until calm and sanity returned" (Jelin and Kaufman 2002, p. 37).

To counter years of military propaganda, talking in the public sphere about the fate of the *desaparecidos* has required that families deliver their testimonies in such a way that they are seen to be credible and legitimate by governments, media and international agencies (Gordon 2008). Their narratives have had to "minimise the ambiguity, complicity, imagination and surreality that necessarily characterize the theatre of terror" (Gordon 2008, p. 79). As a result, the language that has been used in survivors' testimonies has tended to be referential, and has avoided expressions of hatred or taking on an epic tone (Basile 1989). The testimonial format used in creating the CONADEP report, *Nunca Más*, and the judicial trials that followed have thus set a precedent for the form in which oral testimony has subsequently been sought and legitimated in Argentine memorial culture.

---

[7] *Memoria Abierta,* based in Buenos Aires, is a coordinated group of human rights organisations that works to raise social awareness and knowledge about the years of the military dictatorship 1976–1983 in Argentina. It has established an audiovisual archive that houses some 650 testimonials and a photographic archive that contains more than 16,000 images (www.memoriaabierta.org.ar).

This intermittent pattern of showing emotion, but then stopping short of fully entering into an emotion when remembering details from the past, gives the impression to those listening that the full details of the violence and horror that individuals have lived through cannot be told fully in their entirety (Jelin and Kaufman 2002). I began to wonder about the affective impact of this withholding, and sought to question the role emotions and affects might play in accounting for the politics of memory in modern-day Argentina. What role might affect play in the country's seemingly intractable ideological polarisation between memories of individuals affected by military repression and memories of individuals affected by armed guerrilla violence? I wanted to explore their potential in deepening the understanding of the ways in which the women's traumatic memories could be a fragmentary force, and as such were sustaining Argentina's deeply polarised memorial communities.

By engaging emotions and affects in this way, I wish to contribute to the ongoing conversation about the way affective memory flows from private to public domains and back, transforming both of these domains in the process. Publicly sharing their narratives ensures that the women's oral testimonies reach out to the masses; in this way, the circulation of the women's traumatic stories, and their accompanying emotions and affects, results in the shaping of the contours of the public space they inhabit (Ahmed 2004a). If we come to understand how emotions and affects work to align individuals with communities, we can then explore the crucial role they play in the materialisation of collective bodies, including the "body of a nation" (Ahmed 2004a, p. 27), by considering how remembering sustains both forms of antagonism and solidarity within memorial cultures (Rothberg 2009).

In the second half of this book, then, I turn my attention to the affective trails and residues of the personal memories of trauma of the women I interviewed. I explore the ways in which troubling memories of the past—often neglected in memorial culture—continue to affectively reverberate in the present. I aim to deepen our understanding of how the women's traumatic memories are "lived, felt, practiced" (Ahmed 2000, p. 15); the ways in which the women affectively make sense of their experiences of loss; and, with this in mind, how they position themselves within broader public historical narratives. I explore the ways in which the women's memories of trauma can assert their "disintegrating claim" over the women's ability "to certify belief, establish closure, or achieve certainty" about their traumatic past (Langer 1995, p. 22, 15). The research suggests that these memories serve as a vital force, driving the women to remember their traumatic past.

In talking about affect, I wish to not only talk about the private domain of remembering, but also to discuss the relationship between private and social forms of remembering. In analysing the affective transmission of memory, I seek to develop ways of thinking about how emotions and affects can shape encounters between people and permeate public spheres of remembrance. Engaging affect in this way means I look at "not *what* something is, but how it is—or, more precisely, *how* it affects, and how it is affected by, other things" (Gregg and Seigworth 2010, p. 14). It is important to explore, advises Sara Ahmed (2004a), what emotions and affects actually do and how they circulate between bodies. In my research, I consider how emotions and affects are crucial to the multiple ways in which bodies surface in relation to each other, "a surfacing that produces the very effect of collectives" (Ahmed 2004a, p. 39). I want to extend Ahmed's theory as a way of understanding how the women's feelings of deep pain, uncertainty, guilt and anger linger after they have talked about their shared pasts—how, in the process of remembering, these feelings can seep into the public sphere. I explore this notion of affective contagion in terms of how it can alter individuals' understanding of themselves and others, as well as their relation with the past (Probyn 2010).

The research findings detailed in this book problematise juridical and general notions about how we think history needs to be settled, and in particular a whole series of ideas about "overcoming" or "reconciling with" traumatic memories. Rothberg (2009, p. 5), for example, encourages us to think of the public sphere, in which collective memories are articulated, as a "malleable discursive space in which groups do not simply articulate established positions but actually come into being through their dialogical interactions with others". Yet, he does accept that there are some contexts in which models of competition and exclusivity prevail at the expense of solidarity (Rothberg 2009). I would argue cautiously that present-day Argentina is one such context, in which the transcendence of pain and hatred through a shared memorial culture and the unifying narrative of the past is not necessarily possible.

I believe that our desire to see history settled stops us from hearing important stories about the ways in which countless individuals continue to live with, and be defined by, their experiences of atrocity within transitioning democracies. While survivors of political and state violence, not only in Argentina but in many other contexts, bear witness to the traumatic events in their lives, we—the international community—as listeners can be at pains to recast their memories "as wounds to be healed, insults to be paid for, pains to be forgotten, deaths to be transcended or redeemed" (Langer 1995, p. 19). I suggest that the powerful sensory imprints of women's affective memories of violence and loss, and the ways in which these imprints transform the diffused public sphere in which articulation and transmission of public memories takes place, complicate the idea that history could be settled in Argentina. After all, the women "carry an impossible history with them, or they become themselves the symptom of a history that they cannot entirely possess" (Caruth 1995, p. 4–5). An in-depth engagement with affective memories shows us how histories can stay alive in the present, even when not consciously remembered (Ahmed 2004a), and reveals the multiple consequences of their ghostly presence in a society such as Argentina. We cannot eschew affect if we are to produce enduring visions of justice, if we are to ask how and to what end the deep pain that comes from experiencing extreme violence can be transformed.

1.3 Ethics and Interviewing

The book is based primarily on twenty interviews I conducted in 2009 with two groups of women: those whose family members were kidnapped and murdered by the armed political groups from 1973 to 1976; and those whose family members were kidnapped, disappeared or murdered by the military government from 1976 to 1983. The women I interviewed included grandmothers, mothers, wives, partners, sisters and daughters of missing and killed family members, as well as survivors of clandestine detention centres. The women came from a variety of professional backgrounds, and included housewives turned political activists, social workers, psychologists, anthropologists, lawyers, human rights workers and journalists. I made contact with the women through three local human rights organisations based in the Argentine capital of Buenos Aires: (1) Las Abuelas de la Plaza de Mayo (Grandmothers of the Plaza de Mayo); (2) Las Familiares de Desaparecidos y Detenidos por Razones Politicas (Families of the Disappeared and Detained for Political Reasons); and (3) El Centro de Estudios Legales sobre el Terrorismo y sus Víctimas (Centre for Legal Studies on Terrorism and Its Victims). A call for individuals willing to participate in this study was made through the three organisations, and the interviewees were then able to contact me to arrange an interview.

The organisation Las Abuelas de la Plaza de Mayo was founded when a group of mothers emerged among the relatives of the *desaparecidos*. Despite their different backgrounds, beliefs, geographical locations and social and economic classes, the mothers of the *desaparecidos* began to organise themselves to demand the truth about their children's fate (Foss and Domenici 2001). Due to the fathers of the disappeared having to earn a living, and the risk of them losing their jobs, the mothers began searching for their missing children (Navarro 2001a). Women were also less likely to be disappeared than men and young people—particularly in the first years of the military junta—in a society that glorified motherhood and lauded women as domestic beings (Navarro 2001b). For the most part, the mothers were housewives with no political affiliation or prior experience with the political militancy of their children (Agosin 1990).

On 30 April 1977, at a time when public demonstrations were forbidden, 14 mothers wearing white headscarves braved the terror that was prevalent on the streets and met to *hacer la ronda* (circle) in the Plaza de Mayo in the heart of Buenos Aires (Agosin 1990). The white headscarves, symbolising a baby's nappy to help them feel closer to their children, were initially used so the mothers would be able to identify each other in large crowds (Bouvard 1994). Originally, the names of their disappeared sons and daughters were not written on the scarves for fear of further endangering them. Only later did they write the names, dates of birth and imprint photos of the disappeared on headscarves. The women continued to meet in the Plaza every Thursday at 3.30 pm from then on, always wearing white headscarves, to demand answers about the fate of their loved ones (Agosin 1990). The group of women eventually became the organisation Las Madres de Plaza de Mayo (Mothers of the Plaza de Mayo).

Their weekly demonstration in La Plaza de Mayo marked a new form of social organisation in Argentina, one that gradually grew in numbers and strength (Brysk 1994). During Las Madres' weekly gatherings, some of the mothers began to realise that the abduction of their pregnant family members was more widespread than originally thought and their search also extended to the fate of their missing grandchildren (Arditti 1999). In October 1977, 12 mothers established Las Abuelas de la Plaza de Mayo and organised themselves around one specific demand: that the children who had been kidnapped or born in captivity as a method of political repression by the armed forces, be returned to their families (Arditti 1999). Las Abuelas engaged in public appeals as to the whereabouts of their grandchildren, and focused on legal activities that, while unavailable to them as a course of action during the dictatorship, lay the groundwork for advancing proceedings and reforms after the return to democratic rule (Brysk 1994).[8]

The second organisation I engaged with—Las Familiares de Desaparecidos y Detenidos por Razones Politicas—was founded in January 1976 by a group of relatives of the *desaparecidos* who were pressing the government for answers as to the fate of their missing family members in the Argentine city of Cordoba (www.desaparecidos.org/familiares/historia.html). After the military coup in March 1976, family members also began to organise themselves in Buenos Aires and the organisation found a permanent office from which to work in September 1976 (www.desaparecidos.org/familiares/historia.html). While the organisation also demanded answers about the whereabouts of their missing family members, it differed from the groups Las Madres and Las Abuelas in several ways (Brysk 1994). Firstly, male relatives were included in their activities and as such their ritual protests were not centred on the female identity of its members, as was the case with the above two groups (Brysk 1994). Secondly, Las Familiares also included relatives of political prisoners; their work included campaigning on improving the physical and psychological conditions of detainees while in detention, and securing their release (Brysk 1994). Finally, as the organisation name indicates, the group treated repression as a political strategy and its victims as political actors. This contrasts with the focus of other human rights organisations that demonstrated according to "apolitical" principles such as the rule of law or the "sanctity of the family" (Brysk 1994). The group played a less public, symbolic role than that of Las Madres or Las Abuelas, and worked at gathering and publishing information, providing assistance to prisoners and their families, and participating in mass demonstrations (Brysk 1994). The organisation Las Familiares continues its work in highlighting the issue of the *desaparecidos* and in bringing to justice those guilty of human rights abuses.

Lastly, El Centro de Estudios Legales sobre el Terrorismo y sus Víctimas (CELTYV) was founded in 2006 to represent individuals who were kidnapped

[8] As will be further explored in the following chapter, the Due Obedience Law enacted under the Alfonsín administration had a legal loophole, which excluded from its purview those who had assisted or planned the abduction of children of the *desaparecidos*. In a landmark case in 1998, Generals Videla, Massera, Bignone and Nicolaides, together with five lower ranking officers, were charged and jailed for the illegal abduction and adoption of children in seven clandestine centres (Barahona de Brito 2001).

and killed by the armed guerrilla groups which were at their most active prior to the military coup of 1976 (though murders did occur following the installation of the military government). The advocacy organisation evolved as a reaction to the memorial policies of the consecutive governments of Presidents Néstor Kirchner (2003–2007) and Cristina Fernández Kirchner (since 2007). The organisation offers psychological support to the victims of the armed guerrilla movement, and runs publicity campaigns to heighten awareness, both locally and internationally. It also prepares cases and campaigns the government to reopen legal proceedings against those suspected of the murder of the family members that the organisation represents (www.celtyv.org).[9]

Each in-depth interview was conducted in Spanish, lasted between one and a half and three and a half hours, and was tape-recorded with prior agreement from the narrator. Both groups of women were asked the same set of questions. Interviews were held in a private room on the organisations' premises. The interviews were subsequently transcribed by a local transcriber and I analysed the interviews in detail based on the original Spanish transcripts. All interview excerpts included in this book are my own translations into English. Those who participated said they were very clear in their understanding of the way in which their testimony would be utilised in this study and were agreeable to extracts of their testimonies being published for public consumption. In fact, all of the women I interviewed wished to participate in the research project on the proviso that I would make their testimonials public. Through the three organisations contacted, all participants were informed that I was conducting interviews with other groups, and all were made aware of the context within which their testimonies would be examined. The women were very positive about the direction of my work and explicitly declared their wish to be involved.

The interviewees emphasised their preference for disclosing both their names and the identities of their missing/killed family members. For many of the families of the *desaparecidos*, publicly repeating the name of their loved ones at any opportunity is highly significant. As was common practice in the Nazi concentration camps during World War II, names were one of the first things that were stripped of the *desaparecidos* when they entered the military-run clandestine camps. In defiance of this practice, the *Nunca Más* (Never Again) report lists the full names of those who gave their testimonies to the truth commission and also includes the first and last names of the *desaparecidos* as a way of restoring their personal identity (Crenzel 2008a).

All the participants in the research study had previously given oral testimony publicly—some for many years, others more recently (especially those women from CELTYV who officially began to give public testimony in 2006). Many of their testimonies can be found online. Some of the women I interviewed have also testified at legal proceedings, while others have written books about their memories of violence. As such, the women I interviewed were eager that I include both their names and the names of their disappeared and deceased loved ones in my research.

[9] The organisation, though concerned with issues of historical justice, is perceived by the Argentine human rights movement as having an active political agenda.

After I had left Argentina, Graciela, whose partner, Ricardo, was disappeared in 1976, wrote to me saying:

> To not record the identity of the person [disappeared family member] is not the norm for us because for years we have fought for our disappeared [family members]—especially those who were buried [in mass graves]...etc as NN (no name), so their identity is very precious. As such, everybody is named using their first and last names—the disappeared, us etc. So we don't follow the rules or norms that are usually followed for research purposes. So, go ahead and name me .... (Lois 2009)

Given the formula customarily used when soliciting oral testimony in Argentina, the women I interviewed were intrigued and eager to participate in a research project that would allow them to reveal and talk openly about their emotions when remembering. As Cristina, whose husband, Carlos, was disappeared in 1977, told me:

> Although I have given testimony an infinity of times, who knows, but maybe never from this place [exploring the emotions in testimony] but rather from a political point of view, so many times. And when one opens up to an emotion and one looks inside, others [emotions] appear. (Muro 2009)

While the interviews began with a traditional oral testimonial format in which the interviewee recounted details around the specific events of their or their family member's abduction and disappearance, the interviews then followed a life-story approach. The interviews were not structured to produce a coherent set of facts and emphasise the narrative mode to establish an historical chronology of events; rather, I attempted to "unpack" the notion of testimony by exploring how individual women's emotional and affective memories "may be helpful and even necessary rather than inimical to the construction of knowledge" (Jaggar 1989, p. 2). Asking the women how they felt and affectively experienced their traumatic memories allowed them to paint a revealing portrait about how they saw themselves in specific historical contexts, the ways in which they negotiated these memories in order to live with them, how they mediated memories of who they were then compared with who they were now, and what it meant for them to remember. Though I predominantly focus on exploring the women's memories of trauma in this book, the women also spoke at length and with great enthusiasm about their memories of political activism and resistance.

The women were able offer great insight into the ways in which their traumatic memories had shaped their current thoughts, attitudes and behaviours. Argentina has one of the highest rates of psychiatrists per inhabitant in the world; many of the women I interviewed had passed through years of counselling and demonstrated a highly developed capacity for understanding and assimilating past traumatic events. Due to the interviewed women's experiences with psychoanalysis, they were able to elaborate and vividly construct their memory of the past without totally immersing themselves dangerously in the violence of that past. Anthropologist Veena Das (1997) reminds us that women are not passive objects—in this case, in the giving of oral testimony—for they control the articulation of their grief. By giving, to use Das's words, "pain a home in the body", this book explores how Argentine women make efforts to actively engender the transformation of pain into language, and contribute to what Das has called a "genre of lamentation" in which they are afforded control of their bodies and language (1997, p. 78, 68).

In conducting my interviews, I found it critical to steer the women away from the chronological format to which they were accustomed. In presenting narratives of their lived experiences, some of the women began the interview by giving a ritualised repetition of facts that were consistent, cohesive and ironed out; these were well-rehearsed narratives that were palatable for a listening audience. I felt it was important to pay attention to the disruptive and difficult aspects of the women's testimonies as a way of grasping the complexity of what had occurred for them. I also saw it as a way of gaining a more critical understanding of the types of shadows the women's past experiences cast over their present lives. I thus explored with these women their emotional and affective responses to remembering traumatic events as a way of understanding the "potency" of the past rather than merely recalling "what happened" (Middleton and Brown 2005, p. 138).

The open-ended interview style adopted by this research provided a space within which the women were able to express the chaos of their feelings and emotions and to recount their memories as they streamed into their consciousness. This illuminated rather than dulled the testimonies' "texture and imaginative flash" (Hartman 2006, p. 250). The women's oral testimonies solicited in a life story format disclosed the raw, intense and spontaneous emotions evoked by the experience of recounting past events. Unlike the institutionalised, formalised and standardised narratives produced within juridical settings, this approach unearthed a revealing account of the way in which individuals experience and continue to live with their pasts so steeped in tragedy.

Chapter 2
Argentina 1969–1999

2.1 Period of Guerrilla Violence, 1969–1976

In the midst of widespread political turmoil and violence, a military coup took place in Argentina in March 1976. The military government implemented a "Process of National Reorganisation", which involved a systematic policy of clandestine repression to wipe out the main two armed political groups: the Peronist Montoneros and the Marxist Ejército Revolucionario del Pueblo (ERP). For in the years leading up to the military coup of 1976, political violence was widespread (Calveiro 2005; Lewis 2002; Romero 2002; Robben 2005a). There were armed groups on various sides of the ideological divide, including an armed guerrilla movement and paramilitary death squads. The political violence and armed take over of the 1970s is commonly referred to outside Argentina as a "dirty war".[1] The term has been used by both the armed forces, to justify its repressive actions against so-called subversives who threatened Argentina's western, Christian culture, as well as by the guerrilla insurgency, which believed itself to be waging a just fight for a socialist Argentina, free of social inequality (Robben 2012).

The revolutionary impetus for radical social change was strong during the 1960s and 1970s, with guerrilla groups ideologically committed and ready to become the new "authors of history" using armed struggle (Robben 2005a, p. 97). Though Ché Guevara's desire to liberate his native Argentina may have ended with his death in 1967, his ideas about the use of revolutionary violence to fight exploitation and

[1] The term "dirty war", explains anthropologist Antonius Robben (2012), first appeared in an ultranationalist magazine in March 1974, to describe the Marxist guerrilla insurgency. It was later adopted by the Peronist left to denounce right-wing paramilitary death squads. The term again shifted after the military coup of March 1976 when the Montoneros accused the military dictators of war crimes, saying "this is a dirty war, like all wars waged by reactionary armies. It is not just dirty because it uses the people's sons to fight against their brothers and their interests, but because it doesn't even respect the war conventions. The enemy assassinates the wounded, tortures and executes prisoners, and turns its brutality against the people's relatives" (Evita Montonera cited in Robben 2012, p. 307). The term was soon used by the military dictators against the armed guerrilla movement as General Vilas stated, "This is a dirty war, a war of attrition, dark and sly, which one wins with decisiveness and calculation" (cited in Robben 2012, p. 307).

J. Stockwell, *Reframing the Transitional Justice Paradigm*,
Springer Series in Transitional Justice 10, DOI 10.1007/978-3-319-03853-7_2,

injustice continued to flourish (Robben 2005a). The number of bombings carried out by the armed guerrilla movement rose from 141 in 1969 to 654 in 1971, estimates Robben (2005a). The movement also robbed banks, invaded radio and television stations to broadcast political messages, mailed letter bombs to businessmen, kidnapped executives for ransom and threatened their families (Lewis 2002). The guerrilla groups were engaged in urban bombings that claimed scores of victims and mounted attempts on military installations and their personnel (Brysk 1994).

The guerrilla groups were run like a regular army, according to Argentine political scientist Pilar Calveiro (2005). Recruits were assigned a rank and a uniform, and all were made to obey strict rules and to follow military-type discipline (Calveiro 2005). Beyond the mass front lay a broad network of sympathisers—or, as the "Montoneros" called them, the "rear guard of Peronism"—who lived in the neighbourhoods and who were, as the tabloid *Evita Montonera* described them, the "eyes and ears of the people" (Lewis 2002, p. 43–44). Those in the "rear guard" had their fingers on the pulse of the communities in which they lived, and were knowledgeable about all aspects of the lives of police and military officers and their families (Lewis 2002).

While the Montoneros were considered to be by far the larger of the two main guerrilla groups, their actual number remains a mystery (Lewis 2002). The army estimated Montonero troops to be about 30,000 strong, with another 150,000 people active in the mass front organisation and support networks at the beginning of 1975 (Lewis 2002). However, Argentine human rights groups, such as the Centro de Estudios Legales y Sociales (Centre for Legal and Social Studies, CELS), calculate that the combined armed guerrilla forces at the beginning of 1976 numbered between 2,000 and 3,000 combatants (Lewis 2002). General Jorge Rafael Videla, who led the military coup in 1976, reportedly believed that there were around 4,000 armed guerrilla fighters at the time of the army's takeover (Lewis 2002). A former Montonero militant, Juan Gasparini, calculated that the movement lost as many as 5,000 combatants in the first few months of the 1976 military coup (Lewis 2002). In any case, the Montoneros were supported by favourable public opinion and grew in numbers, firepower and organisational complexity in the early 1970s (Lewis 2002).

The origins of the armed guerrilla movement can be found in 1969, when military dictator General Ongania's tight grip on power was shattered, and some of the largest unions led by Trotskyites, Maoists and left-wing Peronists joined students around the country to challenge the regime (Lewis 2002). During this time, the military branch of the ERP was formed and waged a rural insurgency in Tucumán province, northern Argentina. The evolution of the Montoneros soon followed (Robben 2005a). The guerrilla movement saw itself as fighting a "people's war" (*guerra de pueblo*) (Calveiro 2005). Its aim was to "awaken popular consciousness and to show all compatriots the road out of exploitation, hunger and the poverty that our community has been subjected to" (Calveiro 2005, p. 69).

Lewis believes that it was the exiled Perón who, in 1956, initially planted the seed for guerrilla insurrection and the violence that followed among his followers when he wrote to Peronist leaders:[2]

[2] On 20 September 1955, Perón went into exile for the next 17 years. During this time, the Peronist movement was proscribed and Peronist sympathisers were violently suppressed by the military

> We must plan our actions minutely and prepare for their execution by permanent practice and exercises. If it's necessary to use the Devil, then we'll use the Devil as we must. The Devil is always ready for such work. But, it is necessary that the struggle be based on guerrillas. The forces of reaction should never find a place to land a blow, and every day they should feel the force of resistance. (cited in Lewis 2002, p. 11)

A new generation of Peronist resistance emerged, one that was even more combative and aware of the inherent political power than a united labour movement could provide; the movement began to rely on tactics of sabotage and underground propaganda to lay the fertile ground for Perón's eventual return in 1973 (Lewis 2002).[3] Lewis (2002) writes that Perón's genius lay in his ability to keep a close watch on events back home and a tight rein over the Peronist movement, even from a distance in exile. Perón was adept at adjusting his political tactics in response to Argentina's ever-changing political climate (Lewis 2002). For 17 years, even in exile, Perón was able to "exert an almost magical political power from behind the scenes", and "by virtue of his absence, he became a mythic presence" (Feitlowitz 1998, p. 4). Peronist resistance gradually became coordinated as it learned tactics from other similar, international scenarios such as the Cuban Revolution (Lewis 2002). Ernesto "Ché" Guevara was adopted as a cult hero by the movement, and the Peronist underground began to realise, from watching the Cuban experience, that power could be won through armed violence (Lewis 2002).

The power of the armed guerrilla movement grew in May 1969 when the infamous *Cordobazo* uprising took place. Tens of thousands of workers and students fought off the police and army during 2 days of violent battles in Córdoba in central Argentina; this signalled a leap closer to social revolution (Robben 2005a). As anthropologist Antonius Robben (2005a, p. 45) suggests, the *Cordobazo* "marked a watershed in mass mobilization" of ousted President Juan Perón's followers, including a growing band of middle-class students and an increasingly militant working class, who took the initiative in their leader's absence and instigated grassroots street demonstrations. While reflecting the deepening political crisis that began with the overthrow of Perón, the *Cordobazo* was also a more localised version of the worldwide New Left movement of the 1960s, which was rebelling against traditional social institutions and idealising socialism as being ethically superior to capitalism (Lewis 2002). The *Cordobazo* signalled—not only to those in the military and unions but to the

---

government of General Aramburu (1955–1958) (Lewis 2002). Aramburu labelled Perón "the monster", and newspapers of the day called him "the fugitive tyrant" (Robben 2005a, p. 27).

[3] Perón had long been an advocate of the Argentine worker and supporter of the labour movement. It is believed that the founding of Perónism began on 17 October 1945, when hundreds of thousands of workers or *descamisados* ("shirtless ones") walked into the heart of the nation's capital—La Plaza de Mayo—to protest against the internment of Perón. Perón had helped pass labour legislation to improve workers' salaries, conditions and rights and used his authority as then Secretary of Labour and Social Welfare under the military government of Rawson, to unionise workers and strengthen the union movement, especially in rural areas (Robben 2005a). Amid protests from resisters within the military ranks, Perón enforced labour laws that had long been ignored in the country, including laws that delivered an 8 h day, paid vacations and the prohibition of child labour (Lewis 2002). As a result of these enforced changes, Perón was interned by the army in 1945, only to be released 5 days later after fierce protests led by Argentine workers nationwide (Robben 2005a).

revolutionaries themselves—that "the fighting spirit of the Argentine working class remained unbroken despite years of military repression, and that its capacity for resistance had neither been domesticated by the Peronist hierarchy nor paralysed by Perón's prolonged absence" (Lewis 2002, p. 45). It also signalled that there was no alternative to defeating the Ongania dictatorship (1966–1970) except though armed struggle (Romero 2001). For the radical Left, writes historian Paul Lewis (2002), the *Cordobazo* provided an inspiration, and over the next couple of years a number of armed revolutionary organisations emerged as a result. The combined impact of these organisations was far greater than any previous guerrilla attempts.

The Montoneros were the most adept at navigating the political climate and grew in power, eventually absorbing most of the other guerrilla organisations apart from the ERP (Romero 2001). The group triumphed within the Peronist movement by gaining the full support of Perón, thus "winning a space for their autonomous action", and at the same time the recognition of a leader who had become a master in the art of, as he said, 'using his two hands' (the left and right wings of his movement)" (Romero 2001, p. 191). The Montoneros gained support from broad sectors of the urban poor and the Third World priests' movement, and were thus able to mobilise large numbers of volunteers within neighbourhoods, universities and to a lesser extent unions, through the Juventud Peronista (Peronist Youth). Many future Montoneros began their political careers in some of Argentina's elite schools, and as a result high schools became highly politicised (Lewis 2002).

An intellectual new Left emerged, highly influenced by Sartre's existentialism, which argued that "the objective structures of exploitation did not predetermine people's consciousness, but that people were active subjects who produced history" (Robben 2005a, p. 38). A former Montonero guerrilla commander recalls the growing social consciousness of his university days:

> The university begins to embrace Peronism, begins to nationalize itself in the sense that the student breaks with his own isolation, his own environment and begins to develop … a social commitment with his people … We became close to the working class neighbourhoods through social work. (cited in Robben 2005a, p. 38)

Peronists and Marxists joined forces to control the national universities' self-governing institutions and demanded that student bodies incorporate lower middle-class and working-class students, so that the total number of enrolments at Argentina's national universities grew from 82,500 in 1950 to 274,000 by 1970 (Lewis 2002).

Ché Guevara's capture and execution in Bolivia, and the failure of rural guerrilla tactics in other Latin American countries—including Brazil, Paraguay and Guatemala—led to a major tactical overhaul within the guerrilla movement (Lewis 2002). Urban middle-class intellectuals, already too conspicuous in a rural setting and unable to win the support they needed from rural farmers, moved to the cities, where they created chaos and disrupted the economy (Lewis 2002). This was intended to allow the rural guerrillas a free run in the countryside (Lewis 2002). In the cities, while small armed groups (*combatientes*) would do most of the fighting, their actions were supported by mass-action groups of students and workers (*milicianos*), who contributed to the atmosphere of unrest by waging strikes, distributing propaganda, committing acts of sabotage and participating in street demonstrations (Calveiro 2005). While the full-time guerrillas lived underground and engaged in armed combat, those belonging to the front organisations led normal lives, attended classes and held down regular employment (Lewis 2002).

Lewis (2002) estimates that between the start of 1969 and the end of 1975, half of all guerrilla attacks occurred in the nation's capital, Buenos Aires, and its surrounding areas; 30 % of attacks occurred in Córdoba and Santa Fe Provinces; and another 10 % occurred in the other regional centres of Rosario and Tucumán. While many of those killed were police officers and soldiers, other victims included industrialists, merchants, ranch owners, labour union officials, politicians, guerrilla deserters, innocent bystanders and wealthy businessmen—many of whom were held for hefty ransoms (Lewis 2002).

Many individuals who were targeted by the armed guerrilla movement were abducted and kept in "people's prisons" (Lewis 2002). These were rustic cells often located in the dugout remains of old buildings that had no windows and little ventilation, and were invariably so small that captives were forced to lie down or squat (Lewis 2002). During our interview, Silvia Ibarzabal showed me photos of the "people's prison" where her father, Lieutenant Colonel Jorge Ibarzábal, was held captive for 10 months before eventually being murdered. Silvia lived with her family in front of an army base, and remembers the Saturday night when the base was attacked. She told me:

> We had to hit the floor and stay down all night because bullets were being fired into our apartment. The attack lasted practically the whole night, with intense gun fire, bombs, tanks, helicopters that evacuated the wounded and finally … They killed a senior officer, they killed a lady right in front of her children, they killed a soldier so they could enter the room, they wounded other people and they kidnapped my father. (Ibarzábal 2009)

Silvia told me that the ERP, which claimed responsibility for her father's kidnapping, demanded a prisoner swap rather than a ransom. As her father was being transported to another "people's prison" within Buenos Aires, the vehicle in which he was travelling was stopped by police and, rather than surrender the prisoner, the guerrilla guarding Ibarzábal shot him (Lewis 2002). Silvia said that once her father's abandoned body was found, they discovered that he had suffered extreme deprivation; at around 34 kg, his body was severely emaciated. The effect on his children was devastating:

> They not only kidnapped him, but they also took away our [her and her brothers' and sisters'] innocence, our adolescence. They took away our youth. (Ibarzábal 2009)

By 1975, the country was in the midst of widespread violence (Lewis 2002). The right-wing death squads, otherwise known as the Alianza Anticomunista Argentina (Argentine Anti-Communist Alliance) or Triple A, used the hunt for left-wing armed guerrillas as a pretext for the round-up of any ideological opponents of the government (Lewis 2002). Under Isabel Perón's leadership, and for the first time in history, the "eradication" of "subversive elements" was officially decreed on 5 February 1975 (Feitlowitz 1998, p. 6). The decree (no. 265) mobilised the armed forces to "execute military operations necessary to neutralize and/or annihilate the actions of subversive elements in the province of Tucumán" (Crenzel 2008a, p. 200, own translation). The role of the armed forces changed, and their intervention was now considered necessary, "saving" the country from its dangerous enemy (Calveiro 2005). Individuals' disappearances, the use of clandestine detention centres, the torture of prisoners and their illegal detention began during this time (Calveiro 2005).

With President Isabel Perón suffering a nervous condition and being increasingly absent from office, the provisional president, Senator Italo Luder, signed the fateful decrees that expanded the army's anti-guerrilla role (Lewis 2002). The decrees extended the military's authority to "annihilate the activities of subversive elements" Argentina-wide (Lewis 2002, p. 119). What the military might make of such powers was hinted at by General Jorge Videla, who would go on to become President: "As many people as necessary must die in Argentina so that the country will again be secure" (cited in Feitlowitz 1998, p. 6). By mid-March 1976, a cloud of anxiety spread across the political, economical and social arenas. It had become urgent for the armed forces to take action and nobody was about to stop them (Calveiro 2005). Between May 1975 and March 1976, there were 4,324 armed guerrilla attacks recorded around the country (Calveiro 2005). Radical leader Ricardo Balbín declared in February 1976, "I don't know if the government is looking for a coup, but it's doing everything possible for there to be one" (cited in Calveiro 2005, p. 47, own translation). In the early hours of 24 March 1976, a new military junta consisting of (General Jorge Rafael) Videla, Admiral Emilio Massera and Air Force Brigadier Olando Agosti assumed power of the nation and issued the legal instruments of the Proceso de Reorganizacón Nacional (Process of National Reorganisation), by which Videla became president (Romero 2006).

2.2 Military Dictatorship, 1976–1983

The newly installed military regime of Videla, Massera and Agosti presented itself as a "noble victim" (Feitlowitz 1998). Adversaries were publicly demonised and deemed "non-persons", without the right to free expression, citizenship or even to exist (Romero 2006, p. 220). At first, exhausted by the violence and pleading for more order, some individuals welcomed the military coup. This included renowned novelist and poet Jorge Luis Borges, who said "now we are governed by gentlemen" (cited in Feitlowitz 1998, p. 6). From that point, the coup was known as "The Gentlemen's Coup" (Feitlowitz 1998, p. 6). Even prominent and respected Argentine journalist Jacobo Timmerman, who had been threatened by the extreme left prior to the military takeover, cited the "'reserve and welcome modesty' of the 'new authorities'" (cited in Feitlowitz 1998, p. 6), and believed that the new government "would bring Argentina the civilized reparation that it deserved" (cited in Feitlowitz 1998, p. 7).

Argentine historian Ludmila da Silva Catela (2009) writes that even some of the families of the *desaparecidos* initially welcomed the coup in 1976, hoping it would put an end to the chaos that had gripped the country. Catela (2009) believes that, over the years, the population had become so accustomed to the military intervening in crumbling governments *a poner orden* (to restore order) that it was thought this coup would be similar. For example, one of the women that I interviewed, Cristina, recalled: "During that time, the newspapers were saying that this [violence] had to be dealt with. They talked of a coup as if it was something traditional in Argentina" (Muro 2009). It was commonly thought that Videla would be able to bring a quick end to the violent battles that had been waged in various parts of the country (Romero 2002). All three junta generals were more than ready to take up that challenge in the name of "Western, Christian civilization" (Feitlowitz 1998, p. 7), believing discipline, obedience and a strong hand were the secret ingredients for doing so (Calveiro 2005).

The leaders of the military junta proved to be masterful orators, and language was a "precious weapon" in their hands; the regime controlled the discourse during its reign through a torrent of speeches, proclamations and interviews that appeared in various media (Feitlowitz 1998, p. 32). Described by Marguerite Feitlowitz (1998, p. 20) as an "echo chamber", the "official rhetoric of the Dirty War drew much of its power from being at once 'comprehensible', incongruous, and disorienting" (Feitlowitz 1998, p. 20).[4] The regime had manipulated language to "shroud in mystery its true actions and intentions", while saying "the opposite of what it meant" (Feitlowitz 1998, p. 20). One of the mothers from Las Madres, René Epelbaum, explains the effect this strategy had on her: "It made you psychotic. We could barely 'read', let alone 'translate' the world around us. And that was exactly what they wanted" (cited in Feitlowitz 1998, p. 20).

The regime consistently denied the existence of the *desaparecidos*, particularly when addressing foreign governments and reporters. Videla was quoted as telling a British journalist in 1977:

> I emphatically deny that there are concentration camps in Argentina, or military establishments in which people are held longer than is absolutely necessary in this … fight against subversion … I live with my family in a military zone and am certain that I don't live in a concentration camp. (cited in Feitlowitz 1998, p. 28)

In the early years of the dictatorship, many in Argentine society were largely unaware of the state's involvement in the disappearance of its civilians. Even when journalist and Montonero Rodolfo Walsh wrote and published a letter to the military junta on the first anniversary of the dictatorship in March 1977, openly denouncing the state's systematic disappearance of individuals, families of the *desaparecidos*

[4] The period of military rule, 1976–1983, has been described using a variety of different terms, each inferring different causes and conditions. The military applied terms such as dirty war, anti-revolutionary war and the fight against subversion. Human rights groups used names for this period such as state terror, repression and military dictatorship. Guerrilla groups talked about this period in terms of a civil war, a war of liberation and an anti-imperialist struggle (Robben 2005a). The term "dirty war" was coined by the military junta to suggest that "dirty" tactics were needed, as distinct from those normally used in warfare, in order to fight a war against an enemy that "remained hidden, fought from ambush, and used terrorist tactics to subvert institutions" (Lewis 2002, p. 2).

believed the disappearances to be the work of para-police or para-military groups, operating independently of the state (Crenzel 2008a).

Some families of the *desaparecidos* found themselves making excuses for the disappearance of their family members. The sister of a *desaparecido,* Eliana, told me:

> At one stage I thought "this can't be happening". I always held the hope that they were living somewhere overseas or that they'd lost their memory [and had forgotten where they lived]. (Carreira 2009)

In fact, many were unaware of the state's involvement until the families of the missing began to meet each other in the halls of government offices when filing for *habeus corpus*, and started to put two and two together (Muro 2009). Though the majority of abductions occurred in front of witnesses, the captivity, torture and murder of the *desaparecidos* were, for the most part, clandestine (Crenzel 2008a). The operations of the armed forces' task groups were covert—so covert that one woman militant I interviewed, whose colleagues were disappearing and who happened to take refuge in an apartment building directly opposite *La Escuela de Mecanica de la Armada* (ESMA), saw no evidence of what went on at the institution during her 2 year stay in hiding there (Boulliet 2009*)*. Until 1978, almost no *desaparecidos* survived the ESMA camp to testify to their clandestine detention there (Feitlowitz 1998). Nenina, whose partner, José, was disappeared in 1977, said:

> I knew that they [colleagues] were being held somewhere but we didn't know about the ESMA ... I didn't see anything. What I did see was the coming and going of trucks loaded with food-stuffs ... I would lie down on the balcony next to the kitchen and I would watch, for anything strange. Everything seemed normal. (Boulliet 2009)

However, after bodies from the "death flights" began washing up on the shores of Uruguay, Videla made an about-turn on the issue of the disappeared. In 1979, on the US television, he admitted that some of the deaths were "excesses" committed by his troops:

> We must accept as a reality that there are missing persons in Argentina. The problem is not in ratifying or denying this reality, but in knowing the reasons why these persons have disappeared. There are several reasons: they have disappeared in order to live clandestinely and to dedicate themselves to subversion; they have disappeared because the subversive organizations have eliminated them as traitors to the cause; they have disappeared because in a shootout with fire and explosions, the corpse was mutilated beyond identification; and I accept that some persons might have disappeared owing to excesses committed by the repression…. (Videla, cited in Feitlowitz 1998, p. 28)

The *desaparecidos* were officially neither alive nor dead, but were, according to General Viola, the military junta's second president (March–December 1981), "absent forever"; their "destiny" was to "vanish" (cited in Feitlowitz 1998: 13). Viola's explanation of what had happened to the thousands of Argentine citizens whisked off the streets during the military dictatorship was both vague and "resoundingly final" (Feitlowitz 1998, p. 49)—even during the 1978 Soccer World Cup in Argentina, when the state was pressured by the world's media for information on reported disappearances, the practice of torture and the revelation of clandestine detention camps. The junta brazenly responded by mobilising those sympathetic to the regime to walk the streets while wearing badges that read "*Los argentinos somos derechos y humanos*" (We Argentines are right, we Argentines are human) (Feitlowitz 1998, p. 36). The signs began to propagate, and appeared in the windows of apartment buildings, on briefcases and handbags, and in the arrivals lounge of Ezeiza International Airport (Feitlowitz 1998). Las Madres de la Plaza de Mayo, who demanded "*aparición con vida*" (bring them (the disappeared) back alive), responded by talking with foreign journalists, who had come to see the mothers *haciendo la ronda* (circling) in La Plaza de Mayo (Boitano 2009). However, as Lita, whose son, Miguel Angel, and daughter, Adriana, were disappeared in 1976 and 1977, respectively, told me:

> We spoke with the journalists who didn't want to believe us. Few of the [Argentine World Cup Soccer team] players believed us either. Very few. We were the madwomen, the madwomen who screamed. (Boitano 2009)

Romero (2002, p. 220) argues that the "military government's propaganda, massive and overwhelming, picked up traditional themes of Argentine political culture and took them to their final, terrible consequences." Though the military junta repeatedly appealed to family values and deployed the concept of the family as central to its ideology, the repression carried out by the state destroyed entire family units (Franco 1992). For the families of the *desaparecidos*, no mother, father, grandparent or child was immune (Franco 1992). The military believed that families, while being the cornerstone of Argentine morality, were also sites of dissidence; this helps explain the severity of their attacks against many families of the *desaparecidos* (Franco 1992). The families became "dangerous" to be around and thus increasingly isolated; close friends learned to stay away and families no longer knew who to trust. Some cut all ties with friends and colleagues, and attempted to blend in with their surroundings. Hoping not to attract the authorities' attention, the families maintained the search for their loved ones and worked to support young families. Cristina told me:

> There were days that, for example, I had to spend in the zoo. He [her husband] left me there in the morning with my oldest son, and I was pregnant, with a bag ready in case I went into labour or if my husband didn't return…if something happened to him. And I stayed all day at the zoo with little money, sitting down, watching who was around, looking at the animals, until the hour that someone came for me, and I could breathe again. Because I never knew if my husband would be able to come back for me or not. I never knew what was going to happen. (Muro 2009)

Despite the growing resilience and courageous actions of Las Madres, the junta skilfully used language to not only cover up its real actions and intentions but to instil guilt, terror and confusion among the population (Feitlowitz 1998). For example, with the aid of media, the Ministry of Education directed a linguistic campaign at parents: "How to Recognize Marxist Infiltration in the Schools" (Feitlowitz 1998, p. 37). The manual informed parents about the sorts of words, such as "dialogue", "exploitation", "structural change", "socialism", "uprising", "rebellion", that would signify that their children were involved in "subversive" activities (Feitlowitz 1998, p. 37). Just as the military apparatus "watched over" parents, it also urged parents to do their part by regularly checking up on their children's homework and extracurricular activities (Feitlowitz 1998, p. 37). Mothers were particularly targeted by the junta's media campaigns, with daily broadcasts on radio and on television asking: "How have you raised your children?" and "Do you know what your children are doing, *right now*?" (Feitlowitz 1998, p. 37). The military alluded to the fact that maybe the "subversive threat to Western, Christian civilization" they feared was the fault of the Argentine mothers (Feitlowitz 1998, p. 38).

In its propaganda campaigns, the military apparatus made it abundantly clear who could be a part of society and who could not (Feitlowitz 1998). The junta encouraged Argentine citizens to denounce individuals whose appearance, actions or presence seemed "inappropriate" (Feitlowitz 1998). In a front-page article of one newspaper at the time, the junta warned that "the people must learn to recognize the 'civilized' man who does not know how to live in society and who in spite of his appearance and behaviour harbors atheist attitudes that leave no space for God" (cited in Feitlowitz 1998, p. 23). Proper identification was to be carried at all times, and Argentine society was given a six-point set of rules for navigating public space, including how to act on approaching military checkpoints (Feitlowitz 1998). So confusing and terrorising were these warnings and rules that it took very little for innocent citizens to be mistakenly targeted or shot at, and taken to one of the military's clandestine camps. As one woman recalls: "You got to a point where you didn't dare to direct your gaze, you were no longer *able* to focus" (cited in Feitlowitz 1998, p. 149).

By perpetuating the "public secret" of disappearance, the junta "simultaneously announced terror's power and normalized the impossibility of living in a constant state of fear" (Gordon 2008, p. 75). Under the regime's protective mantle of official denial and impunity, the public sphere shrank and society was paralysed with fear (Barahona de Brito 2001). The military's official rhetoric worked "to conquer the mental space of Argentine citizens" by turning a " 'normal' setting into a bizarre, and disorienting, theatrical" (Feitlowitz 1998, p. 151). Going about one's normal daily actions such as catching a bus home from work could render one a powerless witness to the violent kidnapping of a passenger mid-journey by armed gangs (Muro 2009). The terror inflicted by the armed forces, explains Feitlowitz (1998), required a setting that was largely undisturbed, for if the setting was radically changed, how could one assimilate what was happening? Feitlowitz (1998, p. 151) also suggests that: "If the missing were eerily present by virtue of their absence, in what sense were those present really *there*? Space was manipulated to make one thing clear: It was strictly forbidden to get one's bearings." What appeared to be normal could easily turn into a deadly spectacle.

Such was the military's power over public opinion that many citizens began to blame the *desaparecidos* for their own disappearance by saying, *por algo sera* ("there must be a reason") or *estaban en algo* ("they had their hands in something") (Feitlowitz 1998). While civilians were eye-witnesses to kidnappings, many were reluctant witnesses, denying what they had seen for the sake of their own safety and that of their families, including those who had been disappeared (Feitlowitz 1998). For example, Eliana told me:

> I mean, we had made two missing persons requests and then my brother, who's a lawyer… they [police] told him not to make any more missing persons files because it would make things worse because it prejudiced her [missing sister's] case. These types of rumours were passing around—don't ask because the danger is that they'll kill them [the disappeared]. Later they killed them anyway, with or without having filed a missing persons case. (Carreira 2009)

Even the Organization of American States (OAS) Human Rights Commission paid a visit to Argentina in September 1978, to verify for itself claims that had been made by exiled Argentines about the armed forces' practice of the systematic disappearance of individuals (Brysk 1994). Its findings were rejected not just by Videla, but by many of the families of the *desaparecidos*, who were unable to believe that their loved ones had been treated in such a way by the state (Crenzel 2008a). The families questioned how survivors could still be alive if the military's plan had been to kill the *desaparecidos* all along (Crenzel 2008a). These survivors were thus accused of having collaborated with the military junta (Crenzel 2008a). However, they rose above these attacks saying, "many disappeared colleagues, thousands, aren't dead bodies, they're alive, permanently abducted, and are probably still being tortured, but they're alive. For this reason, their rescue must be one of the central objectives of our fight" (Crenzel 2008a, p. 43, own translation). Not long after this, Amnesty International also published a document based on the testimonies of survivors Oscar González and Horacio Cid de la Paz, who were kept in various clandestine detention centres where they had seen around 800 *desaparecidos* (Crenzel 2008a). Like the survivors of the ESMA before them, the two men braved not only their own survivor guilt and the trauma of reliving painful memories to describe their detention and torture, but also withstood stigmatisation by the regime and a society that could not and did not wish to hear them (Crenzel 2008a).

2.3 CONADEP and the Trials of the Military Juntas, 1983–1985

Argentine society struggled to re-evaluate the military's actions from a critical perspective following the return to democratic rule (Calveiro 2007). This was due to the regime's monopolisation of the public space and its unrelenting system of intimidation, fear, denial of the clandestine camps, and demonisation of the *desaparecidos* and their families (Calveiro 2007). Survivors and the families of the *desaparecidos* were therefore left to contest the junta's human rights abuses within a society that for years had been indoctrinated by such a proficient propaganda machine that people doubted the veracity of their claims. Having pledged to investigate and legally address the abuses of the military regime, President Raúl Alfonsín was faced with the task of creating a memorial culture that could turn the tables on the junta's imposed silence and manipulation of the truth. He sought to draw a new vision of democracy—one that was based on peace, legality and human rights (Brysk 1994). In his opening speech to the legislature, Alfonsín proclaimed:

"[Today] the government resumes its tradition as the defender of the rule of law and civil liberties" (cited in Brysk 1994, p. 64). Alfonsín's administration needed to impose measures that could counter an 8-year period of the military junta's monopoly on "the truth" in Argentine society. To do this, he had to formulate a plan for delivering to society an account of the full magnitude of the military's violence despite an absence of material evidence, since all documents had been destroyed in the last days of military rule (Barahona de Brito 2001). He was also required to navigate a fragile transition and avoid military rebellion; it was necessary to address calls by the victims of repression, human rights groups and opposition groups for "truth telling" to counteract years of military denial on the one hand, while managing the military and their allies' strong opposition to any "settling of accounts" on the other (Barahona de Brito 2001).

In response to both the call for a truthful reconstruction of the past and claims that the *desaparecidos* were still alive and held captive in secret detention centres, Alfonsín created the Comisión Nacional sobre la Desaparción de Personas (CONADEP), an independent commission set up to investigate the disappearances of individuals carried out under the direction of the military dictatorship in the years 1976–1983. CONADEP's brief was to receive depositions and evidence, and to pass this information on to the courts where responsibility for crimes would be determined (CONADEP 1986). There were some initial misgivings about the Commission's decision to involve the military courts and wariness about the inclusion of some Commission members, owing to their actions during the period of military rule; however, members of key non-governmental organisations turned over their extensive files to the Commission, and individual family members came forward to give their testimony about those who had been disappeared (Crenzel 2008a).[5] The Commission was given a period of 6 months to receive depositions of disappearances, search for abducted children and issue a final report (Crenzel 2008a).

Some months into its investigation, CONADEP made a decision that changed the course of its inquiry: It came to the conclusion that the only way to find out what had happened to the disappeared was to identify those responsible and to bring them to account in a legal setting (Crenzel 2008a). The construction of the truth during the period of military rule thus took on a legal purpose (Crenzel 2008a). Such was the vast volume of testimonies received by the Commission that it needed to extend its timeframe in order to process all the submissions it had received (Crenzel 2008a). By steering the inquiry towards the identification of perpetrators, the Commission's mandate was extended from that of an intermediary, which received accusations, to an officially sanctioned body that served a legal purpose and referred perpetrators to court (Crenzel 2008a).

[5] Ernesto Sábato, one of Argentina's most renowned writers, initially praised President Videla after meeting him. However, he later led the Movement for the Recovery of Disappeared Children (Crenzel 2008a). See Crenzel (2008a, 2008b) for an analysis of the contribution of CONADEP to transitional justice and the construction of "new public truth" in Argentina.

A total of 8,960 testimonies were collected by CONADEP, including those of the families of the disappeared and survivors of the clandestine camps. The Commission travelled extensively throughout the country, taking testimonies from individuals predominantly living in the major centres, but also from those living in remote areas, some of whom were reporting disappearances and torture for the first time since the country's return to democracy (Crenzel 2008a). Those who had been exiled during the military dictatorship returned to Argentina to testify (Hayner 1994). Testimonies were also taken in foreign embassies and consulates for those who remained abroad (Hayner 1994). The fact-finding mission occurred in a climate charged with tension, not only due to the logistical enormity of the task at hand, but also because the Commission brought the extent and nature of crimes committed under the military's leadership into the public sphere for the first time (CONADEP 1986).

The first-hand narratives of human rights violations experienced under military rule were collected by CONADEP and published as *Nunca Más*. *Nunca Más* not only became a bestseller in Argentina, but was also used as the prosecution's key resource in the civilian trials that convicted nine of the military juntas" ex-commanders in 1985 (Feitlowitz 1998). *Nunca Más* became the authoritative text on the military junta's human rights violations committed by the military; it succeeded in constructing a "new public truth" about individuals' disappearances and the abuses that occurred in some of the 560 secret detention centres scattered across Argentina (Crenzel 2008b, p. 174). It also established a clear difference between the insurgent violence of the period 1973–1976 and the disappearance of individuals that occurred from 1976–1983, thereby highlighting the responsibility of the dictatorship for the latter (Crenzel 2008a). The report stated that, "the armed forces responded to the terrorists' crimes with a terrorism far worse than the one they were combating, and after 24 March 1976 they could count on the power and impunity of an absolute state, which they misused to abduct, torture and kill thousands of human beings" (CONADEP 1984, p. 7).

Nunca Más reconstructs, blow-by-blow, the gruesome and harrowing details of how individuals were disappeared at the hands of the infamous *patota* or task groups, and the treatment of survivors inside the clandestine detention centres. Individuals were abducted by around five or six heavily armed men calling themselves *la patota* (the gang), who burst into the homes of suspects (Feitlowitz 1998). Most of the abductions took place during the night or in the early hours of the morning, and usually towards the end of the week so that some time would have passed before the victim's relatives would be able to take action (Feitlowitz 1998). The gangs threatened those they were looking for, their families and any neighbours who stepped out of their doors to intervene (Feitlowitz 1998). More often than not, there were witnesses to these abductions, particularly when they were carried out in workplaces or in the middle of the street (Romero 2002). The abductions of individuals were carried out in coordination with local police units, and were implemented in such a public way that others knew what was happening (CONADEP 1986). Following the abductions of interested persons, *la patota* then took them to one of the 560 clandestine detention centres or *chupaderos* (which literally translates as a place where people were sucked up), scattered around the country (Romero 2002). These secret locations were sometimes located within military installations, such as ESMA and Campo de Mayo, but were also generally found on police grounds (Romero 2002). On entry to the *chupaderos*, prisoners were stripped of their identity and allocated a number that was called when it was their turn to be tortured (CONADEP 1986). Detainees were permanently hooded, and were left without sufficient nutrition and adequate medical care (CONADEP 1986).

The Commission was able to accumulate a vast body of evidence based on the memories of the survivors of the camps. This included detailed evidence of perpetrators and fellow captives still missing, the movements of prisoners from one clandestine centre to another, as well as in-depth, sketched layouts of the secret detention centres; many of these centres had been significantly altered or demolished in an attempted cover-up of the junta's clandestine activities (CONADEP 1986). CONADEP carried out inspections of detention centres with the assistance of former captives who, blindfolded in captivity, were often required to rely on their bodily memories to recreate the layout and infrastructure of the centres as well as identify perpetrators who were still among the employed personnel (Crenzel 2008a). As in other international contexts, this presented an enormous challenge for those survivors who returned to the site of their torture, often coming face to face with those who had inflicted the violence (Crenzel 2008a). Military and police officials attempted to prevent the inspections, and aggressive threats were made to witnesses in an attempt to prevent them from testifying (Crenzel 2008a).

Hundreds of military and police detention centres that had harboured the disappeared around the country were added to the list of already identified larger clandestine detention centres where the majority of the disappeared had been kept, including the ESMA, Campo de Mayo and El Vesubio in Buenos Aires, and La Perla in Córdoba (Crenzel 2008a). Testimonies that were gathered in these detention centres confirmed the movement of the disappeared from one centre to another, and thus proved that the centres had all been part of a systematic plan of the state (Vezzetti 2002). By visiting these newly discovered detention centres, the Commission was able to take testimonies from some of the individuals who had been involved in the disappearances, including on-duty officers and policemen (Crenzel 2008a). This confirmed the existence of the clandestine detention centres and the activities that occurred there (Crenzel 2008a). Other, involuntary witnesses to disappearances emerged to give their testimonies; they included neighbours who had witnessed abductions, doctors and nurses who had assisted pregnant disappeared women while in detention, and morgue workers who had buried dozens of corpses (Crenzel 2008a). CONADEP used the oral testimonies it had gathered to give materiality to the disappearances and to expand on existing information that identified perpetrators (Crenzel 2008a). The work of the Commission became an exercise in public remembrance, or what Argentine sociologist Elizabeth Jelin calls *los trabajos de la memoria* ("labours of memory") that enabled the expansion of knowledge about the military's clandestine activities (Jelin and Kauffman 2002).[6]

[6] Jelin's notion of "labour of memory" refers to the will of those reminiscing over the past as opposed to memories more generally, which happen spontaneously (2002).

Rather than presenting a technical summary of events, the Commission decided the report should instead present a vivid account that included testimonial evidence, photographs and descriptions of illustrative cases to strengthen the report's narrative, to gain greater credibility, and to reach a mass readership (Crenzel 2008a). Most social sectors in Argentina viewed the disappearances with a degree of denial and disbelief; therefore, the Commission needed to present the testimonial evidence as irrefutable, to let the facts convince the reader without any need for interpretation (Crenzel 2008a).

The names of both survivors and perpetrators were included in the testimonies, except where reasonable doubt existed (Crenzel 2008a). As well, rather than reveal their political affiliations, the report presented the disappeared as human beings whose human rights had been grossly violated under the dictatorship (Vezzetti 2002). The report constructed its narrative around a "moral contrast" between the innocent civilians and the oppressive state authorities (Robben 2012, p. 308). Instead, victims were classified according to their social or professional qualifications (e.g. students) as a way of illustrating how the armed forces had targeted certain sectors of society (Crenzel 2008a). In a bid to emphasise the hypocritical nature of a regime that espoused Christian values and purported to protect the family as an institution, the report also highlighted categories of victims, including children, pregnant women, entire family units and the disabled, to illustrate the inhumane nature of the military's actions (Crenzel 2008a). The report—a massive undertaking—was written from the viewpoint of the victims of state violence, and described in detail what had happened to the *desaparecidos* and how it had occurred (Crenzel 2008a).

The text of *Nunca Más* succeeded in achieving three important objectives. First, its narrative tone and the inclusion of vivid, detailed testimonies have ensured its continued relevance to, and role as a legacy for, future generations (Crenzel 2008a). Second, it succeeded in creating a "new public truth" about the crimes that the military government committed during the period 1976–1983, and included strategic information about the repressive techniques and methods adopted by the junta (Crenzel 2008b, p. 173). Lastly, it was adopted as the prosecution's key evidence in the trial against the military juntas, as well as in more recent prosecutions against other perpetrators (Crenzel 2008a). The work of the Commission was crucial in symbolically legitimising the claims of those affected, as well as condemning those who were responsible (Jelin and Kauffman 2002). Most importantly, the report gave a name and a voice to individuals who had been silenced during the dictatorship, and in such a way that their existence could no longer be negated (Jelin and Kauffman 2002). By so doing, it overcame the endemic public secrecy surrounding the fate of the disappeared (Jelin and Kauffman 2002). The result was the establishment of a memory culture that denounced terror and deception, and demanded truth and justice (Sarlo 2005).

Over a number of years, the military had cast all those who had disappeared—whether or not they played a violent or non-violent role—as "subversives", and thus enemies of the state. *Nunca Más* succeeded in re-establishing the humanity of the *desaparecidos* by describing the individuals according to their names, ages, sex and occupations, thus reshaping the identity bestowed upon them by the military dictatorship as guerrillas or terrorists (Crenzel 2008a). Disappeared individuals were presented as innocent victims and as apolitical, so that their political affiliations would not provide public opinion with a basis for justifying the military's violations (Crenzel 2008a).

CONADEP and *Nunca Más* were of great international and historical significance. The efforts of the Commission succeeded in radically influencing the course of international transitional justice. As the director of Human Rights Watch wrote in 1989, Argentina's CONADEP was "the most successful effort of the decade anywhere in Latin America, and perhaps worldwide, to hold accountable those who committed gross abuses of human rights" (cited in Hayner 1994, p. 614). The work of the CONADEP Commission and the *Nunca Más* report were toted as models for nations entering the democratisation process, and became the cornerstone for the creation of subsequent "truth commissions" in neighbouring Latin American countries as well as in those nations further afield, such as South Africa. Locally, the Commission's report shattered the collective silence that had supported the terror during the years of military rule; members of the general population were faced with asking themselves how they could possibly not have known what had been happening around them (Jelin and Kauffman 2002). For the first time, the victims of the military's actions and their families felt their voice was being heard and their testimony validated (Jelin and Kauffman 2002).

During his election campaign, Alfonsín promised that he would prosecute all those responsible for human rights violations during the military dictatorship, including the torturers as well as those who gave the commands (Lewis 2002). True to his word, and despite enduring weeks of bitter debate to make major changes to Argentina's judicial laws, Alfonsín annulled the military's self-amnesty National Pacification Law of April 1983, which it had passed immediately before the transition to democratic rule (Barahona de Brito 2001). This paved the way for the prosecution of the heads of the military juntas by the Supreme Council of the Armed Forces, and "marked not only a change of regime, but a fundamental change in the character of political life" (Brysk 2004, p. 61).

The trials of the junta in 1985 were the first opportunity afforded to the victims of repression and the families of the *desaparecidos* to reveal, in an institutional setting, the harm they had suffered. It is worth mentioning again that since military records were mostly destroyed during the transition to democratic rule, the oral testimony of witnesses played a vital role in constructing historical and legal proof (Jelin and Kaufman 2002). The fact that the courts allowed oral testimony as proof of that which could not be shown meant that the experiences of those individuals who had directly suffered were accepted as legal evidence (Jelin and Kaufman 2002). The power of *Nunca Más*, therefore, lay in its ability to replace legal and bureaucratic documents with legitimate voices that could oppose the symbolic power of the state (Taylor 1997).

Vezzetti (2002, p. 109, own translation) writes of the trials: "Few images have impacted so much on the awareness of a change in the times as that of military senior officers marching in as defendants before the Federal Criminal Court in the city of Buenos Aires." The power of the law was demonstrated ceremoniously and obeyed by those military leaders who, until recently, had enjoyed absolute power (Vezzetti 2002). The trial hearings were intended to break the spirit of triumph and exaltation that had nourished the imagination of the military government (Vezzetti 2002). As there was no proof that the nine military junta members had personally committed specific acts of violence, the prosecution presented evidence to help argue that there had existed a systematic nationwide strategy of illegal detention, torture and disappearances; this approach was designed to prove that the ex-commanders had organised and ordered the kidnappings, torture and killings of individuals (Jelin and Kaufman 2002).

As part of a painful ritual, more than 800 witnesses faced up to court to give oral testimony and identify the perpetrators (Vezzetti 2002). Compelled to relate the horrors they had survived but that others did not, the witnesses reconstructed what had happened as those in the courtroom listened to the first-hand experiences of suffering during the trials of the ex-commanders (Sarlo 2005). The first-hand narratives began to circulate and became indispensable to the public restoration of human rights in Argentine society (Sarlo 2005). Under military rule, the disappeared no longer existed and their human rights were negated; in contrast, the court recognised the victim as a human being who deserved the full protection of the law (Jelin and Kaufman 2002). As one witness stated: "The trial eliminated the spectral nature of the testimonies that were moving around in society … It presented the victims as human beings, giving them equal standing with the rest of humanity" (cited in Jelin and Kaufman 2002, p. 37).

The testimonials that were presented at the trials of the military commanders and detailed in *Nunca Más* broke the military's monopoly on the truth (Brysk 1994). It was widely thought that the stories that were recounted by the witnesses would finally lead to an overhaul of the narrative that had been shaped to fit the needs of the military during the dictatorship years (Brysk 1994). The evidence provided in the testimonials rewrote history by framing the human rights abuses of the past within the legitimacy of democratic justice (Brysk 1994). Brysk (1994, p. 87) argues further that the "reforms inaugurated a new level of institutional legitimacy by submitting the military to equal justice and seeking procedural justice for the losers of an ideological struggle for the first time in Argentine history." Nine Junta members were tried in the Federal Court of Appeals in Buenos Aires in 1985 (Jelin and Kauffman 2002). The trial's aim was to establish whether the rule of law could impose itself on the rule of force (Jelin and Kauffman 2002). Victims became witnesses, repressors became the accused, political actors became the "observers" of the actions of the judges who themselves were "neutral" authorities appointed to define the events according to pre-established legitimate rules (Jelin and Kauffman 2002). After 5 months of hearing testimonial evidence, five of the nine commanders were found guilty (Jelin and Kauffman 2002).

The ethical and moral imperative to remember in Argentina closely resembled Holocaust labours of memory, and the memory of what Hanna Arendt terms "administered massacres" based on witness accounts (Vezzetti 2002, p. 111, own translation). As with the 1961 Eichmann trial in Jerusalem, the trials of the Argentine generals meant the witnesses had become "an embodiment of memory (*un homme-mémoire*), attesting to the past and to the continuing presence of the past" (Wieviorka 2006, p. 391). The "era of testimony" meant that, unlike sober documents, oral testimony was able to provide "a living record of a gigantic human and national disaster" (Hausner, cited in Wieviorka 2006, p. 390). In the case of Argentina, where the extent of the human rights abuses were incomprehensible to the general public because of the deceptive calmness of public life during the dictatorship, testimony played a key role in conveying the individual horror that so many lived through to those who had not personally been touched by the violence. (Robben 2005a) The "truth" about the clandestine and violent actions of the military junta came to be equated above all else, with the testimony of those who were "directly affected" via the narratives of the relatives of the *desaparecidos* (Jelin 2008). Witnesses were now able to reconstruct the past for the listening audience in a way that essentially made the unbelievable accounts they had heard rumours about believable.

2.4 Addressing the Legacy of Military Dictatorship and Guerrilla Violence, 1983–2003

On taking office in 1983, Alfonsín initially attempted to lay the blame for the violence in the early to mid-1970s with both the military and the armed guerrilla movement, by introducing a *dos demonios* or "two demon" theory. He initially sought to draw a moral equivalence between the violence of the military junta and that of the armed guerrilla movement (Vezzetti 2002). Alfonsín claimed that two parties had been responsible for the escalating violence prior to the 1976 military coup (Vezzetti 2002). He consequently sought to submit both the leaders of the armed guerrilla movement and the leaders of the armed forces to simultaneous legal proceedings (Vezzetti 2002). Alfonsín prepared two executive decrees for Congress to ratify—one that required the Supreme Military Council to initiate criminal proceedings against all those who had participated in the junta from the beginning of the coup right up to the appointment of the last military dictator Reynaldo Bignone, and another that ordered the civil courts to begin proceedings against the top leaders of the Montoneros and the ERP for crimes committed after 25 May 1973, the first day of the last civilian-backed government (Lewis 2002). By advocating the *dos demonios* theory, Alfonsín was attempting to fulfil his election promise to prosecute all those who were responsible for human rights violations both in the lead-up to and during the dictatorship (Lewis 2002). By putting both the perpetrators within the military and the armed guerrilla groups on trial, he was also seeking to create the foundations of legitimacy that would secure the continuation of his administration and define a new political identity, distinct from that of the previous military regime (Booth 2006).

Alfonsín was required to manage a delicate balancing act to deter an agitated and unrepentant military from again seizing power in the future (Mallinder 2009). Above all, he wanted to re-establish democracy and to guard its future (Feitlowitz 1998). When Alfonsín was elected, opinion polls indicated that 60 % of Argentines believed the military would soon be politically active once more (Mallinder 2009,

p. 53). Alfonsín made attempts to remove supporters of the junta from the armed forces to prevent this from occurring; at the same time, during the trials, the military was still promoting individuals who had committed abuses during the regime (Feitlowitz 1997).[7]

The *dos demonios* theory, explains anthropologist Antonius Robben (2007), was fiercely criticised by most human rights organisations. They countered that the struggle had instead been between an idealistic, young generation and a repressive military apparatus (Robben 2005). Nonetheless, Congress ratified Decree No. 157, which held the Montonero and ERP leaders criminally responsible for insurrection and violation of the amnesty of May 1973, and Decree No. 158, which held the leaders of the first three juntas—Videla, Viola, Galtieri, Massera, Lambruschini, Anaya, Agosti, Graffigna and Lami-Dozo—accountable for multiple counts of illegal detention, torture and homicide (Robben 2005a).[8] The verdict was announced on 9 December 1985 (Robben 2005a). Videla and Massera were given life sentences, while Graffigna, Galtieri, Anaya, and Lami-Dozo were acquitted (Robben 2005a). Agosti, Lambruschini and Viola were sentenced to four and a half years, 8 years and 17 years in prison, respectively (Robben 2005a). A judicial truth had now been established, and was added to other competing narratives (Robben 2005a). This revived disputes about interpretations of the past, and opposing memory constructions again vied for attention in the public arena (Robben 2005a).

By 1985, more than 2,000 complaints had been made about 650 officers (Robben 2005a). Feeling it had been singled out for prosecution and disconcerted by the sheer number of legal investigations building up against it, the military began to refuse to testify (Robben 2005a). Bomb attacks ensued, and a number of attempts to

[7] In the mid-1990s, Nunca Más was no longer regarded as a legal instrument, after the impunity laws passed by Menem blocked any further trials. Instead, the report became seen as a vehicle for the transmission of memory. Some social groups edited the original report to incorporate their own interpretations of this period of the country's history. Then, in 2006, at the urging of Nestor Kirchner's administration, a new official interpretation of the report was made, with the addition of a new prologue written by the National Secretary of Human Rights (Crenzel 2011). It was critical of the explanation given for the political violence in the original report, stating that it was "unacceptable to attempt to justify State terrorism like a sort of game of counteracting violences, as if it were possible to look for a justifying symmetry in the action of individuals faced with the Nation and the State's estrangement from their proper goals" (CONADEP 2006, own translation). As Crenzel (2011) explains, the new prologue failed to place the political violence in its historical context, and did not establish civil and political responsibilities for the violence. Taking on a social justice tone, the report excluded any mention of guerrilla and political activity from the lives of the disappeared, and talked instead of the human rights movement's thirty-year struggle for "truth, justice, and memory" (Crenzel 2011). The new prologue was met with criticism by former members of CONADEP, including journalist Magdalena Ruiz Guinazú: "It is a grave historical mistake to think that the report was an apology for the theory of the two demons" (cited in Galak 2006). Alfonsín concurred, saying the prologue addition showed "a dangerous tendency to re-invent history that was beginning to alarm Argentines" (cited in Galak 2006).

[8] Decree Law 158 stipulated that prosecution would be extended only to the commanders-in-chief of the armed forces, and not to those who had obeyed orders. Trials were eventually held in the civilian courts after the military courts failed to initiate proceedings in the allotted time period (Barahona de Brito 2001).

destabilise the government began to shake the Alfonsín administration (Mallinder 2009). In December 1986, concerned about the destabilising threat that a status of never-ending trials posed to an already rocky democratisation process, Alfonsín pursued measures to limit the number of prosecutions (Mallinder 2009). He placed a 60-day statute of limitations on criminal complaints against the military officers, which became known as *el Ley de Punto Final* (Final Stop Law) (Mallinder 2009). However, the courts worked tirelessly to process claims, and managed to file charges against 280 officers as well as two former junta leaders, Leopoldo Galtieri and Reynaldo Bignone, who had been acquitted and exempted from the junta trials (Mallinder 2009). Despite this, and much to the chagrin of the human rights organisations that had submitted a vast amount of evidence to the courts, the Under Secretary of Justice publicly stated that those who had not been charged would be "innocents forever" (cited in Mallinder 2009, p. 61).

Relations between the Alfonsín administration and the military became further strained. Despite the government's attempts to limit the prosecutorial strategy, a number of lower-ranking military officers became increasingly anxious about the forthcoming prosecutions (Mallinder 2009). Following internal rifts within the military (with many junior officers losing faith in their superiors, believing they had been made scapegoats, and dissatisfied with the government's policies on the armed forces), a group of officers, who became known as the *Carapintadas*, began a rebellion and launched another wave of bombing attacks and threats against members of the Argentine judiciary (Mallinder 2009).[9] Despite promises that he would not negotiate with the rebels, Alfonsín—faced with the prospect of losing control over the armed forces—introduced the controversial *Obediencia Debida*, or Due Obedience law, in June 1987 (Feitlowitz 1997). This law allowed lower-ranking officials to claim they had been "following orders" (Feitlowitz 1997). Though Alfonsín himself was displeased with having to pass the Bill, he "regarded it as necessary for the survival of Argentina's fragile democracy", for the country was again "on the edge of a civil war" (Mallinder 2009, p. 64).

One human rights publication estimated that 450 pending cases were reduced to fifty following the application of the law (Brysk 1994). As a result, lower-ranking criminals were never charged, and instead kept their jobs in the military and police, as well as in businesses and civilian institutions (Feitlowitz 1998). Outcry came from all corners of the human rights movement. Las Madres put out a statement saying that "those who asked for this amnesty are those who have raped, tortured and killed. We do not want vengeance, but we shall continue seeking justice" (cited in Mallinder 2009, p. 64). A number of sentences were overturned on the basis that the convicted individuals were following orders. Most distressingly for the human rights movement, this included those of some high-profile perpetrators such as Miguel Etchecolatz, who had been sentenced up to 25 years in prison for torturing prisoners (Mallinder 2009). Miguel Etchecolatz was eventually sentenced to life imprisonment in 2006. The case was not without controversy, however. Jorge Julio

[9] The *Carapindadas* (painted faces) refers to an elite group of officers who used camouflage paint to cover their faces as a symbol of their opposition to the army high command (Mallinder 2009).

López, one of the key witnesses in the trial against Etchecolatz, was disappeared and magistrates received threats and intimidation. Despite a high-profile campaign by the human rights movement, López remains disappeared (www.cels.org.ar).

Alfonsín was placed in the difficult position of balancing demands for impunity on the part of the armed forces on the one hand with demands for justice on the part of the survivors of detention facilities, families of the *desaparecidos* and their supporters on the other (Roniger and Sznajder 1999). Ultimately unable to confront the legacy of authoritarianism through institutional channels, Alfonsín set in motion a precedent of impunity that consecutive administrations, though wishing to dissociate themselves from the issue of human rights violations during the period of military rule, have had to deal with time and again (Roniger and Sznajder 1999).

Families continued their fight for full accountability and justice, and against policies of oblivion and forgetting, when Alfonsín's successor, Carlos Menem, assumed office in July 1989. Menem further rolled back prosecutions by extending pardons to all military officials with human rights prosecutions pending, as well as dozens of officers who had been involved in the military rebellions and a handful of former leftist guerrillas, to symbolise that it was "time to turn the page" (Feitlowitz 1998, p. 113). These pardons were also extended to the former junta leaders already convicted of human rights violations (Brysk 1994), thus completing the regressive phase of policies that had been initiated under Alfonsín (Roniger and Sznajder 1999). In a televised broadcast, Menem advised Argentineans to follow the course of national reconciliation and to refrain from attributing significance to the human rights abuses of the military when he said: "Argentina will not be possible if we continue tearing apart the old wounds, if we continue fomenting hatred, distrust among conationals, on the basis of the false grounds of discord" (cited in Roniger and Sznajder 1999, p. 148).

Between the *Carapintada* revolt during the Presidency of Alfonsín and Menem's policy of impunity, the country lapsed into a political stalemate in which two distinct camps of remembrance emerged, "whose views of the recent past were so divergent as to present two irreconcilable histories" (Lewis 2002, p. 241). It was only once Néstor Kirchner came to power in 2003, followed by Cristina Fernandez de Kirchner in 2007, that the claims for recognition of the families of the *desaparecidos* were politically, socially, legally and culturally endorsed. Kirchner sought to distance himself from the corruption of previous administrations, and thus focused on human rights as a result, claiming that he would exercise power "without rancour but with memory" (Rohter 2003b, p. 4).

In May 2003, Kirchner implemented a presidential decree to remove three-quarters of Argentina's highest ranking military officers—a move, it was suggested, to purge the armed forces of human rights violators (Mallinder 2009). Then, in June 2003, Kirchner proclaimed Decree No. 222 to regulate the process for appointing Supreme Court justices (Mallinder 2009). The Supreme Court had lost much of its legitimacy, and was seen as yet another institution that was corrupted by the policies of impunity adopted during the Menem era (Mallinder 2009). Kirchner appointed new members of the court in a procedure that permitted civil society participation (Mallinder 2009). Shortly thereafter, Kirchner signed Decree No. 420

in July 2003, which returned decisions about extradition back to the control of the judiciary (Mallinder 2009).[10]

Then, in August 2003, Kirchner signed the law that declared that *Punto Final* and *Obediencia Debida* laws were null and void, although the pardons given by Menem were left unaffected (Mallinder 2009). The retroactive annulment of the amnesty laws was highly controversial, with lawyers and politicians arguing that Congress had exceeded its powers (Mallinder 2009). The various policies adopted by the consecutive Kirchner administrations have been condemned by those groups that represent victims of the armed guerrilla movement. These groups argue that victims of the armed guerrilla movement have been excluded from the Kirchner government's political memory agendas.

Since Argentina's return to democratic rule in 1983—and in the face of the repeated impunity bestowed on those guilty of human rights violations and the public marginalisation of the issue of human rights abuses—oral testimony has been a major way for both the families of the *desaparecidos* and the victims of the armed guerrilla movement to address a lack of judicial, political and social accountability that has become "undeniably a part of the popular and political *imaginario* (imagination)" (Barahona de Brito 2001, p. 157). Traumatised by each consecutive government's shifts in policies on justice, the families of the *desaparecidos* and the victims of the armed guerrilla groups have poured their frustrations into a continual struggle over the politics of remembering. In the following two chapters, I discuss the different sorts of issues for each group that have arisen from the way in which collective memorial culture was created during the period of re-democratisation. I explore the collective and individual frustrations and tensions that the two groups have experienced in response to successive administrations' policies of remembering and forgetting. I consider political, legal, social and cultural factors that precipitate an "eternal return" to these historical issues, and that shape the current visions and decisions of both groups of women.

[10] Shortly before he resigned in 2001, then President Fernando de la Rúa signed Decree No. 1581, which established a general refusal to petitions from foreign courts, using the argument that local courts should try crimes committed in Argentina (Mallinder 2009).

Chapter 3
Politics of Remembering: The Military Dictatorship and Its Aftermath

3.1 Disappearance and the Politics of Mourning and Melancholia[1]

There has been a long history to reclamation rights in Argentina since the end of military rule. This began with a plurality of mechanisms used by the first democratic government of Alfonsín in 1983 in an attempt to have the magnitude of the issue of the *desaparecidos* recognised (Roniger and Sznajder 1999). It is only since 2003, however, that official recognition of the *desaparecidos* came about when Néstor Kirchner came to power and endorsed new cultural models of collective remembrance and commemoration. For the first time since the early days of the return to democratic rule, the Kirchner government embraced the traditional discourse of human rights by consecrating the idea of memory as a "national duty" (Sosa 2009, p. 251).

Elizabeth Jelin (2003) tells us that political changes and times of transition can give a boost to activities that previously were censored in the public sphere, allowing for a new wave of stories and narratives to emerge. "Such openings", Jelin writes (2003, p. 29), "create a setting for new struggles over the meaning of the past, with a plurality of actors and agents who express a multiplicity of demands and claims." In their role as "memory-crafter" since 2004, the successive Kirchner administrations have created such an opening. They have inscribed a new narrative on society through cultural forms of collective remembrance, and have confronted

[1] Robben (2005b) explains that individuals respond to loss through normal mourning, pathological mourning or melancholia. Normal mourning "unravels the emotional attachment to a deceased person by relegating this relation to the past as remembrance". Pathological mourning "is characterized by reactions such as the inability to accept the death, feeling responsible for it, or displaying aggression towards the deceased person". Melancholia "is a process in which a person does not understand what he or she lost when death or destruction undid the relation; the attachment is not unraveled but incorporated into the person's self, thus leading to a continuous sense of loss and a suicidal depression" (Robben 2005b, p. 126). Mourning and melancholia are not two separate states of bereavement, but form a continuum, according to Robben (2005b). In Argentina, psychological studies have shown that relatives of the missing have displayed a wide array of reactions to enduring loss, ranging from impeded to chronic mourning, from acceptance to denial, and from normal to pathological mourning (Kordon, Edelman y equipo de asistencia psicológica de Madres de Plaza de Mayo 1986 and 2007).

J. Stockwell, *Reframing the Transitional Justice Paradigm*,
Springer Series in Transitional Justice 10, DOI 10.1007/978-3-319-03853-7_3,

the legacy of human rights violations by the armed forces by providing monetary reparations to victims and victims' families, and reclaiming the physical scars of terror held in former sites of repression. The reclamation of sites of repression has meant that the families of the *desaparecidos* have been able to sustain the memory of their loved ones, particularly the thousands whose fate is still unknown. The families have been able to place their painful memories in the bricks and mortar of these traumatic sites, thus claiming their ongoing role as "a living collective memory and ethical collective consciousness" (Roniger and Sznajder 1999, p. 222). Cristina tells me how impacting it was for her to revisit the clandestine detention centre where her husband was last seen alive:

> I managed to go to ESMA because in 2004, they [the navy] gave ESMA back to the human rights organisations, and we could enter and retrace [the steps of our loved ones], and I could go to the place where my husband was kept in isolation, because one of the survivors [of ESMA] who had seen my husband [detained in ESMA], had told me exactly the place [where he was held], and it was so shocking to go up and down the stairs, knowing that that is where he [husband] had gone up and down, where they [military] had punched him, shackled him, attacked, tortured, mistreated [him], desperate and alone…totally alone. The memory that comes to me is the feeling of this final image of his last days alone, mistreated, desperate…who knows…dying with dignity. (Muro 2009)

Following years of being questioned about their individual involvement in armed guerrilla activities, and dealing with consistent institutional denial—particularly under the Menem government—survivors and families finally felt they were being acknowledged under the successive Kirchner governments. Receiving the moral and political recognition of their traumatic memories had initially an enormous impact on all of the female relatives of the *desaparecidos* with whom I talked, particularly partners of the missing. Noemi, whose partner, Eduardo, was disappeared in 1977, told me:

> I'm not going to talk about politics; I'm going to talk about this government. For me the first part of this government [time of Nestor Kirchner]…of its recognition, of its public expression [of talking about the horrors committed by the military], what it did had a sense of repair for me internally that was very important. Not because it particularly touched me; I continue in the same situation, I don't know what happened to my partner; but he publicly said, "this happened and this was how it was", without hiding anything, without bias. What all the governments up until this one have done is to avoid the issue, and to say no, a little bit of the law but a little bit of something else. This for me personally, had a tremendous healing affect…it allowed me to say…it helped me internally. (Ciollaro 2009)

Noemi continued:

> Because for many years, it [lack of recognition] took a lot; where you had to prove who you were all the time; that a lot of other women lived through what you lived through…that your children were legitimate, and not illegitimate until the law was passed that recognised children born out of wedlock. This cost a lot of women, children and families. And still 20 years later people would ask you, "but are you sure you don't know where he is? Are you sure he didn't just run off with another woman?", really crazy stuff. For the children…for the children…it was something symbolic; for the children to see the president of the nation speak about this history, and to speak and teach…because in one form or another, we have always been on the outer of our laws. (Ciollaro 2009)

With the successive Kirchner governments speaking out publicly in support of the victims of the military and the families of the *desaparecidos,* individuals such as Noemi no longer have to face societal doubt about abuses they suffered under military rule. Despite this relatively new-found public and official recognition for survivors and the families, however, questions about the fate and the whereabouts of thousands of missing individuals remain unanswered by those responsible in the armed forces. Through the efforts of Comisión Nacional sobre la Desaparición de Personas (CONADEP), various human rights organisations, and the testimonial narratives of individual survivors of the military's clandestine camps as well as a few perpetrators, we now know a good deal about collective disappearance in Argentina. However, exactly what happened to each and every individual following their abduction by members of the security forces remains a complete mystery for most families. Noemi Ciollaro, who has written about the female partners of the *desaparecidos,* has no knowledge about where the remains of her partner lie. She told me how devastated she was on hearing the story of one woman who knew about her partner's final moments:

> When she told me that friends of her partner told her about his final moments, when they [repressors] took him away, I couldn't write about this testimony because it was too shocking for me that someone could know of the final moments, and where and how...The rest are all disappeared. For some there are clues, for others nothing. For some, dates came out, but only dates, nothing else. It astonishes me that it is so widespread, that they are disappeared, completely disappeared, where you know nothing, not even where they were, nor when, nor how, nor when or how they were killed, nothing. For someone who...was disappeared and then all of a sudden was shot, and you have a body or you find their remains and you can bury them; there's a big difference between one and the other. (Ciollaro 2009)

Despite the political recognition and legitimacy of their memories in the public sphere, the relatives of the *desaparecidos* continue to demand that the military provide a full public disclosure of what happened to their loved ones. No woman I talked with, however, believed that the military would ever break ranks to reveal what really happened to each individual *desaparecido*. Graciela, whose partner was disappeared in the early days of the military dictatorship, told me:

> There are those in this country who stand up against what they [the military] did; they're a minority. We have won respect. We have continued on with the fight...That they [the military] haven't told us where they [remains of loved ones] are, that they're not going to tell us, they haven't told us up until now so I don't think they're going to tell us. It would be fortuitous if we could find archives to help us [know what happened to the bodies], to keep finding information, little bits of information, that build the memory...all this to keep reconstructing [memory], we could possibly recuperate more bodies, remains and identify them. This would be a triumph; to be able to identify everyone that has been found to date. Because I understand, here again I'm putting on my militant hat, that as a mother, to die without knowing where my children are is horrendous. It's terrible. (Lois 2009)

The *desaparecidos* are not lost or vanished, insists Avery Gordon (2008, p. 75), but each—living or dead—"is in a very real place as a result of a real series of decisions taken and implemented by real people. *Someone* does know and, more importantly, is responsible." Aware that someone in the military ranks knows what happened to each individual has been a source of enormous frustration for the searching families. Cristina relayed her frustration:

> What I want is to one day see them [husband's repressors] at trial, and for them to tell me to my face, like they did the day they took my husband away, where he is, what they did to him. (Muro 2009)

The military's systematic disappearance of individuals "disavowed their death as a loss to society, a loss which could not be commemorated by relatives and comrades" (Robben 2005a, p. 269). The families of the missing—many of whom had already been traumatised by the abduction and permanent disappearance of their sons and daughters or husbands and wives—were also traumatised by an inability to bury their loved ones' bodies. Without a body, families of the *desaparecidos* have fixated on keeping their family members' memories alive to prevent the possibility of their disappearance a second time (Richard 2001). For the women I interviewed, to not undergo the daily ritual of publicly remembering their loved ones would be a betrayal of the memory of the 30,000 individuals who disappeared during military rule. Graciela said:

> They [the military] didn't count on us, or they thought that if we lost everything…they didn't count on us keeping memory alive. They never foresaw, I suppose, that we would do everything we have done, from [reclaiming] spaces, monuments to the victims and the recuperation of ESMA. (Lois 2009)

As such, prolonging the memory of the *desaparecidos* has become a matter of upmost importance for those remembering. In giving oral testimony, the continual repetition of the names of disappeared individuals has been one way for the families to "exorcise forgetting from the name invoked", and to use the pain they have felt when remembering those they have lost as a way of giving them back life (Richard 2001, p. 12, own translation). Naming the *desaparecidos* is not just an inducement to fill gaps in historical knowledge; the naming process is a way for the families to remember those who suffered at the hands of the military regime and to fill in what James Booth (2006, p. 115) calls "a morally unacceptable void".

Derrida reminds us that the name persists even when the corporeal body has vanished (cited in Morris in Eng and Kazanijan 2003). He suggests that, "the disjuncture between the name and the thing named contains within itself the very possibility of the thing's memorialization through its name" (cited in Morris in Eng and Kazanijan 2003, p. 33). Never having recovered her husband's bodily remains, Cristina told me how significant it was for her to name her husband in order to keep his memory alive:

> Therefore the trials keep going ahead, they will keep naming the guilty, they will continue to recognise the identity of the disappeared because the first thing they did [the repressors] was take away their names. When they entered the clandestine camps, they de-robed them, covered their eyes so that way they were exposed, stripped bare, and naked. They prohibited the use of their names and gave them a number. So for us, this is what we transmit all the time, we give them back their names. My husband was Juan, he had a life, he had two children, he had a wife, he had dreams, plans, and things, he had a family, he had a mother, brothers and sisters, school friends, neighbourhood friends knew him and could…this is what should never be forgotten, that each of them was a person who had a life…. (Muro 2009)

The *desaparecidos* have lost all social and political identity: no bureaucratic records exist. There can be no funerals; there are no bodies. In the early years of the dictatorship, many *desaparecidos* faced firing squads, and their bodies were dumped in unmarked mass graves (Lewis 2002). These deaths were reported in the daily newspapers at the time as "subversives" being shot in the midst of armed conflict or while trying to escape (Lewis 2002). As time went on and the possibility of reporting deaths as a result of armed combat decreased due to the almost non-existent clashes with the enemy, new ways of dealing with the deceased had to be invented. This included the "death flights" where hooded prisoners who were selected "to fly" were taken to the basement in ESMA, injected with a powerful sedative (sodium pentothal), hauled into waiting trucks and driven to a military airport where they were then loaded on to planes (Feitlowitz 1998). Prisoners were given another shot of the sedative by a doctor onboard, stripped of all their clothing and thrown out to sea (Feitlowitz 1998). Retired navy Captain Adolfo Scilingo, who admitted to participating in two of the weekly "death flights", calculated that during his 2 years at ESMA, over "a hundred Wednesdays, between 1,500 and 2,000 people" were thrown into the Rio de la Plata (Feitlowitz 1998, p. 196).

Gordon (2008, p. 80) tells us that a central aspect of state-sponsored disappearance "is precisely the elaborate suppression and elimination of what conventionally constitutes the proof of someone's whereabouts". The families of the *desaparecidos* continue to live with the military's legacy of suppression and elimination of thousands of individuals. As a result, feelings of anguish and uncertainty about what happened to their loved ones never leave them. According to one relative:

> The disappearance inserts you into a very large and dense fog from which one cannot escape because one assumes rationally the certainty of death, but some hope survives permanently in the unconscious. (cited in Robben 2005a, p. 274)

Even when perpetrators of human rights abuses have confessed to crimes committed in the past, the uncertainty with which the families continue to live means such first-hand accounts have been very difficult to hear. For example, though survivors had told of the death flights to CONADEP and at the 1985 trials of the ex-commanders, it was not until the tenth anniversary of the trial of the ex-commanders, when Navy officer Adolfo Scilingo confessed his direct participation in the death flights in Horacio Verbitsky's book *El Vuelo* (1995), that this crime was accepted as public truth. Scilingo participated in two death flights (Feitlowitz 1998). He testified that death-flight duty was rotated to virtually all naval officers (Feitlowitz 1998). His confession, which appeared in the book *El Vuelo,* became an immediate best seller (Feitlowitz 1998). Following Scilingo's testimony, a handful of other ex-military men directly involved in kidnapping, torture and murder in the clandestine camps came forward with their version of events (Feitlowitz 1998). The emergence of testimonies of others who were complicit in the violence during the period of the military dictatorship became known as "the Scilingo Effect" (Feitlowitz 1998, p. 193).

The mother of seven disappeared family members, Laura Bonaparte, said of Scilingo's confession:

> What Scilingo showed me was that in the deepest recesses of my spirit, I still hoped my children and grandchild were alive. Hope was my secret, even from myself. It was terrible to discover and, I have to admit, terrible to let it go. (cited in Feitlowitz 1998, p. 193)

The recovery of knowledge about what happened to the *desaparecidos,* and making this knowledge public through the giving of oral testimony, have been crucial activities in recovering the past for human rights organisations and families of the *desaparecidos*.[2] For many, what is of upmost importance now is the identification of their loved ones' remains. Graciela told me:

> Reality for me is that today without identifying the remains signifies that everything that the military did wins. Because their [the military's] intention was to make them disappear and to disappear in a way that they couldn't be found, that is…they're nothing. So if one doesn't manage to rescue [their remains], they will have won. (Lois 2009)

The recovery of the remains of the *desaparecidos* has been a contentious issue for many in the human rights movement, to the extent that it contributed to a split within Las Madres organisation in 1986. One group, Las Madres-Linea Fundadora (Founding Line), decided to recuperate and bury the remains of their missing children when found (Lewis 2002). The organisation presents itself as non-hierarchical, and focuses on gathering data, creating memorials and challenging the state to bring to justice those guilty of human rights violations (Lewis 2002). The group is interested in identifying and discovering the particular cause of death for each individual killed during the military dictatorship (Foss and Domenici 2001).

Meanwhile, the other group—La Asociación Madres de Plaza de Mayo, a more hierarchical and radical group led by Hebe de Bonafini as the first and only president (Bouvard 1994)—chose to refuse exhumations of mass graves, thus signalling its refusal to accept the death of its members' children (Lewis 2002). The group emphasises the political and social commitments of the *desaparecidos,* and continues the fight for the truth about what happened (Lewis 2002). It prefers to concentrate on preserving the cultural memory of the actions of the military, and insists that the disappeared should not be considered dead until the fate of each individual is accounted for (Foss and Domenici 2001). To do otherwise, it argues, would be to close the book on the atrocities that occurred that have never been accounted for (Lewis 2002).[3] The group also rejects any economic reparations, saying that "a human life can't be given a monetary value", since "this signifies the burial of the dead" (cited in Lewis 2002, p. 239). However, many of the women with whom I spoke believed the recovery and the process of identifying the remains of their loved ones would assist them in releasing the deep pain that came from years of living with uncertainty. Cristina told me:

> I believe that the theme of human rights and of the disappeared today, for me, is focused on the truth, justice, the trials, and in some ways the work of the anthropologists. For me, this [work of anthropologists] is extremely important. Because what are we left with today? A group of old people that are all going to die. For me, I would like to find the remains of my husband and finish with this, close it, let go of the pain, not because I will forget, because I will never forget, even when they recuperate the remains, because it's a lifetime commitment. (Muro 2009)

---

[2] It is by no means certain that all paper documentation was destroyed. In April 1977, former navy officer Adolfo Scilingo stated that secret files on the disappeared were hidden in a Swiss bank in 1983 by orders of the then commander-in-chief of the navy, Admiral Ruben Franco (Arditti 1999, p. 210). However, no proof of such lists has ever been found.

[3] The two groups of Madres emphasise that they are not opponents. but have different approaches to remembering the *desaparecidos*. Rather than focusing on their differences, the groups have decided to be "in agreement on things that matter" (Foss and Domenici 2001, p. 238).

The women's attention to discovering what happened to the *desaparecidos,* and to being unable to find or refusing to find the bodily remains of their loved ones, has placed them in a state of internal suspension. It has generated a politics of mourning and melancholia that encompasses the individual and the collective, the psychic and the social, and the aesthetic and the political (Morris, in Eng and Kazanijan 2003). As Noemi Ciollaro told me: "This story is without an ending" (Ciollaro 2009). The military "are masters, if not of spirits, then of knowledge about the dead", and it is their possession of such knowledge that makes the names of the *desaparecidos* continue to circulate (Morris, in Eng and Kazanijan 2003, p. 48). The women's insistence on naming the *desaparecidos* until such time as the military confesses to the whereabouts of each individual has furnished a state of melancholia without end.

3.2 The Politics of Identity

During the dictatorship, the Argentine military introduced a new form of human rights abuse in Argentina: the kidnapping of children. During the dictatorship, babies and infants were also kidnapped, along with their parents. In addition, babies who were born in the clandestine detention centres were routinely taken from their kidnapped and illegally incarcerated mothers and given to military families or to those with close military ties. These babies, with forged birth certificates, were thus given whole new identities (Donda 2010). Many of these "babies"—now in their mid to late 30s—are being tracked down by the organisation Las Abuelas de Plaza de Mayo (Grandmothers of the Plaza de Mayo).

One of the women I interviewed, Raquel, works tirelessly as a spokesperson for Las Abuelas. On her son's birthday in 1976, a group of six individuals dressed in civilian clothes came to Raquel's house and asked her son, Andrés, and daughter-in-law, Liliana, who was 4 months pregnant, for a box of books they suspected was stored in the house. When Raquel's daughter-in-law gave them the box of books, they took both her and Raquel's son away and promised to have them returned home within 2 h. Raquel was never to see her son and daughter-in-law again. For 32 years, she has had no news of their fate. She told me:

> I have never known anything, nothing of them…But nothing…nothing. I'm looking for my grandchild who would be by now 32 years old, but all of the grandmothers in general are looking for their grandchildren. We want to know where the remains of our sons and our daughters-in-law or our daughters and sons-in-law are. For this, we will never stop searching. (Marizcurrena 2009)

I spoke with Raquel at the head office of Las Abuelas. Raquel gives oral testimony frequently as one of the spokespersons for the organisation, and throws herself into the daily search for the grandchild she suspects was born in captivity, as well as information regarding the fate of her son and daughter-in-law. Over the years, Las Abuelas has combined moral appeals with information-gathering exercises, and has succeeded in locating hundreds of illicitly taken grandchildren and in legally restoring several dozen to their biological families. Together with the group's awareness-raising activities, and the Kirchner government's change in policy towards the advancement of human rights discourse, doors have opened for the organisation. This has allowed the grandmothers to take more concrete steps to find their missing grandchildren. As of August 2004, over 400 children were recorded as missing (www.abuelas.org.ar). However, the organisation estimates that approximately 500 children were kidnapped. As of April 2011, a total of 103 kidnapped children have been found and reunited with their biological families (www.abuelas.org.ar). Raquel acknowledges the impact the change in government policy has had for the organisation:

> Now, even though I haven't found my grandchild or know where the remains of my son and daughter-in-law are, I am supportive of this government…The government has helped us a lot, in the sense that…because they have joined together many children with their families, small children, that have documentation, while before, in those first months, in those first years, we couldn't get any sort of birth certificate from anybody. But on the contrary, with this government, we ask for birth certificates and they give them to us.
>
> They [the Argentine government] have opened the doors such that we can carry on with our work, to find out what has happened to the young [who were kidnapped], who come [to the office of Las Abuelas] to search for their identity. For the young who come to search for their identity [voluntarily], it's much easier to recover it. (Marizcurrena 2009)

The organisation advocates for the right of appropriated children to know their true identity, and believes that individuals need to know who they are (www.abuelas.org). The legal team of the organisation states that:

> the kidnapping and subsequent cover-up of minors born in captivity and those who disappeared after being born was part of a systematic plan that included murders, tortures, forced disappearances of adults, kidnappings, and other crimes committed by members of the security, police, penitential, and armed forces. (www.abuelas.org)

In its searching over the years, Las Abuelas has faced tremendous legal obstacles. Some judges have advocated that the organisation has not possessed sufficient evidence to prove that the kidnappings were part of a systematic plan by the military authorities, and were not simply a "matter of chance" (www.abuelas.org). The organisation claims that other members of the judiciary have resisted attempts at restitution because they have found that abducted children have been living in "good socio-economic conditions" with those who appropriated them (www.abuelas.org). Through the organisation's participation in the International Convention on the Rights of the Child, Articles 7, 8 and 11—which refer to the right to an identity and are known as the "Argentine clauses"—were included (www.abuelas.org). For Las Abuelas, the process of locating and establishing the identity of the missing children, and reuniting them with their biological families, is not only a matter of justice but is also imperative if Argentina's damaged social equilibrium is ever to be restored; "otherwise, a kind of social insanity will continue" (Arditti 1999, p. 140).

Alejandro Ramiro Gallo—grandchild number 101 to have been found by Las Abuelas—found out only at the age of 32 that his real name was Francisco Madariaga (Martinez 2010). Francisco was raised by his violent "father", who was an intelligence official with the Argentine army (Martinez 2010). Francisco told the media when asked how he knew he was living under a false identity:

> It's difficult to explain, it's like something [knowledge] that you carry inside you. I never thought like the appropriators, or acted like them. It's also got to do with the fact that I didn't look like them and didn't mistreat others in the way they did. It's true when they say that babies who were robbed were a war toy. He ["father"] always treated me like I was the enemy. (cited in www.abuelas.org, own translation)

Francisco's doubts nagged him for many years until he was finally convinced that the people who claimed to be his parents were in fact not. When Francisco finally found out the truth from Las Abuelas, he said: "It's a gift of life when someone tells you your history. One must fight for the truth. Whoever searches, finds" (Martinez 2010). Many of the appropriated children who were located said their feelings of uncertainty about their identity were so great that they were left with no choice but to confront their inner doubts. While some of the children told of their appropriators being aggressive and violent, others spoke of close and loving relationships that they had, and in some cases continue to have, with the "parents" who raised them.

Unlike Francisco, however, not all those who discover their real identities have been happy to do so. Buscarita, whose son, José, and daughter-in-law, Marta, were disappeared in 1978, told me that she finally located her 22-year-old missing granddaughter more than 5 years ago. Her granddaughter, Claudia, refused to take a voluntary test, but was legally obliged by a federal judge sympathetic to the family's case to give DNA. The DNA results revealed a 99.9% match between Claudia and Buscarita's family. Buscarita told me that she knew deep inside that Claudia was her grandchild when she first laid eyes on her. After the judge told Claudia the results of the DNA test, as well as her real name, Buscarita gave her some photos of herself as a baby, as well as some video cassette tapes of Las Abuelas marching in La Plaza de Mayo. Lost for words, Buscarita told her grandchild to take a look at the photos because she and her aunts and uncles had been searching for her for 22 years. According to Buscarita, Claudia responded angrily, saying: "I don't need anything from you" (Roa 2009). Buscarita told me that her son—Claudia's uncle—made various attempts to make contact with Claudia, who was hostile and resistant each time attempts were made. Finally, after many failed attempts to establish contact, Claudia agreed to meet with her biological uncle. During these discussions, Buscarita's son explained to Claudia the work of Las Abuelas, since:

> she had been raised by the military and she wasn't aware [of the work of Las Abuelas]. She was never able to know what was going on around her because the Colonel [her father] would turn off the television or change channels when something would come on about this [the children of the disappeared]. They didn't read newspapers at home either. (Roa 2009)

Buscarita told me that it was not until much later that Claudia could finally be persuaded by her uncle to visit the family home. The relationship was extremely tenuous, Buscarita told me, and had to proceed very slowly; it took Claudia 5 years to reach out and give Buscarita a hug. Not long after finding out about her kidnapping, the truth of Claudia's real identity was confirmed to her within her abductor's home. When the military had ransacked her biological parents' house, they had taken with them family photos that were then given to Claudia's abductors to hang on their wall at home. One of the photos that hung on the wall in her abductor's house was a replica of a photo given to her by Buscarita. When she saw the photo, Claudia finally accepted that she was the daughter of *desaparecidos*. Years later, Claudia admitted that when she saw the photograph of her biological mother breastfeeding her, she held not even the slightest doubt that the photo was of her.

While Las Abuelas treats each located grandchild as its own, the uncertainty and anxiety that accompanies the endless waiting for news of their own biological grandchild can be too much for some women to talk about. This was true for Abuela Raquel. The grandmothers asked to be interviewed together and Abuela Raquel found it particularly difficult to talk too intimately about the pain of her loss. *Abuela* Buscarita explained this to me further:

> When one is missing a grandchild like her [Raquel], you're always with the hope that the grandchild will be found. Because here [in Argentina] strange things happen, so that whether it be morning or night, one of them [grandchildren] can appear, and it could be her [grandchild]. So in this moment, she [Raquel] is suffering a lot inside, but at the same time, still holds a lot of hope. It is this that she cannot…[tell you about]. (Marizcurrena 2009)

The road travelled by members of Las Abuelas to locate their missing grandchildren has certainly been arduous and emotionally taxing. After the return to democratic rule in 1983, the grandmothers were placed in a difficult situation. Although they believed they had located abducted grandchildren through their own investigative efforts and anonymous tips from concerned citizens, they were unable to prove the children's identities in a way that would stand up in a court of law (www.abuelas.org.ar). In conjunction with US scientists, the organisation developed an "index of grand-paternity" that would enable them to discover the biological identity of missing children in the absence of their disappeared parents (www.abuelas.org.ar). The Argentine National Genetic Data Bank (www.abuelas.org.ar) was thus created in 1987. The Data Bank, which has the power to perform analyses without legal intervention, stores DNA samples from family members. These samples can be used to compare with samples of potential grandchildren in order to reunite them with their biological families. In the early days after the return to democratic rule, the Data Bank provided Las Abuelas with the scientific expertise it required to legally prove the real identity of abducted grandchildren (Arditti 1999). When the DNA bank was established, Las Abuelas successfully located and reunited over 50 grandchildren with their biological families—though usually after enduring lengthy and challenging legal battles (Gandsman 2009). Given the Argentine average life expectancy, it is estimated that the kidnapped children of the *desaparecidos* will be able to use the Data Bank until at least the year 2050 (Arditti 1999). At any point in their lives, these grandchildren will be able to be tested.

As the missing grandchildren grew older and custody no longer posed an issue because the children were of legal age, Las Abuelas realised it needed a change of tactic (Gandsman 2009). The new strategy was based on the belief that the missing grandchildren would harbour an almost natural suspicion that the individuals who raised them were not their biological parents, and would thus hold a desire to discover their real origins (Gandsman 2009). Las Abuelas was banking on the notion that fundamental to a person's concern for being "real" is a longing for authenticity (Hartman, cited in Gandsman 2008). Believing the abducted grandchildren would have a longing for authenticity, Las Abuelas launched a very public media campaign and created cultural activities that promoted the theme of identity. For example, the organisation created campaigns such as *Teatro por la Identitdad* (Identity Theatre) and *Tango por la Identitdad* (Tango for Identity) to raise awareness of the issue of abducted children and to urge "those with doubts about their identity" to contact them (www.abuelas.org.ar).[4] The purpose of the organisation's publicity campaigns was to help kidnapped individuals question what they may always have taken for granted, and to actively generate doubt where it did not previously exist (Grandsman 2009).

Las Abuelas has faced a great deal of aggressive resistance over the years from certain sectors within Argentine society. When I spoke with members of the organisation in 2009, they had just participated in a 13-part radio series that included interviews with the grandmothers and relocated children. They had received a number of telephone threats as a result of this broadcast. Raquel told me:

> Before there was a time—now it has calmed down, but in the beginning when we found a grandchild—we would [publicly] announce that we had found a grandchild for example in the morning, and by midday the phone insults would begin. They called us everything. (Marizcurrena 2009)

There have been some contentious cases, including high-profile cases where the suspected children of *desaparecidos* have refused to voluntarily carry out DNA testing. A recent legal case ruled that the twin son and daughter of the owner of the Clarín media group, Marcela and Felipe Noble Herrera, both 34 years of age, were to give DNA samples to the National Genetic Data Bank. The Noble Herrera siblings do not trust the National Genetic Data Bank, however, because it is under the control of the office of the President Cristina Fernandez. Presumably adopted in 1976 by perhaps the richest woman in Argentina, the young heirs to the Clarín media conglomerate have been caught up in a tit-for-tat between their adopted mother and the government of Cristina Fernandez de Kirchner. Clarín has been a staunch critic of the Kirchner administration, focusing on allegations of political corruption, while the government organised a raid by 200 tax inspectors of the Clarín offices in 2009 to investigate the company's books (Goni 2010). No irregularities were found (Goni 2010). Fernandez de Kirchner believes those in the Clarín group are "media generals" who are plotting her overthrow (Goni 2010). In cases such as that described, Las Abuelas has waged controversial legal battles that have obligated the child in question to give their DNA to the National Data Bank and not to the Cuerpo Médico Forense (Medical Forensic Body)—the preferred agency of the abductors for soliciting DNA samples (www.abuelas.org.ar). Las Abuelas accuses the Cuerpo Médico Forense of corrupting DNA evidence by tainting samples (www.abuelas.org.ar).

Argentine right-wing media commentators have criticised Las Abuela's strategy of compulsory DNA testing, drawing parallel connections between the compulsory

[4] *Las Abuela*'s campaigning also involves educating the Argentine public about the important differences between appropriation and adoption of children. The argument made by the political Right—that the abducted children had been well cared and provided for with their appropriators—did not constitute mitigating circumstances, stressed Las Abuelas. The organisation educates the wider public of the damage such thinking could do to a child's psyche and to society as a whole (Arditti1999).

measures adopted by the organisation with those of the military during the dictatorship (Gandsman 2009). While any attempt to draw such moral equivalence between the two entities is entirely offensive, Ari Grandsman (2009) suggests that Las Abuelas has skilfully used the military's tactic of producing uncertainty and doubt among Argentine citizens as a way of generating introspection and self-contemplation in modern-day society. However, this application of uncertainty and doubt is very different from the military's application of these emotions, stresses Grandsman (2009). The military used these emotions as tools of state terror, aimed at paralysing family members from taking any action (Gandsman 2009). Las Abuelas argues that its tactics are based on the notion that missing children have an obligation to know who they are, whether they want to or not: "people need to know who they are", urges the organisation (cited in Gandsman 2009, p. 445). Identity, as used by Las Abuelas, is a task in "making memory" for all Argentine citizens (Gandsman 2009, p. 445).[5] In the organisation's words, "a society needs to define its identity. To construct it is the obligation of everyone" (Gandsman 2009, p. 455).

In the course of its work, Las Abuelas has become "a national reference point" for the violent events experienced by Argentine society during the military dictatorship (Grandsman 2009, p. 443). Its campaigns target young people who have doubts about their identities, but also aim to actively generate doubt within general society (Gandsman 2009). These public campaigns have succeeded in transforming individuals' doubts about their identities into collective doubts about national belonging (Gandsman 2009). "The individual and embodied truths of these individuals (their own 'certainty of knowing who they are')", writes Grandsman (2009, p. 443), "become the foundations for the construction of the country's collective historical truth about the dictatorship. In such a way, children of the disappeared who have recovered their identities are transformed into cultural models for Argentines to follow." What was in the early stages of the organisation's formation a search for biological grandchildren has transformed itself into a search for national belonging (Gandsman 2009).

Ana Maria Mariani believes that the right to an identity belongs not just to the children of the *desaparecidos,* but to every citizen. She writes:

> Who are we? Where do we come from? Where are we going? These three questions will continue being foundational for human beings. If whoever among of [sic] us cannot calmly and truthfully respond to them, then it would be impossible for them to live. (cited in Grandsman 2009, p. 448)

While this statement is a normative rather than an empirical one, according to Grandsman (2009, p. 448), one of moral philosophy's leading contemporary advocates, Harry G. Frankfurt, is of the opinion that "we really cannot live without truth. We need truth not only in order to understand how to live well, but in order to know how to survive at all" (cited in Grandsman 2009, p. 448). Frankfurt argues that truth is intimately related to self-knowledge (cited in Grandsman 2009). If one were to

[5] "Making memory" is a phrase frequently used in Argentina by human rights organisations in reference to truth and collective memory (Jelin 2003). However, while human rights groups talk about the construction of memory in these terms, right-wing groups contest this, accusing the human rights movement of advocating "partial" or "half" memories (Gandsman 2009).

refuse to live with the truth, then it follows that one would also refuse to live with self-knowledge (Frankfurt cited in Grandsman 2009).

In Argentina, the human rights concepts of truth, justice and memory are all built around uncertainty (Grandsman 2009). The grandmothers' identity campaign strives "to turn individuals into self-conscious subjects" by generating an environment for self-reflection and self-contemplation that extends beyond the cases of appropriated grandchild and reaches out to all of Argentine society (Grandsman 2009, p. 461). Through its cultural activities, Las Abuelas make its audiences realise that they too could be children of the disappeared. The publicity materials circulated by Las Abuelas include an important slogan: "If you have doubts about your identity or think that you are a child of the disappeared, get in touch with the *Grandmothers*" (www.abuelas.org). While being the child of a *desaparecido* is confined to a certain sub-set of the population, by including the word "or" in the slogan implies that the doubt promoted by Las Abuelas applies to everyone (Grandsman 2009). This tactic is reflected in all the organisation's cultural activities as Las Abuelas strive to provide a space for the construction of a collective Argentine identity (Grandsman 2009).

Neither Abuela Buscarita nor Abuela Raquel believes the group has as much public support as previously. They told me that they consequently concentrate their educational efforts on Argentina's youth, who they hope will carry on their fight for identity. Raquel expressed her dismay at the public waning of interest in their struggle for memory:

> We have, over time, had a lot of support from the Argentine people and from people coming from overseas as well. The years have passed, and now we don't have as much support as before. People are tired [of hearing about their fight] and there are only a few that support us. (Marizcurrena 2009)

Raquel's observation tells us how the passage of time has shaped both the Abuelas' struggle to recover their missing grandchildren, and societal responses to their raising public awareness of the issue of stolen and falsified identities. Raquel tells me that 33 years on, her children have spent more time disappeared than alive, and that she can still think of nothing else. Fighting for the memory of her son, she says, is something she will do until death; she sees it as the only reason to keep living. The morning I arrive to interview her, Raquel tells me she had been at Las Abuelas' head office in Buenos Aires alone since the early hours. Even when reading the newspaper, her head is full of thoughts of her missing children and grandchild. Raquel says that every day is the same: She comes daily to the office to escape the entrapment of her own thoughts alone at home. She tells me how it feels to live with the uncertainty of not knowing the fate of her grandchild:

> Even though time passes, the wounds never heal themselves totally, especially that of the heart. A wound here [pointing to her arm] heals quickly, but a wound inside here [pointing to her heart] never heals because one's missing a child or a grandchild or someone very loved. It is exhausting because every time the Grandmothers find a child, I think it could be her [grandchild]. So I'm suffering so much inside for my loss but at the same time I hold so much hope [of finding her granddaughter]. (Marizcurrena 2009)

Raquel tells me that repeating her painful story time and again is not an easy thing to do. She believes that the heart condition she has developed is a result of the ritualised repetition of loss she feels when giving oral testimony. Raquel tells me that she gives testimony to fight against collective forgetting of the military's appropriation of babies, and to keep memory alive for future generations. She fears that the organisation's hard-fought gains would be for nothing should the next government take a different approach to collective remembrance:

> We're sometimes preoccupied by what's happening politically because we are living a moment in which we've had a lot of luck with the opening of many things. We've recuperated clandestine centres; we've recuperated places where they tortured our children. We're very afraid that we would lose all this if another government comes to power and they'd leave us with nothing; like has happened before. This is our worry. (Marizcurrena 2009)

Las Abuelas have challenged the endemic silence and denial over what happened to appropriated babies and children by focusing on the politics of memory and on the distortion of the historical record (Arditti 1999). They realise that the first steps in recovering the truth about what happened to their loved ones involve personalising the *desaparecidos* and naming perpetrators (Arditti 1999). By publicly sharing their narratives of loss and hope, and by implementing highly emotive and visual publicity campaigns that personalise the disappeared, name perpetrators and recuperate appropriated children, Las Abuelas continues its fight to keep alive and relevant the issue of justice and accountability within a society that is occupied with other "pressing" matters. The devastating impact the appropriation of a child can have on the level of family disintegration is enormous. According to Las Abuelas, such a violent rupture within the family unit will affect the next three or four generations of Argentine families (Arditti 1999). The legacy left by the work of Las Abuelas, as well as stories told by young individuals who have recovered their true identities, will continue to challenge society's leaning towards historical amnesia, and ensure that the collective memory of the *desaparecidos*—both big and small—will continue to be transmitted for generations to come.

3.3 Witnessing and Justice

Since the return to democratic rule in 1983, various governments' policies of oblivion and impunity have made it possible for countless perpetrators to fly under society's legal radar. Even in cases where prosecutions occurred, perpetrators' connections within the legal power structure, together with lengthy judicial delays, have meant that many of these cases have been dropped (Arditti 1999). In 1994, the Menem government offered financial reparation to the families of those murdered or disappeared during the military dictatorship, which some human rights organisations, including Las Abuelas and Las Madres-Linea Fundadora, accepted (Arditti 1999). While these organisations believed this to be an indication of the government's acknowledgment of the "genocide" perpetrated by the state during the dictatorship, no legal sanctions were planned by the Menem administration for those responsible for the crimes committed (Arditti 1999). As a result, a culture of impunity flourished in Argentina during the decade 1989–1999. The dictatorship's unpunished crimes created an environment in which police violence, a lack of an independent judicial system and government corruption were treated as part of everyday Argentinian life (Arditti 1999). Being part of a society that legitimated crime and denied reality had serious consequences for both individuals and families already suffering from psychosocial trauma. For example, Abuela Raquel told me:

> The justice system has been very unjust with us. For many years we have wanted to know what happened to our children and grandchildren. For many years, the justice system has not allowed us [to find out]. But I don't believe it has just been because of the justice system but also for the bad governments that we have had in the past, that wouldn't allow us to open lawsuits that should have been opened. They would not punish the kidnappers or the assassins of our children. Some of them [kidnappers/assassins] are dying, without telling us what happened [to our children]. So for us, the justice system has been unjust and we have had an opening where we have been able to condemn some of the assassins thanks to the government we have in power. If not [for the current government], none of this would have ever happened. (Marizcurrena 2009)

However, there have been doubts about the kind of punishment the justice system has really meted out to convicted perpetrators. Abuela Raquel continues:

> And now we have trials and they're not even prisoners; they are comfortably living in places that are like country resorts; splendid places where you can go swimming, sports, see a doctor, with everything they need, all the comforts. So what kind of justice is this? (Marizcurrena 2009)

When I ask them how this makes her feel, Raquel responds:

> It makes you feel as if all these years we have been fighting have been for nothing. It makes you feel very bad; it makes you feel very troubled. But unfortunately we can't do anything because during all of these years we have done everything we could, but there is always something up with the justice system. (Marizcurrena 2009)

The military's refusal to accept responsibility for human rights abuses, and the degree of injustice and impunity that the families of the *desaparecidos* have had to face ever since the return to democratic rule in 1983, were emphasised by Graciela:

> He [The Secretary of the United States Embassy] told me about a theory that the military had, various theories, but I remember that he spoke of the pendulum theory. And I asked him, "What is the pendulum theory?" It's time. The pendulum is time. The time passes, people get old, they die and the protest ends. This is what one sector of the military thought. What I believe they haven't taken into account is another thing. It's certain that the mothers [Las Madres de la Plaza de Mayo] will die in time, we will all die, but what they perhaps haven't banked on is that we have triumphed as far as how much the world knows about this theme and that they [the world's citizens] are with us. (Lois 2009)

In talking about those mechanisms that have impeded the development of democracy in Latin America, Uruguayan writer and novelist Eduardo Galeano uses the expression "the kidnapping of history":

> For those who are starving, the system denies them even the nourishment of memory. So that they don't have a future, it steals their past. Official history is told by, for, and of the rich, the white, the male, and the military. (cited in Arditti 1999, p. 162)

In defiance of attempts by political actors to "kidnap history", the families of the *desaparecidos,* survivors of the clandestine detention centres and the human rights movement have continually demanded "truth, memory and justice". These groups have, over a number of decades, used expressive modes of collective action to do so. These include mass mobilisations and consciousness-raising activities to create a "counter hegemonic culture of resistance" to the impunity and public secrecy that continue to surround the clandestine activities of the military apparatus in the years 1976–1983 (Brysk 1994, p. 22).

In particular, the human rights movement has creatively enacted *escraches,* or public "outings", which attempt to expose the identities of torturers and assassins, and to condemn the human rights abuses of those who had benefited from the amnesty laws of previous political administrations. Organised by the group Hijos y Hijas por la Identidad y la Justicia contra el Olvido y el Silencio (HIJOS) (Sons and Daughters for Identity and Justice against Forgetting and Silence), demonstrators surround the house or apartment block where known torturers live. When assembled, the group gives speeches, stages street performances, plays music and, most importantly, distributes flyers that list facts about the individual being *escrachado* ("outed"): a photograph of the known perpetrator, his/her name, address and the role played during the military dictatorship are all listed. The group then "marks" the torturer's residence by painting slogans with red paint on the sidewalks and on the building's outside walls. This acts as a symbol of the blood of those who suffered at their hands (Kaiser 2002). These demonstrations, according to Susan Kaiser (2002, p. 500), represent "a new and dynamic twist in the public challenge to impunity and political amnesia". The group brings back the past in such a visual way that society cannot help but be faced with its failures of administering justice for human rights violations (Kaiser 2002).

In his play *The Maiden and Death,* Ariel Dorfman explores the sorts of dilemmas faced by a population when a government has embraced impunity and policies of forgetting in the name of national reconciliation:

> How can the repressors and the repressed live in the same land, share the same table? How to heal a country that has been traumatized by fear if that same fear continues to do its silent work? And how to reach truth when we have become used to lying? Can we keep the past alive without becoming its prisoners? And can we forget that past without risking its future replication? Is it legitimate to sacrifice truth to assure peace? And what are the consequences for the community if the voices of that past are suppressed? Is it possible that a community should search for justice and equality if the threat of military intervention remains ever present? And, given these circumstances, how can violence be avoided? In what sense are we all responsible in part for the suffering of others, for the great errors that led to such a terrible clash? And perhaps the most tremendous dilemma of all: in what ways should these questions be confronted without destroying the national consensus, which is the basis of any democratic stability? (Dorfman, cited in Roniger and Sznajder 1998, p. 142)

Dorfman's observations highlight some of the long-lasting and wide-ranging problems posed for individuals who were directly affected by the repression and violence of the 1970s and 1980s. In Argentina, fear is still doing its silent work. In a sense, survivors of the military's clandestine torture centres who were made to "live" with their repressors, as well as those whose family members were killed by the armed guerrilla movement, are still required to live among those who committed violent crimes in society.[6] Political prisoners and repressors lived together in some of the clandestine detention centres. For example, the secret detention centre, the ESMA, was "a complex sociospatial universe", writes Robben (2005a, p. 250). The detention centre comprised three floors (Robben 2005a). The first floor housed the officers of the ESMA task group, while the private quarters of the naval officers were located on the second and third floors (Robben 2005a). Prisoners were also kept on these floors, though they were forbidden from entering the officers' private quarters (Robben 2005a). Living in the same building where they worked meant that even during their time off, torturers often sought out the company of the political prisoners: "Both parties seem to feel some need of the other: for the torturer, it is a sense of omnipotence, without which he'd find it hard perhaps to exercise his profession—the torturer needs to be needed by the tortured; whereas the man who's tortured finds in his torturer a human voice, a dialogue for his situation, some partial exercise of his human condition—he asks for pity, to go to the bathroom, for another plate of soup, he asks for the result of a football game" (Timerman 1981, p. 37–38)

Living side by side with the dictatorship's *repressores* (a term ascribed to those who tortured and killed on behalf of the state) has become, over the years in Argentine society, a part of "normal", everyday life. Many *repressores* are free to circulate in public areas, become democratically elected politicians and appear as guests on talk shows. One of the best-known cases of amnesia was the re-election of General Antonio Bussi—a renowned torturer and murder—as governor of the northern Argentine province of Tucumán only 20 years after he had committed crimes against his own people (Rohter 2003a).

Maria told me that she would never know whether she has crossed paths with some of the men who tortured her, since she was continually blindfolded. The odd sensation she has felt on passing someone in the subway or on the street has made her terribly ill at ease, with the knowledge that while she may not recognise former *repressores,* they could well remember her. She worries for the future of her children and grandchildren:

> I'm worried for the youth today; it's a thing that I…I'm really worried; I'm worried about their freedom, their way of thinking but I'm always thinking about the beasts that are still around. (del Socorro Alonso 2009)

---

[6] Political prisoners and repressors lived together in some of the clandestine detention centres. For example, the secret detention centre, the ESMA, was "a complex sociospatial universe", writes Robben (2005a, p. 250). The detention centre comprised three floors. The first floor housed the officers of the ESMA task group, while the private quarters of the naval officers were located on the second and third floors. Prisoners were also kept on these floors, though they were forbidden from entering the officers' private quarters (Robben 2005a). Living in the same building where they worked meant that even during their time off, torturers often sought out the company of the political prisoners: "Both parties seem to feel some need of the other: for the torturer, it is a sense of omnipotence, without which he would find it hard perhaps to exercise his profession—the torturer needs to be needed by the tortured; whereas the man who is tortured finds in his torturer a human voice, a dialogue for his situation, some partial exercise of his human condition—he asks for pity, to go to the bathroom, for another plate of soup, he asks for the result of a football game" (Timerman 1981, p. 37–38).

Since 2010, some 280 judicial trials of those in the military and security forces accused of human rights violations during the dictatorship have commenced. However, many in Argentine society are fearful that these very recent and hard-fought political and judicial gains to bring those accused of human rights abuses to trial could be lost with a change of government. Equally pressing is the sense of injustice the families of the *desaparecidos* continue to feel, which will not magically "disappear" just because of the political and legal gains they have received since 2003. Cristina told me:

> Justice would be that one day my husband would reappear and that he wasn't disappeared, that none of this would have ever happened, because it is not just what happened. It's unjust. But given the circumstances, because this is unreal and could never happen, justice would be that one day the repressors would tell us the truth about what happened. That would be justice. I know that the trials are important because they show society that what we've been saying these last 30 years has been true…For me justice would be that they [the military] tell us publicly everything they did and where the bodies are so we could recover them… So for them [the disappeared] justice is what we do every day; we say their name, their life, their history, so that others may know them, so they know who they were; this is also justice because it is that which they [the military] tried to take away from them. (Muro 2009)

Many of the women with whom I spoke held little faith in a justice system that previously had failed them and that, in their view, continued to accommodate corrupt and biased judges. Having given her oral testimony in court, Maria told me:

> There are judges who are aligned with the dictatorship, so if you have to go and give testimony, you know that the judge is, is a friend of such-and-such; there are judges that get together and later immediately become lawyers for the repressors. (del Socorro Alonso 2009)

She continued:

> There is no motive to kidnap someone and then kill them. It's a crime. Here they [the judges] search everywhere for a reason, you see…. (del Socorro Alonso 2009)

Eliana also confirmed Maria's perception of a corrupt legal system in Argentina:

> It was so coarse, so gross, that it made you realise that the judge was on the take, and this gives you terrible venom. (Carreira 2009)

"Memory is the ultimate form of justice", writes Roger Errera (cited in Booth 2006, p. 117). The family members of the *desaparecidos* act as guardians of memory of state violence and repression as a way of countering corruption within the judicial system. In so doing, they work against the "erosion" of memory caused by not only the passing of time and the nonchalance of a society preoccupied with other pressing concerns, but also by the counterefforts of those trying to forget (Booth 2006, p. 122). Lita told me:

> We say, "Memory, truth and justice"; memory we are making; truth, we don't have; and justice, little by little. All of this makes us very tense. And it has brought discussions, fights among us, and satisfaction. But at the moment it's tough. And apart from this, I believe that…as the [Argentine] people have never really been with us, and there are a lot of people who are not interested and, if they know [about the injustice], they're not concerned about it; I don't think we're the centre of the world. (Boitano 2009)

Through their truth-telling and awareness-raising activities, the women seek a justice that is the "moral inversion of time" (Améry, cited in Booth 2006, p. 117). Jean

Améry's notion of justice as the "moral inversion of time" can be thought of as "the will's resistance to (or revulsion at) the pastness of the past" (Booth 2006, p. 117). By publicly remembering their loved ones, the women call into being those who are no longer present, but call out to be made so; they reclaim and restore the humanity of those individuals whom the military regime attempted to leave in the absences of memory (Booth 2006). Justice cannot repair what was broken, bring back those who are lost or reverse time to return society to the earlier status quo (Booth 2006). However, the women's "labors of memory-justice" are, at their core:

> forms of resistance to the counter-moral course of time, to a force that constantly threatens to erase the events and persons of the past and to wash away whatever traces, whatever footprints in the sand they have left. (Booth 2006, p. 114)

While justice is the "inversion of time" because it is retrospective, it also acts on the past by making it present and thus attempts to overcome the void created by the crime (Booth 2006). Not only does justice cast its light on the past but, by bearing witness and bringing the facts "from their refuge in the past" into the present, it restores the "moral truth" of the past (Booth 2006, p. 115). The women's labours of memory-justice act as a bridge between time past and present; they become a moral response, purging the past of its injustices and restoring justice to the parties—both present and absent (Booth 2006).

Booth believes that the work of memory-justice "keeps alive the passion for revenge and retribution, fuels an inextinguishable resentment, chains the will to the 'it was'" (2006, p. 122). The women with whom I spoke do not hold on to feelings of revenge, but they do maintain a deep resentment towards individuals in the military and security forces. This deep resentment motivates them to give oral testimony despite the emotional pain involved in doing so. Persistence and resentment find their outlet in the endurance of the women's work of memory-justice. These qualities work to address a void that nothing can fill (Booth 2006). Punishing perpetrators and receiving legal and moral recognition for the loss of victims is, for the families of the *desaparecidos,* to see repair insofar as it is possible (Booth 2006). Maria told me:

> This produces a…it's a thing, that is like…it presses on my chest. No? That no…I can't, I can't accept it…I can't accept it. I think I'll die without accepting it. That all these guys and girls aren't here. (del Socorro Alonso 2009)

Memory work guards a sense of moral outrage, which is the core of resentment (Booth 2006). It is this that Booth believes is at the heart of doing justice:

> Justice's revulsion, bound up with its unrelenting memory, is directed not at becoming, at the passage of time, but at the way in which the absences thereby created tend to erase the crime, shelter the perpetrators, and deny the victims their due measure of retribution. The preservative function of memory here is the work of justice against that process of obliteration…. (2006, p. 122)

The memory-justice work carried out by the families of the *desaparecidos* is not an attempt to heal their wounds; in their minds, this would deny justice its due. Instead, the families give oral testimony to ensure that the crimes committed by the military continue to have a "moral reality" within Argentine society (Booth 2006, p. 122). In the face of so much uncertainty, they wish to be at least certain that the truth of what happened to their loved ones does not become separated from the passage of time, acting as a force that exonerates perpetrators (Booth 2006). The women with whom I spoke were committed to publicly naming every single individual disappeared by the military until their own death, to avoid "the winds of forgetting extinguish[ing] the names" and thereby to fulfil their obligation to the dead (Booth 2006, p. 139).

Chapter 4
Politics of Remembering: Armed Guerrilla Violence

4.1 Politics of Recognition

While the testimonial narrative of *Nunca Más,* as well as that heard at the trials of the ex-commanders, established what had happened during the years 1976–1983, it also sent a clear message about that which should be left behind or forgotten (Crenzel 2008a). In what was a new constitutional cycle in Argentina's history from 1983, victims of the armed political movement during the 1973–1976 period were not included in the Comisión Nacional sobre la Desaparición de Personas (CONADEP) report. The right-wing sectors of society therefore challenged the report, alleging that it did not make mention of these crimes (Vezzetti 2002). CONADEP leader Ernesto Sabato was forced to respond to accusations of partiality—of denouncing only one side of the events while remaining silent about the "terrorism" that occurred prior to the military takeover in 1976 (CONADEP 1986). Sabato wrote:

> It was not our task to look into the crimes committed by those terrorists, but simply to investigate the fate of the disappeared, whoever they were, and from whichever side of the violence they came. None of the relatives of the victims of that earlier terror approached us because those people were killed rather than "disappeared" (cited in CONADEP 1986, p. 6).

"In truth", write Argentines Elizabeth Jelin and Susana Kaufman (2002, p. 31), "political and ideological conflict in the early 1970s was extreme in Argentina". While it was not the Commission's central role to investigate the violent activities of the armed guerrilla groups during the period 1973–1976, the omission of the testimonials of their victims meant that certain groups' experiences were not included in what was a new democratic chapter of Argentine history (Crenzel 2008a).[1] According

[1] Other groups' claims were also omitted. The Commission initially received hundreds of reports from family members about disappearances that occurred prior to the military coup in 1976. However, President Alfonsín baulked at investigating the involvement of the Peronists in the disappearances that occurred in the years leading up to the military takeover. The Commission believed that opening up discussions around responsibilities of the political leadership could trigger a series of cross-accusations that would diminish the legitimacy and impact of the report. Fearing a confrontation with the Peronists, and thus the possibility of diverting attention away from creating a smooth transition to democratic rule, CONADEP's leader, Sábato, was intent on clarifying that the Commission's report

J. Stockwell, *Reframing the Transitional Justice Paradigm,*
Springer Series in Transitional Justice 10, DOI 10.1007/978-3-319-03853-7_4,

to Argentine author Hugo Vezzetti (2002), the *Nunca Más* report stood as the first institutional representation of the Alfonsín government's new approach to justice. However, because the report has been so influential and foundational to the creation of a "new public truth" within society (Crenzel 2008a), and has subsequently been used as the principal reference point for memory issues in Argentina, the omission of some groups' experiences has had serious implications for the entrenchment of ideological divisions within cultures of memory. While the report repudiates the political violence in the lead-up to the military coup, it is confined to the prologue, and as such ignores this period of Argentina's past (Crenzel 2008a). While the prologue alludes to the political violence being a result of ideological extremes, it fails to delve into Argentina's national history to provide any historical–political origins for this (Crenzel 2008a).

In the years since the return to democratic rule, family members have made attempts to come to a sense of peace about their memories of a violent past. However, in more recent times the families have rallied together to fight against perceived moves by the current government to remember one side of history while forgetting another. Victoria, whose father, José, was kidnapped and killed in 1974, told me:

> There were more than 21,000 terrorist attacks. And today, the effort required to make some listen and to take this into account is monumental. Because from the government down, the situation is used for political means. So the hurt from 30 years ago comes back to the point that we talk about it every single day in my home (Paz 2009).[2]

She continued:

> What makes a human being act this extremely? I also ask what becomes of a society that ignores these acts, that only looks at one side of history; and of a justice system that does not repair these wounds? (Paz 2009).

The families of individuals kidnapped and killed by the armed guerrilla movement told me they felt ostracised, marginalised and discriminated against as a result of a society that did not recognise their articulations of memory or claims to victimhood within the creation of Argentina's public memorial culture. They told me that their feelings of victimisation had been reignited since the governments of Néstor Kirchner and Cristina Fernández Kirchner took office in 2003 and 2007, respectively. In their view, the consecutive Kirchner administrations began to make the memories of loss and violence of the families of the *desaparecidos* more politically relevant than those of the families of the victims of the armed guerrilla movement. The Kirchners have played a powerful role in the shaping of the judicial memory work by deciding what constitutes a crime, whose injuries will be recognised and how individuals' suffering should be addressed. As Gladys told me:

---

would be a "report" and not a "black book" that only served to out perpetrators (Crenzel 2008a). The title of the report—"*Nunca Más*", or "Never Again"—thus represented a rejection of the dictatorship and a desire to find closure for the historical period being investigated (Jelin 2003).

[2] "During the 1970s, Argentina was torn by terror from both the extreme right and the far left" (CONADEP 1986, p. 6).

> This married couple [Nestor and Cristina Kirchner] opened wounds from the '70s but from only one side. Both of them speak of the 1970s, of human rights and they reward all the subversives. But they don't acknowledge that there was subversion. Yes they talk about repression, but for them subversion didn't exist (Echegoyen 2009).[3]

Both the consecutive Kirchner governments have made attempts to align state policy with the victims of the military dictatorship. For example, since they took office in 2003, the anniversary of the 1976 coup d'etat—24 March—has been transformed into a "National Day of Memory, Truth and Justice" for the families of the *desaparecidos,* and public ritualised expressions of grief have been officially approved and sanctioned (Sosa 2011). The propaganda espoused by the armed forces monopolised the public sphere during the military dictatorship; following the return to democratic rule in 1983, human rights organisations have been able to practically monopolise the public space on 24 March. They have traditionally campaigned on this day to call for institutional answers as to the fate of the *desaparecidos,* and to demand moral and legal recognition of their experiences of state terrorism and repression (Jelin 2003, p. 37). Meanwhile, Vittoria Villaruel—who founded El Centro de Estudios Legales sobre el Terrorismo y sus Victimas (the Centre for Legal Studies of Terrorism and Its Victims) (CELTYV) in 2006 to represent Argentine victims of the armed guerrilla movement—said her organisation had been forbidden from participating in the marches held on 24 March in the capital of Buenos Aires. She said the organisation has been told they did not belong (Villaruel 2009). The organisation instead commemorates the 'victims of guerrilla terrorism' on 5 October each year. They rally in the Plaza San Martín, a square within central Buenos Aires, and organise both civilian and military speakers to address claims of past injustice. The date chosen for the mass demonstration commemorates the victims of the attack of the group, the *Montoneros,* on the 29th Infantry Regiment in the province of Formosa (www.victimasdeargentina.org).

Villaruel also told me that the organisation was refused on-site representation at La Escuela de Mecanica de la Armada (ESMA) in 2007, when it requested inclusion in the site's future plans to carry out memory work on behalf of civilians killed by the armed guerrilla movement. She told me that she delivered a petition to various government bodies when discussions about ESMA's future as a national site of memory took place. In the petition, Villaruel requested access to two office spaces on the premises of the 17-acre site. She presented it to three official bodies: the Argentine government, the Buenos Aires City Council and the organisation El Espacio para la Memoria. The national government never replied to her submission, the local council denied her request, and El Espacio para la Memoria denied access on the grounds that ESMA was a space for remembering the victims of state terrorism.

The Argentine state has defined the purpose for ESMA to teach "present and future generations the irreparable consequences that are brought by substituting the rule of law with the application of violence by those who exercise state power" (cited in Seri 2008, p. 9). El Espacio para la Memoria asserted that it did not consider

[3] "Subversive" (in Spanish, *subversivo*) is the term that the political Right gives to describe *los desaparecidos*.

individuals affiliated with Villaruel's organisation to be victims of state violence. However, Villaruel countered: "If it's going to be a museum of memory, it needs to include all innocent victim, including those victims of the armed guerrilla groups" (Villaruel 2009). Villaruel claimed that in modern-day Argentina, some victims were valued more highly than others by the government. She said she believed that, for the members of CELTYV, the sense of societal alienation had been made even worse when those who had absolutely nothing to do with the conflict of the 1970s were treated as non-entities: "How can a bomb that killed twenty-four innocent victims not be considered a crime against humanity?" she asked (Villaruel 2009).[4]

In talking with Lorenza, I gained a clear sense of the societal alienation about which Villaruel was talking. Lorenza told me of her struggle to find a reason to keep on living because the sadness and the sense of loss she experienced on a daily basis were overwhelming. She told me that the memory of seeing her only daughter, 19-year-old Laura, critically wounded by a car bomb that exploded outside the gates of her university in 1975 never leaves her:

> We all went to the hospital with the hope that it wasn't serious … We waited until the doctors came out. I think the operation on her head lasted about four hours … The doctors came out and talked with my husband and my husband said to me, "I have to tell you that Laura's gone." We wanted to take her with us but they wouldn't let us … her head was completely blown to shreds. When she [Laura] was in the coffin, her head was completely bandaged, she looked like a mummy. Can you imagine the damage that was done to her head? (Ferrari 2009).

Lorenza told me that the struggle she has faced to live with such traumatic memories has been compounded by a sense of "imposed oblivion" (Passerini 2003, p. 247) and a never-ending struggle for the moral and legal recognition of her memories in the public sphere. Being forgotten, she told me, only increased her pain and sense of denigration. Lorenza continued:

> Right now is when I feel saddest, I feel forgotten, I feel … not forgotten really because I don't want anyone to remember me but I feel … discriminated … I'm not saying that others' pain should be ignored but they [government] are ignoring mine [pain] completely, completely (Ferrari 2009).

Michael Pollak (1989) suggests that when nation-states propel one version of history into the public sphere of remembrance, "they are more or less conscious efforts to define and reinforce feelings of belonging that aim to maintain social cohesion and defend symbolic borders" and to also "provide reference points for framing the memories of groups" (cited in Jelin 2003, p. 27). Rather than playing a role in expanding social patterns of recognition, the current government's political approach to collective remembrance of the period of political violence during the 1970s has possibly contributed to the social and cultural conditions that foster feelings of marginalisation, ostracism, resistance and anger among the families of victims of the

[4] The National Chamber of Criminal Appeal declared that crimes committed by armed guerrilla organisations during the dictatorship did not qualify as crimes against humanity, citing that "what distinguishes crimes against humanity is a crime committed by a government or quasi-governmental organisation against groups of civilians under its jurisdiction and control" (*Pagina 12* 2011).

armed guerrilla resistance. Lorenza and others believe the combined actions of political and societal interest groups have created a scenario of competitive remembering and victimhood by making distinctions between different groups' histories of victimisation within the public sphere. Gladys told me that the sense of victimisation felt both by her and other families has been amplified in recent years because the state has promoted the remembrance of one version of history over another. She described the impact this has had on her:

> I was peaceful, having overcome the pain and everything. But when this government came [into power], it all came alive again, not hatred but it makes me angry to think that they've emphasised one part while they talk about the 1970s. They're the only ones to have rewarded the guerrillas, the only ones to have rewarded them (Echegoyen 2009).

Like all narratives, according to Jelin (2003), political attempts to promote certain narratives and exclude others are selective, and often emphasise the heroic actions of some while silencing others. This means, however, that along the way the errors of those heroes are sidelined (Jelin 2003). Following the publication of *Nunca Más,* the human rights movement worked tirelessly to recover the past by reclaiming the identity of the *desaparecidos* as citizens (Brysk 1994). As a result, the *desaparecidos* gradually assumed the identity of innocent victims within Argentine memory debates (Calveiro 2007). One way in which they did this was by printing an eight-page newspaper supplement on the eve of the 1983 transition elections, which resembled pages from a voter roll (Brysk 1994). It listed thousands of names of the *desaparecidos,* under the caption "WHERE WILL THE DISAPPEARED VOTE?" (Brysk 1994, p. 127). The human rights movement refused to distinguish among classes of victims, including whether or not they had been engaged in violent or non-violent activism (Brysk 1994). It was only once the Kirchner administrations came to power and bestowed moral and legal recognition on the *desaparecidos,* and the full blame for the violence of the 1970s and 1980s solely with the state, that narratives about the actions of the armed guerrilla militancy began to emerge (Calveiro, in Lorenzano et al. 2007). "It was not by chance that precisely when society was able to assume legal reparation and financial support [for the victims of the military], between 1998 and 1999, that a militant memory could also emerge", writes ESMA survivor and Argentine writer Pilar Calveiro (in Lorenzano et al. 2007, p. 56, own translation).

Once this "new memory" emerged, active militants began to reappear—the same ones who previously had denounced the violence of the state, though themselves having committed violent actions when with the armed guerrilla movement (Calveiro, in Lorenzano et al. 2007). In 1997, Las Madres de Plaza de Mayo-Linea Fundadora organised an exhibition, *Esposición por la identidad del detenido-desaparecido,* which publicly explored the personal identities of the *desaparecidos* (da Silva Catela 2009). The exhibition, held in various locations throughout Argentina, depicted intimate information about the *desaparecidos* as well as those who had been detained by the military (da Silva Catela 2009). The aim of the exhibition was to reveal the personal characteristics of lives that were violently interrupted by the military dictatorship during the period 1976–1983 (da Silva Catela 2009).

It was hoped that such an exhibition would attract the attention of young people, some of whom might be the children of the disappeared and might recognise their true identity within the pictorial depictions of their parents (da Silva Catela 2009). Photographs, letters, birth certificates, personal objects and details of individuals' political affiliations were all on show (da Silva Catela 2009). As Argentine scholar Ludmila da Silva Catela (2009) explains, the exhibition threw up questions about which aspects of the lives of the *desaparecidos* the families wished to show and the kind of truth they were searching to transmit.

Due in large part to these exhibitions, the *desaparecidos* became predominantly identified publicly as "*militantes populares*" or popular militants (da Silva Catela 2009, p. 232). The reappearance of the militant figure as part of social memory signalled the recuperation of a memory more political and, in a sense, more loyal to the actions of the insurgents and those of the state (da Silva Catela 2009). Little by little, memories of militancy within the political–military organisations that were active prior to the military dictatorship began to come to light (Tello Weiss 2006). This broke the silence around the activities of the armed guerrilla movement that had prevailed since the publication of *Nunca Más* (Tello Weiss 2006).

Slowly but surely, one of the most controversial and least discussed aspects of the period of political and state violence began to be discussed publicly by the militants themselves. Written *testimonios* of former guerrilla members began to appear on bookshelves, and documentary films were released depicting the heroic actions of individuals who fought against the military apparatus. *El Centro de Estudios Legales sobre el Terrorismo y sus Victimas* (CELTYV) recently decided to reopen a case against the armed guerrilla group, the Montoneros, based on testimonials included in a book written by Montonero Juan Gasparini. In the book titled *David Graiver: El banquero de los Montoneros,* Gasparini (2007) writes that Mercedes Benz paid \$ 4 million to secure the release of one of its executives, Heinrich Franz Metz, who had been kidnapped by the Montoneros in 1975 (CELTYV 2012). He also admits to knowing about the sum of \$ 60 million demanded by the group for the release of another high-profile capture of two brothers, Juan and Jorge Born, who were heirs to an Argentine multinational corporation, and the deposit of this money in a US bank account (CELTYV 2012).

In 2004, a periodical titled *Lucha Armada* (Armed Conflict) sought to bring the armed guerrilla past out into the open, and to renew discussion around the relationship between politics and violence (Calveiro 2007). The first edition's editorial asserted that:

> the experience of the armed conflict is still waiting for its historical re-evaluation from a critical perspective, in which its rich political wealth might be broached without prejudice. It stands out instead a clear tendency towards a self-legitimising history … The lack of a critical perspective imposed a mould where justification substituted the analysis of the circulation of ideas (*Lucha Armada*, cited in Calveiro 2007, p. 56, own translation).

Calveiro (2007) believes a memory that functions in a political sphere should be analysed from its political coordinates. She argues that the disappearance and elimination of many of the main protagonists, and their public identification as innocent civilians, has resulted in the idealisation of those *desaparecidos* who were involved in armed conflict (Calveiro 2007). Films and speeches delivered by the human rights organisations began to shift the identity focus of the *desaparecidos* from one of "victims" to one of "revolutionary heroes" who died in the struggle for a better world (Calveiro 2007, p. 57, own translation). For example, a documentary drama was made in 2008 about the life and death of prominent Montonero leader Norma Arrostito, who was sought by the armed forces for her role in the kidnapping and killing of Army General Aramburu, a former de facto president of Argentina. Even the slogan adopted by the organisation HIJOS (children of the *desaparecidos*) reads, "*Reivindicamos la lucha revolucionaria de nuestro padres y sus compañeros*" (We vindicate the revolutionary fight of our parents and their comrades) (Calveiro 2007, p. 57, own translation).

This scenario, Calveiro (2007) argues further, has been convenient for some of the survivors of the armed guerrilla movement. She believes it has freed them from assuming responsibility for the political violence in the lead-up to the 1976 military coup (Calveiro 2007). Such a shift in the public remembrance of the *desaparecidos* and the glorification of their violent pasts in popular culture has infuriated the families of the victims of the armed guerrilla movement. Beatriz Sarlo (2005) writes that survivor testimonies must not become untouchable, encased and crystallised in the past. This, she notes, risks sidelining other important and pertinent narratives that do not fall within the relevant timeframe, but again offer the only way of accounting for crimes that occurred in the lead-up to the dictatorship (Sarlo 2005). Gladys, feeling sidelined by a government which has ignored crimes committed by the armed guerrilla movement, and which has instead rewarded them with financial and legal reparation, told me:

> They have never given me a peso. I'm not interested [in compensation] but then I see that they've paid a fortune to the other side, to those who were in the ESMA and had been guerrillas who killed a number of officials, civilians, workers … but this has intensified the anger I feel … What is one meant to do in front of so much power? (Echegoyen 2009).

Gladys and others described experiencing feelings of social rejection because they felt excluded from the right to moral and legal redress within Argentine society. Despite being fully fledged participative members of society, the women were confused and angry about why their individual claims to victimhood were continually treated with suspicion by society, and ignored and denied by the state apparatus, particularly when those on the political Left were admitting so publicly to their violent past. Victoria questioned:

> I wanted to know why … I wanted to understand how a person could enact such cruelty. In the case of my father, it was a despicable act because it was an attack of 19 people on an unarmed civilian. What happens when a human being arrives at such an extreme? And I've been asking myself what happens to a society, which refuses to acknowledge these acts? I feel such pain because I cannot understand the actions of human beings. We have lost so many people during these years in Argentina. To me, this is such a lack of humanity … at such a deep level (Paz 2009).

Victoria's questioning of a society that refuses to acknowledge past violent acts points to a need to explore the "moral" dimensions to historical struggles (Honneth 1995). Honneth describes a "good society" as one in which individuals have the opportunity for "full self-realization", and in which:

> common values would match the concerns of individuals in such a way that no member of the society would be denied the opportunity to earn esteem for his or her contribution to the common good (1995, p. xvii).

The women with whom I spoke perceive that their memories of violence have been excluded from political and societal representations of past violence; this has generated negative emotional reactions including poor self-confidence and self-esteem. Honneth (1995, p. xviii) tells us that, "in pluralistic and mobile societies, it is difficult to maintain self-esteem in the face of systematic denigration from outside one's subculture." He (1995) stresses that every civilian in a society is owed recognition of and respect for his/her status as an agent capable of acting on the basis of reasons, as the autonomous author of the political and moral laws to which he or she is subject. He warns that we miss the "moral grammar" of conflicts if we fail to see that claims to recognition can only be met through greater inclusion (Honneth 1995).

Almost all contemporary theories of identity are based on the notion of recognition (Oliver 2001). Generally, the term "recognition" is understood to mean a sense of ourselves as active agents—or, in other words, our individual identity, which we develop through the recognition we gain from others (Oliver 2001). Honneth expands upon the link between an individual's self-esteem and the gaining of recognition from another:

> [T]he reproduction of social life is governed by the imperative of mutual recognition, because one can develop a practical relation-to-self only when one has learned to view oneself, from the normative perspective of one's partners in interaction, as their social addressee (1995, p. 92).

Lorenza told me that she feels herself "coming undone" in her social interactions with others, as she fails to gain a sense of mutual recognition of her memories of her daughter, Laura. She told me of the difficulties she encountered to maintain her self-esteem in the face of the social devaluation of her memories of trauma:

> With the passing of the years, I keep going, seeing things every day, listening every day to so much injustice. I am coming undone and I don't want … I don't want to lose the will to resist, to fight, to hope. One day, someone has to explain this torment because if not, I'll go completely crazy (Ferrari 2009).

Honneth (1995) argues that human beings are constitutively dependent on the experience of recognition, and that in order to maintain a positive relationship with the self, one requires the intersubjective recognition of one's experiences and accomplishments. Honneth (1995) advocates that individuals see themselves as autonomous only when they perceive a positive relationship with others; it is only after feeling they have earned another's trust and respect that individuals can trust and respect themselves as autonomous agents.

In having their claims of social recognition ignored, the women with whom I spoke have used the sense of injustice this brings and channelled it as a force for political resistance. Configuring feelings of injustice into a force for resistance is further explored by Honneth:

> For each of the negative emotional reactions that accompany the experience of having one's claims to recognition disregarded holds out the possibility that the injustice done to one will cognitively disclose itself and become a motive for political resistance (1995, p. 138).

Silvia told me that she had channelled her feelings of frustration into a fight to have her father's memory legitimated in the public sphere of remembering:

> As I told you before, we're also living in a special situation in this country where all of these things have come afloat again and they [the government] deny us the victims of terrorism [the right to talk about the deceased], so, I have started to work with some people in an attempt to be heard and to have our stories known because well, those who are younger than forty have no idea about what happened, so … To attempt to make our story known has a sense of reparation because what will make me feel good or better is that my father—I'm searching for moral reparation—is that he takes the place in history that he deserves, and that he isn't just counted as another dead, but that he takes his place in history that he deserves (Ibarzábal 2009).

The sense that her father's memory has been marginalised within society has been a strong impetus for Silvia's own public articulation of her personal, traumatic memories. Compelled to talk about her painful and traumatic experiences in the public sphere as a way of breaking the collective silence over the actions of the armed guerrilla movement, Silvia has stepped out of the refuge of her personal memories and has embraced a form of open resistance (Scott, cited in Jelin 2003). Despite doing this, Silvia continues to feel as though she is a second-class citizen in Argentine society. She does not perceive that her memories are afforded the same level of respect as that of other victim groups in the public sphere. What Silvia is experiencing is further explained by Honneth:

> What is specific to such forms of disrespect, as exemplified by the denial of rights or by social ostracism, thus lies not just in the forcible restriction of personal autonomy but also in the combination with the feeling of not enjoying the status of a full-fledged partner to interaction, equally endowed with moral rights. (1995, p. 133).

Lorenza tells me how she does not feel she is "equally endowed with moral rights" in Argentine society:

> When I have the opportunity, when I see there's an injustice, then I will talk about my pain. I won't go—for this I say I'm not the type to go out waving a flag or being political—but if someone asks me, or if I hear something, without offending anyone, I will defend mine [story]. I don't know if I've explained myself. You can have a deep sorrow and I will respect that but you need to listen to mine too. I believe that I'm in my rights, no? (Ferrari 2009).

Because she feels her rights/claims are denied a hearing within the public sphere, Lorenza's intersubjective expectation to be recognised as an equal citizen fails, and her sense of self-respect diminishes. Honneth assumes that recognition is something that others confer on an individual for that individual to gain a sense of self-respect. However, Kelly Oliver (2001) argues that we need to go further and ask, "Who is the individual in the first place that has this intersubjective view of the oppressor and the oppressed?" We need to go beyond addressing only the symptoms of a deficiency of self-respect, argues Oliver (2001), and instead go deeper into the causes behind such feelings. The need to demand recognition of one's memories from the dominant group within memorial culture could be seen as a symptom of the pathology of oppression, whereby feelings of oppression create the need for recognition in the first place (Oliver 2001).

Oliver (2001) builds upon Frantz Fanon's work on understanding recognition among colonised and oppressed people. Fanon examines the way white domination creates a paradox of identity for the black or colonised population, which as a result sees itself as inferior and evil (in Oliver 2001). This struggle for recognition by the oppressed population, Fanon suggests, creates a scenario of dehumanisation (in Oliver 2001). Feelings of dehumanisation can then create an overwhelming desire for recognition from the dominant culture (in Oliver 2001). This process, however, only reinforces the place of dominance of the oppressor and the subordination of the oppressed within society (Oliver 2001). Fanon's theory can help understand Lorenza's narrative as she describes how any interaction she has had with the Kirchner government in recent years has only compounded her sense of abandonment and invisibility, not only as a victim of violence but also as a citizen of Argentina. Lorenza told me that she sent three letters to the President of Argentina, asking for an explanation about what had happened to her daughter, Laura. She received no reply but, many months later, was deeply confused when she was sent a card from the President wishing her a "Happy New Year." She told me:

> The president won't talk with me—Dr Kirchner, to whom I sent three letters, and she never replied to me. If I'm not mistaken, I know that when letters arrive [to government offices] they are archived in a computer together with [the person's] address, first name and surname. Once they mistakenly sent me a new year's card. It was addressed to me. So I say to myself, they have a heart. So I sent another letter explaining once again what happened to her [Laura] and they didn't answer. I sent another three letters, if I'm not mistaken, and they never replied (Ferrari 2009).

Lorenza reveals the extent to which she is locked psychically into the dependence on the state for recognition of her traumatic memories. She continues:

> I have never received an explanation [of who killed Laura]. I can never receive an explanation when there's so much silence and so much forgetfulness. The pain I feel is already bad enough but this is what makes my pain so much worse. Completely … Terror touched me. And this, I don't know, is abandoning someone, really abandoning someone (Ferrari 2009).

Vittoria Villaruel from CELTYV stressed that the organisation had initiated thousands of lawsuits over recent years. Many of the families feel they have been denied justice because the state, though having an obligation to investigate the claims, has refused to do so. Lorenza concurs:

> In recent years [I feel the injustice] a lot more. Before there was always a little hope, that there would be more justice. That is to say that … But now, I despair that there could ever be justice. Today, and today more than yesterday, and for certain tomorrow more than today, I ask for justice. I want to know why … For me, every day, when I hear the difference that is being made between the dead, it's like being stabbed [in my heart]. It's like being stabbed because it's another foot that is pushing Laura into the ground … Justice is blindfolded. Justice is blind [in Argentina] because it doesn't see that which it should (Ferrari 2009).

Who is entitled to considerations of justice is a present-day concern, according to *Scales of Justice* author Nancy Fraser (2009). Fraser describes such present-day debates about justice as having a "freewheeling character", and believes that presuppositions about justice lack any form of structured shape of normal discourse (Fraser 2009, p. 49). Within a "normal" understanding of justice, whoever belongs to the citizenry of a bounded polity can expect and deserve equal consideration in judicial matters; however, Fraser (2009) notes that within the case of "abnormal" justice, three principal nodes are missing. First, there is an absence of a shared view of the "what" of justice—in other words, how justice is conceived: "Where one party perceives distributive injustice, another sees status hierarchy, and still another political domination. Thus, even those who agree that the status quo is unjust disagree as to how to describe it" (Fraser 2009, p. 53).

The second node that is absent in "abnormal" justice is a shared understanding of the "who" of justice—in other words, whose claims and needs deserve consideration (Fraser 2009). And third, a scenario of "abnormality" reflects a lack of shared understanding of the "how" of justice. Fraser (2009) describes further that the "how" of justice is the criteria one uses to resolve disputes about the "what" and the "who". While Fraser discusses the positive side of "abnormal" justice, insofar as it expands the possibilities for contesting injustice, she also tells us about its negative sides. First, since expanded contestation cannot overcome injustice alone, a stable framework needs to be in place within which judicial claims can be equitably vetted; and second, institutionalised agencies and a means of redress are needed (Fraser 2009). In the case of Argentina, while current political circumstances are such that the levels of contestation have been expanded by the families of the victims of the armed guerrilla movement, there is no means for them to corroborate and redress the injustices they face. Victoria discusses present-day notions of justice in Argentina:

> This is not just an ideological conflict. It seems to me that it is a conflict that goes further than that of ideology … I think it goes deeper than that in that, are we agreed that the system in which we are going to discuss our ideologies is a democratic system or not? To me, it seems that the word "democracy" is used for methods that are very anti-democratic. That in some way, I see these methods related to those methods used in the '70s and '80s where justice was metered out by whoever had the most power at the time and that justice wasn't based in an institution of the Republic (Paz 2009).

Victoria perceives that the present-day Argentine public sphere has failed to perform its democratic function. She does not believe the public sphere is open to everyone potentially affected by the period of political and state violence. Nor does she think it is currently one that generates legitimate public opinion which is in the interest of all concerned. The struggle for the families of the victims of the armed guerrilla groups to be part of a larger memorial picture within Argentina comes from a need "to be accepted as normal or natural rather than different and therefore abnormal" (Oliver 2001, p. 154). Lorenza described feeling like she is forced to exist on the edge of society, in a no man's land, because her daughter Laura, who was apolitical, was in the wrong place at the wrong time when a car bomb that was planted by the armed guerrilla movement exploded. She told me: "These were political ideas that weren't mine, that weren't of my family, that weren't of Laura. And we were victims of these political ideas" (Ferrari 2009).

Lorenza told me she has sought support from CELTYV, not because she has ever been affiliated in any way with the political Right, but because her daughter was killed in an attack by the armed guerrilla movement. With the current government disinterested in her claim for recognition, she feels she has nowhere else to turn for support. Though not affiliated with the political Left or Right, Lorenza still finds herself caught up in the middle of competitive remembering. Her story shows how someone who is apolitical can be co-opted into a political discourse because they have nowhere else to turn. Lorenza was angry because she was ostracised by Argentine society simply because her daughter was killed by "the wrong crowd". She told me:

> Today I know there are Montoneros still alive, some of whom, I want to tell you clearly because I have nothing to hide … if I have something to say I will say it … some of them are in today's government. As a political idea, I'm not saying they were Laura's killers, but as a political idea, they are in government and they are the same ones that won't acknowledge what happened to me and to others. That's to say, the military have someone to defend them, the Montoneros have someone to defend them. But who's going to defend me? Me, my son, my husband, nobody has come near us; no government has ever looked after our mental health because I'll tell you, insanity is waiting at the door. It only has to open it (Ferrari 2009).

Lorenza's story circulates within a grey area of the politics of remembering. Her sense of vulnerability increases when she is publicly called to account for her daughter's death, as if she herself is to blame for what happened, or as if her daughter had some role to play in her own death. Judith Butler (2003) describes just how easily we can be undone by another when our experience is called into question:

> I might try to tell a story here, about what I am feeling, but it would have to be a story in which the very "I" is called into question by its relation to the Other, a relation that does not precisely reduce me to speechlessness, but does nevertheless clutter my speech with signs of its undoing (2004, p. 13).

In the telling of her story, Lorenza exposes the degree to which she is gripped and undone by her need for recognition from others (Butler 2004). Her story shows how our grief and rage can undo us and "implicate us in lives that are not our own, irreversibly, if not fatally" (Butler 2004, p. 25). Butler suggests that grief in particular can show us the degree to which our relations with others can hold us:

> in ways that we cannot always recount or explain, in ways that often interrupt the self-conscious account of ourselves we might try to provide, in ways that challenge the very notion of ourselves as autonomous and in control (2004, p. 23).

Lorenza's notion of herself as "autonomous and in control" was challenged by an interviewer during a television broadcast in which she participated some years ago. The commentator—a well-known lawyer, writer, university professor and supporter of the political Right, Mariano Grondona—stated that both the military and the armed guerrilla movement needed to assume shared responsibility for the political and state violence of the 1970s and 1980s. Lorenza told me she became infuriated by his comments while on the air:

> I asked him, "Doctor, why must I take responsibility? Because I'm not from the military or from a family of the terrorists". He couldn't answer me; he just kept saying, so much pain, so much pain. And I got up and left and he didn't say anything to me; there was nothing more to say. What explanation could he give me? Tell me how I'm to blame? Now that you know this story, I don't know if I explained clearly enough that Laura was not involved in politics, that she went to a private university for tranquillity and peace, to be able to study, and then she was hit by a terrorist car bomb and she lost her life. And I have to take responsibility for that? (Ferrari 2009).

In understanding how a political community is shaped from our ties with others, Judith Butler (2003) questions whether there is a way to struggle for autonomy while considering the demands placed upon us in a world of human beings on whom we are subjectively dependent. Butler writes that:

> This way of imagining community affirms relationality not only as a descriptive or historical fact of our formation, but also as an ongoing normative dimension of our social and political lives, one in which we are compelled to take stock of our interdependence (2003, p. 16–17).

Perhaps, however, we create an impossible situation by seeing ourselves as separate from another in the first place (Oliver 2001). By presuming that we are separate from others, we remove the ability to connect—despite our best efforts, at times, to bridge such an abyss (Oliver 2001). If we presume that relationships are fundamentally hostile, any attempts to create the possibility of cooperative relationships may be doomed (Oliver 2001). Vittoria Villaruel of CELTYV told me of the public hostility and harassment faced by the families she supports on a daily basis. She told me that she herself has publicly been labelled a fascist for demanding human rights on behalf of the organisation's victims. She told me: "We're being called Nazis for defending innocent people" (Villaruel 2009).

Vittoria, along with other women I interviewed, described how it feels to exist on the margins of a society that "lumps" them together with those in the military who committed human rights abuses:

> We are living in a situation of inequality in Argentina; a situation that is lacking in objectivity and impartiality. The state looks after the rights of the civilians from one part of society while the other part has nothing. So these people, when they speak with someone like you, are left with the feeling that they are nobody; that they don't count (Villaruel 2009).

Groups such as CELTYV, which seek legal reparation for crimes committed by the armed guerrilla movement and call on society to remember its victims, are perceived by Ranelletti (2010) as comparing victims of these groups with the victims of the military, and are branded as "negationists". Ranalletti (2010) argues that CELTYV's description of the military's response to the actions of the armed guerrilla movement as a "war against subversion" has restored the military government's original *raison d'être,* and in doing so attempts to justify its repressive actions. Ranalletti (2010, p. 167) sees the organisation's attempt to include in the national calendar a commemorative day for those killed by the armed guerrilla groups as a "new stage of negationism". He argues that certain groups and individuals are dedicated to "manipulating" the past for propaganda purposes, an aim that is shared by the extreme Right sectors in society (Ranalletti 2010). Ranalletti believes that Argentina's negationists are attempting to distort memory of the past with "another" version of the state and political violence of the 1970s and 1980s within Argentine society.

Negationism—most widely associated with denial of the genocide of Jewish individuals during World War II—is the distortion of information and knowledge as a way of possessing the truth of past events (Ranalletti 2010). The term can imply "apologist", "reactionary" or, as Ranalletti suggests in the Argentine case, "nationalist" (Ranalletti 2010, p. 161). Argentine negationists, Ranalletti believes, are:

> an amorphous group of political and cultural agitators, organized in a social network whose main activity consists of appearing in public trying to impose and/or question some event of the recent past. These groups or individuals fragment, mutate, regenerate into new groups or NGOs, and blend into society … (2010, p. 161).

There are those within the political Right in Argentina, including within the organisation CELTYV, who fit the above description. However, I argue that it is important not to conflate or "lump" together those families of innocent civilians who were killed by the armed guerrilla movement with those who committed gross human rights abuses within the military. With a group tag so widely cast, we fail to see individuals as separate entities, and instead apply a group label where it may not be justified. While there are negationists within CELTYV, there are also those who condemn the human rights abuses of the military and feel appalled by what happened to the disappeared. Victoria Paz of CELTYV told me:

> … even though it scandalises a lot of people, I am in complete solidarity with the pain of the families [of the disappeared], of the persons that died because of the actions of the military (Paz 2009).

Victoria was not alone in telling me this; it was conveyed to me by a number of different women. What they do ask, however, is that they also be granted the political, social and legal recognition that they feel they deserve, and that the concept of human rights in Argentina encompass all sectors of society adversely affected by violence during these years.

Judith Butler (2003) critically asks, "What makes for a grievable life?" She asserts that a process of differential grieving can lead to the marginalisation of groups that do not conform to the prevailing norm of the human (Butler 2009). These ungrievable groups are framed as never having been alive at all, and so are already lost from the living (Butler 2009). Perceived as threats to human life rather than as living people, such groups become targeted for marginalisation in order to "protect the lives of the living" (Butler 2009, p. 31). Butler (2004) presents a connection between vulnerability, political recognition and the performative element of community by arguing that violence and the experience of loss are a part of us all: We all have some notion of what it is to lose somebody. She argues that grief can lay bare the "thrall" in which our relations with others hold us; "in ways that often interrupt the self-conscious account of ourselves we might try to provide, in ways that challenge the very notion of ourselves as autonomous and in control" (Butler 2004, p. 23).

Re-actualising the anguish of their experiences when delivering oral testimony within the public sphere is painful for the women I interviewed. However, their sense of deep pain is made even worse when:

> The absence of an empathic listener, or more radically, the absence of an addressable other, an other who can hear the anguish of one's memories and thus affirm and recognize their realness, annihilates the story. And it is, precisely, this ultimate annihilation of a narrative that, fundamentally, cannot be heard and of a story that cannot be witnessed, which constitutes the mortal eighty-first blow (Laub 1992, p. 68).

The women I interviewed gave oral testimony as a way of countering the "amnesia" imposed by various societal and institutional groups around past injustices, and affirming the rupture and new identity of their community (Booth 2006). Bearing witness is a sign of faithfulness, not just to those absent but also to a community with which one has a life in common (Booth 2006, p. 138): "The witness fulfils an obligation to the absent of her community, protests against the effacement of their past, and in so doing affirms the continuity of the community and its core identity." The women's public and private struggles over the meaning of the past ensure that they fulfil their obligation to the dead, but also warrant the continuity of their community across time—a community of which their absent loved ones will forever remain a part (Booth 2006).

Only by testifying to their traumatic experiences do the women with whom I spoke feel they can "reinscribe their subjectivity into situations that mutilated it to the point of annihilation" (Oliver 2001, p. 99). However, in doing so they face the prospect that their testimonies could be forever "on trial", their credibility constantly questioned (Oliver 2001). This is true for any testimony that ascribes to forms of oppression, argues Oliver (2001), so long as the culture within which an individual speaks continues with policies of amnesia. The women's need to seek legitimacy for their memories in such an environment can make the witnessing of their own oppression painful and problematic (Oliver 2001). Despite this, individuals affected by armed guerrilla violence continue to give oral testimony as a way of justifying their status as fully fledged citizens of Argentine society, flying in the face of any attempts to silence the memories of their loved ones.

Chapter 5
Deep Memory

5.1 Reliving Trauma

Anthropologist Veena Das (2001) suggests that a traumatic experience does not just alter one's inner world; it changes it profoundly. The Argentine women I interviewed described various ways in which the traumatic events they lived through had permanently altered their lives. For example, Barbara, who was a young girl when her father was murdered by the armed guerrilla movement in 1974, told me that the trauma resulting from this event had overruled any happy memories of her childhood. Instead, as the oldest in the family, she supported her mother who suffered mentally and physically as a result of the violence through many difficult years. "It was an operation with the aim of assassinating my family; and they managed to", Barbara told me (Tarquini 2009).

The women's narratives illustrated numerous examples of what Susan Brison describes (1999, p. 39) as an "undoing of the self" following the survival of traumatic circumstances. The narratives reveal how trauma extends into the women's everyday physical worlds, stalks their unconscious and causes them to repeatedly relive, both physiologically and physically, the violent events they originally experienced. Their examples lay bare the uncontrollable, unpredictable, unscripted, unsharable and persistent nature of trauma, and show how trauma is "not experienced as a mere repression or defense, but as a temporal delay that carries the individual beyond the shock of the first moment" (Caruth 1995, p. 10). While trauma is a repeated suffering of an experience, "it is also a continual leaving of its site", argues Cathy Caruth (1995, p. 10). Both individual and collective traumas arise out of a collapse of witnessing, which can open up the likelihood of an involuntary reliving of an event (Caruth 1995).

To drill down deeply within the condition of "stuckness" in Argentina, I suggest we need to consider the implications of lives permanently transformed by trauma. Even more importantly, we need to think about the ways in which a consideration of the memorial culture is itself transformed when we emphasise the traumatic—its manifestations, pathways and residues. There is no question that the period of political violence and state terror in Argentina produced a "traumatogenic" environment, which "affected the psychic structures of the self and the systems of attachment and

J. Stockwell, *Reframing the Transitional Justice Paradigm*,
Springer Series in Transitional Justice 10, DOI 10.1007/978-3-319-03853-7_5,

meaning that link the individual to the community" (Hollander 2010, p. 123). While some authors suggest that trauma may not be a universal response to violence but a western construct, Robben (2005a) does not believe this line of argument is relevant in the Argentine case. For example, Argentine psychologist Diana Kordon, who is a member of the Team of Psychological Assistance to the Mothers of the Plaza de Mayo (Equipo de Asistencia Psicológica a las Madres de Plaza de Mayo), has said: "We don't even speak of trauma because that is usually understood to mean an intra-psychic experience. We use the concept "traumatic situation" in order to represent the social sources of the psychological suffering produced by state terror. And we do not speak of victims [*víctimas*] but of individuals and groups that are affected [*afectados*] by political repression" (cited in Hollander 2010, p. 122).

However, Robben argues that psychoanalytic thought has been part of Argentine culture for decades (Robben 2005a). Psychoanalysis has for many years held a prestigious place in the cosmopolitan culture of Argentina's capital, Buenos Aires (Gordon 2008). The practice of psychoanalysis took off in Argentina in the 1960s; by the 1980s, Argentina's psychoanalytic community was the fourth largest in the world (Hollander 1990). Hollander (1990, p. 889) suggests that "in Buenos Aires, where a third of the country's 26 million people reside, there are more psychoanalysts per capita than anywhere else in the world," Psychoanalysis is even embedded in the geography of Buenos Aires, where many analysts are clustered in a neighbourhood popularly known as Villa Freud. Elizabeth Lira (1997, p. 227) is also of the view that the concept of trauma has been the basis for understanding "the subjective impact and the consequences of human rights violations" in Latin America's Southern Cone.

Cristina and Carlos had one boy and Cristina had recently given birth to their second boy when Carlos was "disappeared". On the day of her husband's disappearance, members of the military's security forces paid her a visit at her home. Cristina recalls:

> I began to realise what time it was, I was pacing back and forth, breastfed the baby, made some tea, paced back and forth, until about three in the afternoon more or less. I remember that on television, in black and white during that time, was the film The Last Days of Pompeii, and just at the point when Pompeii was going to be destroyed, I finished breastfeeding the baby, put my top back on, put the baby down in his cot, and looked out the window wondering, "Why isn't Lito back by now?", because he'd been away a long time…He was meant to come back and he didn't come back. He didn't come back…and then I heard a voice behind me say, "Be quiet, raise your arms." (Muro 2009)

The man who grabbed her and threw her to the floor had blond hair, just like her husband's. He asked for her and her husband's names. He then told her that Carlos was "disappeared". At that moment, Cristina realised that nobody would know of her and her children's fate, so she started to scream to alert the neighbours:

> Every time I screamed, they hit me. As I was on the floor, mouth touching the floor, with my legs and arms open, every time they kicked me so that I would stop screaming, they kicked me between my legs…there was blood everywhere because they had busted my stitches. To stop my screaming, I saw that they had my baby, five days old, naked, by the feet, head upside down, with a gun in his mouth. (Muro 2009)

In that moment, Cristina's body responded to the violence she was witnessing:

> It was like I was looking at myself from above, it was very strong, I looked at myself from above and everything around me, but at the same time I was below, screaming and I was asking myself, "Who is this [person] screaming below?" (Muro 2009)

This has not been the only time Cristina has experienced the sensation of leaving her body and looking at herself from above. In fact, the moment in time when Cristina left her body during the violent encounter persists inexplicably in her life. She tells me that when she leaves her body, she feels as if there is some third person acting separately from herself, against her wishes and control. Cristina has been prone to this experience unexpectedly at other times of extreme fear since the end of the military dictatorship; it is a fear that affects her with the same intensity as that she felt during the junta's rule. Cristina describes what it was like to live within an environment of debilitating fear created by the military forces in a way that enabled some individuals to move freely in the public space while restricting the mobility of others:

> It was a permanent feeling of distress…of anxiety more than distress…it was something that made your stomach churn to think that at any moment, something could happen to you. We had to be careful when we walked along the street, in the buses, anywhere we went, to see if anyone was following us…because, I tell you, it was really terrible. (Muro 2009)

When Cristina remembers and relives these violent experiences, she is filled with fear and feels again as if the world is pressing against her body. In Ahmed's words (2004b, p. 69), Cristina's body "shrinks back from the world in the desire to avoid the object of fear". Ahmed (2004b, p. 69) further describes how fear manifests itself: "shrinking the body; it restricts the body's mobility precisely insofar as it seems to prepare the body for flight". Cristina told me:

> For many years, the feelings and the emotions that I had of fear, that I could feel in the middle of my stomach every time I spoke about this…I would be trembling. It's very strong [to remember]. (Muro 2009)

Cristina's experience can be interpreted through the prism of trauma theory. Cathy Caruth (1996, p. 11) describes trauma as "an overwhelming experience of a sudden or catastrophic event in which the response to the event occurs in the often delayed, uncontrolled repetitive appearance of hallucinations and other intrusive phenomena". In psychoanalytic theory, the term "trauma", which literally translates as "wound", refers to an event that is "experienced too soon, too unexpectedly, to be fully known and is therefore not available to consciousness until it imposes itself again, repeatedly, in the nightmares and repetitive actions of the survivor" (Caruth 1996, p. 4). It is the psychic wound that makes us bear witness to the "trauma of the necessity and impossibility of responding to another's death" (Caruth 1996, p. 100). Cristina told me how the trauma she experienced more than 3 decades ago continues to emerge in recurring dreams:

> For a long time I have had a recurring dream; a dream in which my husband would come and I would ask him, "Where have you been all this time? I have been looking for you everywhere." And he would reply, "Didn't I tell you I had to go?" And I wake up totally anxious because I would never know where he had gone. (Muro 2009)

The trauma Cristina lives with has "no beginning, no ending, no before, no during and no after" (Laub 1992, p. 69). Her narrative lays bare the way in which the distressing memory of her husband's disappearance, juxtaposed with her own survival, returns repeatedly through her unconscious, placing her in a perpetual state of torment. Caruth (1996, p. 7, emphasis in original) argues that the "oscillation between a *crisis of death* and the correlative *crisis of life:* between the story of the unbearable nature of an event and the story of the unbearable nature of its survival" is what lies at the heart of a traumatic experience. Her dream suggests that what is terrifying for Cristina is the way in which the event of her husband's disappearance returns in all its fullness in a way that it was never experienced at the time it occurred. When Cristina asks, "Where have you been all this time? I have been looking for you everywhere", one can gain a clear sense of the anxiety she unconsciously feels in being incapable of finding her husband. What also becomes clear is her inability to accept her husband's disappearance and death as permanent and final because she dreams that he finally returns to her. Cristina's memories of trauma in the framework of her dreams show how her "narrative of a belated experience, far from telling of an escape from reality—the escape from a death, or from its referential force—rather attests to its endless impact" on her life (Caruth 1996, p. 7).

The returning traumatic dream was addressed by Freud: "Dreams occurring in traumatic neuroses have the characteristic of repeatedly bringing the patient back into the situation of his accident, a situation from which he wakes up in another fright" (cited in Caruth 1996, p. 59). While trauma can return in an individual's life through repetition and re-enactment, its reality continues to elude the individual who remains in its grip (Laub 1992). Cristina's traumatic encounter with the military's security forces took place outside of the parameters of her "normal" reality (Laub 1992). As such, the repetition of Cristina's dream can be understood as the inability of her mind to avoid revisiting the unwanted event of the disappearance of her husband—an event for which she has been unable to consciously discover any psychic meaning (Caruth 1996). Caruth (1996, p. 7) argues that trauma can act as a double wound through which "a breach of consciousness reappears in acts of self-injury as a repetition of and an awakening to an experience that cannot be assimilated into consciousness, yet cannot be forgotten." What this suggests is that, in trauma, the wound of the mind remains hidden until it resurfaces at later stages in the form of bodily and psychic effects (Caruth 1996).

Freud's theory of trauma relates to the repetition compulsion; however, Caruth goes beyond this focus on the compulsive re-enactment of the past to suggest that it is also important to pay attention to "the moving and sorrowful *voice* that cries out, a voice that is paradoxically released *through the wound*" (1996, p. 2, emphasis in original). This voice can be heard crying out during the repetition of an act, argues Caruth (1996), as a way of alerting an individual to bear witness to a past that he or she is unwittingly repeating. Suffering a deep sense of defencelessness and powerlessness from being unable to prevent her husband's disappearance, as well as being unable to predict at the time what might happen to herself and her children, Cristina has had to find a way of living with the fear, uncertainty and guilt that comes from being a survivor of state terror. Uncertainty can still find a way of paralysing Cristina; however, she told me that she now puts herself repeatedly in danger in order to help others. She explained this further:

> When I see a situation of an abuse of power in a movie, on the street, in some place, I feel very frightened, but I react in the opposite way. I go and place myself [directly in the middle] of what's happening. (Muro 2009)

The voice that Cristina hears—telling her to put herself directly in the way of danger—comes from the original wounding that she suffered: the experience of being unable to save her husband and prevent the violent treatment of her children. Cristina's memory of this violence and the disappearance of her husband is evoked by situations that remind her of the original traumatic situation (Kolk and Van der Hart 1995). In Cristina's case, seeing another individual exposed to an abuse of power triggers her re-enactment of the moment in which she was visited by the military's security forces. The phenomena of re-enactment was first explained by Pierre Janet, the pioneer of trauma research, who argued that trauma could not be remembered as a past event but was instead "retriggered" and felt as a "realtime" experience (Bennett 2002, p. 339). In living with trauma, Cristina has thus been subject in the present to the uncontrolled repetition of behaviour associated with her past; she is provoked into re-enactment by factors in her immediate environment over which she has had little or no control (Tomkins et al. 1995, p. 54). Her interventions to help others in danger may be seen as a way of her redressing the original trauma and revisiting that moment of powerlessness, but in a different state.

Cristina's actions reveal, one way she has found to overcome the powerlessness with which she has lived for so many years. Though not directly placed in a situation of danger in the present, Cristina's response to seeing another in a situation of danger nonetheless stimulates a special reaction in the act of remembering her own past (Kolk and Van der Hart 1995). Dori Laub argues that:

> Trauma survivors live not with memories of the past, but with an event that could not and did not proceed through to its completion, has no ending, attained no closure, and therefore, as far as its survivors are concerned, continues into the present and is current in every respect. (1992, p. 69)

Laub's understanding of trauma suggests Cristina will not transcend or overcome the trauma she experienced, but will rather undergo a ceaseless cycle of repetition and re-enactment of the original trauma throughout her life (1992).

Cristina told me that she is a very different person from the one she was before the traumatic event. "The undoing of the self in trauma", writes Susan Brison (1999, p. 40), "involves a radical disruption of memory, a severing of past from present and, typically, an inability to envision a future." Yet Cristina's life—especially her interventions in others' lives—attests to the ongoing struggle of survivors of trauma to "find ways to reconstruct themselves and carry on with reconfigured lives" (Brison 1999, p. 40). When I asked her to explain how helping other people had affected her as a person, Cristina told me:

> More powerful, that I can undo it, that I can do something. A situation of helplessness makes me ill, my own memory of helplessness and fear makes me feel very bad about myself, so every time I see a situation of this type, I participate and interfere…I get involved

> instinctively…it's like healing my own feelings of fear and absolute loneliness in this situation [her own encounter with security forces]. (Muro 2009)

Cristina has sought to create meaning for her violent experiences through a complex process of "working through" her traumatic memories. In his work, *Representing the Holocaust: History, Theory and Trauma* (1994), Dominic LaCapra reflects upon the processes of grieving and mourning, using the psychoanalytic categories of "acting out" and "working through". By acting out, suggests LaCapra (1994, p. 65), an individual comes to understand that there is a relationship of projection with the past. In this relationship, that which "is not confronted critically does not disappear; it tends to return as the repressed" (LaCapra 1994, p. 65). The process of working through refers to a different relationship with the past, a critical relationship that may allow for historical understanding and the resulting dissolution of the symptom produced by the historically traumatic loss (LaCapra 1994). LaCapra does concede that the process of acting out may never be fully overcome in cases of trauma, and that the idealised notion of full recovery from trauma may in fact be misleading. Nonetheless, he advocates that working through a trauma requires an effort to articulate affect again and again; although that activity may never match the raw experience, it may to some extent, counteract the feelings of "disassociation of affect and representation" brought about by trauma (LaCapra 2001, p. 42).

While Cristina's commitment to repeatedly articulating her experience of trauma through the giving of her oral testimony has assisted her to work through her fear, uncertainty and guilt to a certain degree, it is not necessarily common among survivors of trauma. For many, trauma is carried deep within the psyche and remains inaccessible to willed conscious recall. For most survivors, trauma is uncontainable in language, and as such remains unarticulated and prone to eruptions. There are many important literary works, in particular by Holocaust survivors, bearing witness to the atrocities they lived through in an attempt to "explain the inexplicable" (Delbo 2001, p. 1). These writers have deployed the affective nature of testimonial literature in a bid to convey the affective nature of trauma and "to read the gaps and silences that necessarily accompany the process of testifying" (Bennett and Kennedy 2003, p. 3).

5.2 How Deep Memory Works

One such writer is Holocaust survivor Charlotte Delbo, who wrote extensively about living with trauma and the ways in which she was unable to integrate her experiences of violence into her life narrative. After returning to Paris from the death camps, Delbo (1995, p. 237) wrote:

> My former life? Had I had a former life? My life afterwards? Was I alive to have an afterwards, to know what afterwards meant? I was floating in a present devoid of reality.

In her writing, Delbo explores what it was like, as a survivor of trauma, to live with the challenge of envisioning a future in the midst of the destruction of one's emotional and cognitive capacities (Brison 1999). Delbo explores her traumatic memories of Auschwitz so profoundly, and in such a way that future readers are able to gain insight into how it was to live through those years of "unthinkable" events—even though those events are ones which "no one really wished to reawaken from the slumber of forgetfulness" (cited in Langer, in Delbo 1995, p. xi). Delbo communicates to us, through her exploration of deep memory, the complex ways in which the past continuously and unexpectedly ruptures trauma survivors' reconstructed realities. Her concept of deep memory echoes many of the insights of trauma theory, but Delbo's particular model of traumatic memory, with its emphasis on the survivor's body, resonates deeply with my own research.

My exploration of the workings of deep memory in this chapter draws primarily on Holocaust literature, and in particular on the work of Charlotte Delbo. By engaging with Holocaust texts, I do not suggest that the field of trauma studies is limited to a selection of Holocaust works. I acknowledge that these texts represent a narrow range of traumatic events and histories, and that some scholars have questioned the uses of the Holocaust as a paradigmatic and universally applicable case study within the field of trauma studies (see Bennett and Kennedy 2003). A global scope of other theoretical works on the politics of testimony and trauma has been engendered in a rich range of contexts, including the Australian Stolen Generations testimonies, the South African Truth and Reconciliation Commission, as well as those associated with the Vietnam War, among others. However, I believe the insights and methods deployed to examine the traumatic legacies of the Holocaust can also be productively and meaningfully applied in a context such as Argentina.[1] More specifically, I find that the Holocaust literature, particularly the work of Charlotte Delbo, offers me highly imaginative and sophisticated ways of thinking about traumatic memory. Delbo's work on the Holocaust has been helpful in giving me insight into the phenomenon of "impossible memory" in the oral testimonial encounter within a context such as Argentina. Her writing on the psychic impediments to speaking trauma provides my work with an important framework for engaging with the different layers and levels inherent in the Argentine women's embodied memories of torture and atrocity.

5.3 Living with Deep Memory

Deep memory fulfils a different purpose from what Delbo (2001) terms "common memory": those memories that are constructive, logical and connected with cognition. Delbo used the idea of common memory as a way of attempting to incorporate her Auschwitz experience into a chronology of her life—a process that could free her from the pain of remembering the "unthinkable" (cited in Langer, in Delbo

[1] The human rights movement and certain academic and judicial circles in Argentina compare disappearances that occurred under military rule with the Holocaust. These groups advocate that genocide also occurred in Argentina (Robben 2012).

1995, p. xi). She writes: “I am very fortunate in not recognizing myself in the self that was in Auschwitz…I feel that the one who was in the camp is not me, is not the person who is here, facing you” (Delbo 1995, p. xi). On the other hand, Delbo (2001) uses the term “deep memory” to refer to those memories that record the physical imprint of a traumatic event within the individual. Delbo describes deep memory as different from common or intellectual memory in that it preserves sensations—it is the memory of the senses.

The argument that trauma resists representation and that it involves bodily responses that resist verbal-linguistic representation is now well established (Bennett 2002). Richard Terdiman employs Delbo’s concept of deep memory in a similar way, by suggesting we should think of memory as having two different modalities (cited in Faye 2003). In one type of memory, the past is tamed and disciplined, and is available to the conscious memory as symbolic representation (Terdiman, cited in Faye 2003). In the other modality of memory, the “referent” of the past is carried “as a threatening and malignant excess of language” (Terdiman, cited in Faye 2003, p. 161). Terdiman writes:

> Psychical material (mnemic traces) of past experiences—although in themselves inaccessible to consciousness except through their representational derivatives—persist and betray, through their repetition, the presence of something real and traumatic left over from the past. (cited in Faye 2003, p. 161)

In other words, Delbo’s “common” or representational memory makes the experience of trauma intelligible to the listener; deep memory, on the other hand, “registers a sense of the interior experience of trauma and of its fundamental unintelligibility” (Bennett 2002, p. 335).

In *Days and Memory,* Delbo (2001, p. 1) further explores the state of living “within a twofold being” comprising her Auschwitz self and her post-Auschwitz self. She uses the image of a snake shedding its skin as a way of explaining how the “new” sense of herself in the years since her internment has come about:

> Explaining the inexplicable. There comes to mind the image of a snake shedding its old skin, emerging from beneath it in a fresh, glistening one. In Auschwitz I took leave of my skin—it had a bad smell, that skin—worn from all the blows it had received, and found myself in another, beautiful and clean, although with me the molting was not as rapid as the snake’s. (Delbo 2001, p. 1)

Delbo likens the way in which deep memory works to the regenerative skin of a snake. Like the snake’s skin, memory changes with time and alters together with its representations and transmissions of the past (Grunebaum and Henri 2003):

> …the snake’s shed skin retains its “memory”, that is, the trace of the snake who, meanwhile, retains the memory of the skin through which it has passed and through which it will once again pass precisely because the process of shedding skin is a returning, ritualising occurrence. (Grunebaum and Henri 2003, p. 105)

Grunebaum and Henri (2003, p. 106) suggest that Delbo’s skin metaphor sets up a spatiotemporal construct whereby the more the traces of the traumatic experience become temporally absent in the life of an individual survivor of trauma, the more memory is charged with the onus of “signposting the past”.

Delbo's use of the term "deep memory" is a way of reminding us that her Auschwitz past was not really in the past, and never would be. While a snake's skin may disintegrate and disappear, Delbo's memories of her incarceration in Auschwitz, which Langer describes as the "skin of Auschwitz memory" (cited in Delbo 1995, p. xi), remain, though they may not continuously be felt. Delbo tells us:

> Auschwitz is so deeply etched in my memory that I cannot forget one moment of it—So you are living with Auschwitz?—No, I live next to it. Auschwitz is there, unalterable, precise but enveloped in the skin of memory, an impermeable skin that isolates it from my present self. Unlike the snake's skin, the skin of memory does not renew itself…Thinking about it makes me tremble with apprehension. (1995, p. 2)

The "skin of memory" to which Delbo refers is not renewed like that of the snake. Rather, she suggests that her memories are layered on top of each other and never fade or lose their initial integrity (Soo-Jin Lee 2003). In a similar way to Delbo's deep memories of the concentration camp, Maria del Socorro's memories of torture at the hands of Argentine military repressors are unwelcome intruders in her daily life. Despite wanting to banish them from her mind, her traumatic memories persist and chronically plague her in unconscious ways where she has little control. During our interview, Maria told me about the terrible migraines she suffers—migraines that can leave her in a foetal position for days—on remembering the torture she endured during her incarceration at the hands of military repressors. Only 58 years of age, Maria believes she will suffer physically and psychologically until her death as a result of what she went through. She lives daily with the painful embodied memories not only of torture but also of her miscarriage under the duress of torture and the disappearance of the father of her unborn baby.

Scarry (1985, p. 4) observes that for those in pain, the very act of "having pain" is the most vibrant example of what it is to "have certainty". For Maria, this is particularly relevant during the times she has been asked to testify in legal proceedings against the Dirty War's perpetrators. Her scars offer her a sense of certainty about her memories of past violence in the face of confusing images of former repressors in the present. She tells me of her disbelief on seeing those very perpetrators of violence against her being accompanied to the court by loving family members. It was beyond belief that these people should also appear to be able to love another human being. Eliana, whose sister was illegally incarcerated together with Maria and who attended these proceedings, also registered her disbelief at these public demonstrations of support:

> You would look at them [perpetrators], and it would surprise you that they were people… that they looked like people, or in other words that they weren't monsters with three eyes and four heads. (Carreira 2009)

Maria's physical and psychic pain acts as a constant reminder of the torture she endured at the hands of those who are now humanised. Maria tells me that she will frequently enter into the grip of deep memory when recalling what she endured. This experience can last for days at a time. Maria's deep memories plunge her back into reliving the past in a way similar to Delbo (2001, p. 2), who was fearful should "the camp get hold of me again". To be in the grip of deep memory "is, by definition, to remain haunted by memory that resists cognitive processing" (Bennett 2002, p. 340). Maria's experience of torture also resists cognitive processing. She told me that she was near death twice during torture, and that both times she witnessed her body being brought back to life as her torturers massaged her heart. Maria was confused as to how this was possible:

> I saw them running with my body and they put me on a table and they began massaging my heart. But during the cardiac arrest, I could see this vision of myself that I…I cannot explain intellectually. I can't explain it. I have been fearful of telling this story. I believe this is the first time that I've told this to anyone. I don't know what it is. (del Socorro Alonso 2009)

Maria told me about how anxious she can become as she suffers physically from the injuries she sustained from torture and again comes face-to-face with her own mortality. Maria tells me that the smell of blood from her daughter's cut finger can transport her instantly back into the darkness of those violent days:

> …the smell of blood, the smell of dried blood, because there was blood everywhere. And as I was paralysed, I had to drag myself to the bathroom. I had to drag myself across [other inmates'] blood…. (del Socorro Alonso 2009)

For Maria, in reliving of the horror and trauma of her experience, "the sensory memory that is deep memory replaces the sensation itself and re-places the survivor in the death space" (Grunebaum and Henri 2003, p. 107). Maria is made to recall her vulnerability during torture as she smells the blood from her own daughter's wound and is again plummeted into "the boundary between life and death" (Adams, cited in Takemoto 2001, p. 112). By virtue of her deep memories, Maria is continuously faced with being plunged again and again back into the physical horror of the clandestine camp in which she was held. For Maria, it is as LaCapra (2001, p. 89) describes: "Whether or not the past is re-enacted or repeated in its precise literality, one feels as if one were back there reliving the event, and distance between here and there, then and now, collapses".

Even though the skin enfolding Maria's memories of torture appears to be tough, in Delbo's words (2001, p. 3), it "gives way at times, revealing all it contains". It becomes clear from her narrative that Maria's conscious will hold no such power over her body (Delbo 2001). It is Maria's body that betrays the tough skin of memory by giving way, shutting down and revealing all it contains (Delbo 2001). In those dark moments, Maria sees herself as she was—helpless, bloodied and broken. These sorts of memories never fade or lose their initial integrity for Maria. The physical pain she feels is all too similar to the pain she endured at the hands of the repressors. In these moments, she is unsure whether she will survive, as she once again feels "death fasten" on her (Delbo 1995, p. xiii).

"They broke my neck", Maria told me (del Socorro Alonso 2009). As a result of the torture she experienced, Maria suffers from a degenerative spinal condition and feels like her body is continuously in ruins. When Maria is in the process of reliving the physical and psychological trauma from torture, her children look on helplessly, unable to communicate with her. The splitting and disassociation Maria goes through as she tries to articulate to her children what is happening to her when experiencing an "episode" reveals her struggle with and against language as a condition of trauma (Felman 1992). When Maria is caught reliving these moments, her memory of physical pain "does not simply resist language but actively destroys it, bringing about an immediate reversion to a state anterior to language, to the sounds and cries a human being makes before language is learned" (Scarry 1985, p. 4).

As Maria relives in such a physical way the memories associated with the smell of blood from her daughter's cut finger, we are reminded by Parveen Adams that although a scar may be healed, "it nevertheless opens you up continuously to the previous time of the open wound, a continuous reopening of the wound" (cited in Takemoto 2001, p. 112). For Adams, the signification of the wound is different from a cut, which acts to inscribe the skin with a memory (cited in Takemoto 2001). Instead, Adams believes the wound marks the boundary between life and death, and acts as an "unwriting" of the skin that is not fixed (cited in Takemoto 2001, p. 112). Maria's reaction to smelling the blood from her daughter's wound tells us about the difficult process she must face on a daily basis in dealing with the unconscious and unpredictable nature of deep memory. When I asked Maria how she was affected psychologically by these memories as they arose in the present, she replied:

> And so, I get through the days like this…always…I get panic attacks when I feel the [physical] pain come on…I get very panicked when these moments arise. And in those moments, I'm very fearful because I never know how I'm going to get out of it. (del Socorro Alonso 2009)

When I asked Maria where the panic came from, she told me:

> The panic comes because the pain is so bad when…there are things that I can't do, for example…I can't turn my head to look behind me. I can't look above me…My future is uncertain. (del Socorro Alonso 2009)

What Maria experiences is explained by Jonathan Shay, who writes about the consequences of trauma experienced by individuals who fought in Vietnam:

> Once experiencing is under way, the survivor lacks authority to stop it or put it away. The helplessness associated with the original experience is replayed in the apparent helplessness to end or modify the re-experience once it has begun. (cited in Brison 2003, p. 45)

Argentine psychoanalyst Susana Kaufman also offers her views about what is happening in such a situation:

> At the time of the event, because of the suddenness and intensity of its impact, something becomes detached from the symbolic world, and remains without representation. From that moment on, the event will not be felt as one belonging to the subject. It will remain foreign to him or her, and it will be difficult or impossible to talk about it. The event will not be integrated into the experience of the subject and its effects will be displaced to other spaces that the subject cannot control. The intensity of the event produces a breakdown in comprehension, opening a breach or a void in the subject's ability to explain what has occurred. (cited in Jelin 2003, p. 50)

Following a traumatic "episode", Maria slowly "pieces" herself back together and re-enters her "normal", everyday life. She told me that it may take her days to recover from reliving her deep memories of violence, and "for everything to get shoved back inside memory, and for the skin of memory to mend again" (Delbo 2001, p. 3).

Once this process is complete, Maria is once again able to become herself and to attest to the abuses she suffered without exhibiting or registering anxiety or emotion. However, as Jean Améry writes: "Whoever has succumbed to torture can no longer feel at home in the world" (in Brison 1999, p. 44); the experience of torture leaves survivors like Maria with few bearings by which to navigate their lives. She predicts the long-term impact her violent experiences will have on the rest of her life:

> Yes it's this that happens to me. Because…because well, because I believe I will suffer until the end of my days. So it's impossible for me to forget [the torture]. That's the truth. (del Socorro Alonso 2009)

In Maria's story, she explains how her experience of torture has prevented her from envisioning any sort of "normal" future for herself. Her narrative reveals how, over many years of attempting to resume a "normal" life, her deep memories of violence have assumed a powerful presence in her life. As a survivor, Maria is drawn into what Lawrence Langer (1995) calls the "tomb of durational time", which signifies a death that has not been preceded by a "normal life" or transcended by a "normal" future, for those who remain.

5.4 The Durational Time of Deep Memory

In describing Holocaust survivors' efforts to live with their traumatic memories, Langer (1995, p. 15) reveals that "no one recovers because nothing is recovered, only uncovered and then re-covered, buried again beneath the fruitless struggle to expose 'the way it was.'" Langer (1995, p. 15) draws on philosopher Jean-Francois Lyotard's exploration of "an aesthetics of the memory of the forgotten", which Langer calls an "anesthetics", to address the dilemma survivors face in fighting against the forgetting of the past. In explaining what he means by this dilemma, Lyotard (cited in Langer 1995, p. 15) writes that the Holocaust past is "a past located this side of the forgotten, much closer to the present moment than any past, at the same time that it is incapable of being solicited by voluntary and conscious memory". Lyotard's explanation of the destabilising force of Holocaust memory is what Langer (1995, p. 15) calls "durational memory". Durational memory, Langer explains (1995, p. 15), is "not to be dredged from memory because it is always, has always been there—an always-present past". In what follows, Victoria's narrative conveys how the duration of her deep memories resists the efforts of time to erase her experiences. While her *common* memories may hold hope that her trauma will fade with time, Victoria's *deep* memory resists these attempts and finds ways to remain present.

Victoria told me that she talks about the loss of her father every day with her family, even after 35 years. She decided to begin speaking publicly about the events surrounding her father's death a few years ago to combat the discrimination she felt when her father's memory was silenced within the public sphere. Victoria feels that she is the official keeper of her father's memory, and believes she is one of the few witnesses to the type of person he really was. Over the years, Victoria has assumed the responsibility of transmitting to her younger brothers and sisters her father's values and dreams, as well as her memories of him. Achieving this has been no easy feat. Victoria not only walks in her father's footsteps, but also claims them as her own. This has come at great personal cost. She told me that following her father's murder by the left-wing armed guerrilla group ERP (the People's Revolutionary Army), she tried to remember the days leading up to and immediately after the event. At that time, she became aware of how painful these things were to remember, and decided to form a fragile treaty between her unconscious and the reality of the lived experience:

> In that moment, I realised that what I had to do was to close the door. And I mentally constructed a box of cement. Why cement? Why a box? I don't know. But I do know that I said to myself, "this I can't, I can't think about this, I can't remember, I need to put it away. I will put it away in a cement box." Mentally I imagined doing this. I put everything in there and closed it. (Paz 2009)

Victoria says that she attempted "opening the box" at different times, but when overwhelmed by the demons lurking inside, would again seal it shut. It was not until her first husband was diagnosed with cancer that an analyst who Victoria was seeing advised her "to open the box" and begin processing the impact of losing her father at such an impressionable age. Her body ached 24 h a day, every single day for 2–3 years. Victoria attributes the breast cancer she developed and eventually overcame to the decision to "open the box" (Paz 2009). Like Cristina's dreams, Victoria's experience can be interpreted through the prism of trauma theory, which says that a traumatic experience can be buried deep within an individual until such time as it emerges through a variety of symptoms (Caruth 1995). For Caruth (1995, p. 4–5), a traumatic memory is the memory of an experience that "is not assimilated or experienced fully at the time, but only belatedly, in its repeated possession of the one who experiences it. To be traumatized is precisely to be possessed by an image or event." Victoria's experience is an example of what Caruth calls the "latency" of trauma, or how the past receives its traumatic meaning at a later stage, when an event or experience has the power to make the original experience become defined as traumatic through its being remembered (Faye 2003). Caruth (1995, p. 6) suggests that the "historical power of the trauma is not just that the experience is repeated after its forgetting, but that it is only in and through its inherent forgetting that it is first experienced at all."

Though she made conscious attempts to forget the violence she saw and experienced, Victoria's body functions as a powerful agent in signposting her painful past. In the narration of her testimony, Victoria uses her deep memories of trauma as a way to recuperate the personal and disruptive memories that contest the linear narratives found in shared memory, and as a "symbolic locus for conceptualising the materiality of memory" (Grunebaum and Henri 2003, p. 105). Her deep memories evoke those events that are incapable of being solicited by conscious memory, as they recall the sensory imprint of the traumatic violence she experienced during the 1970s (Grunebaum and Henri 2003). Victoria says her body hurts each time she talks about her father; something she is doing publicly more and more to combat the sense of alienation she encounters within Argentina's collective memorial culture (Paz 2009). Though she is talking publicly about the memories of her father, her body perpetually reminds her that there is no recovery from experiencing trauma because it can only be "re-covered" and "buried again beneath the fruitless struggle to expose 'the way it was'" (Langer 1995, p. 15).

5.5 Discovering Deep Memory in the Testimonial Experience

In exploring with the women what the moments of violence and loss were for them, I was entreated to see, in brief flashes when their unconscious took over, what remained. These flashes of deep memory did not obey the sequential time of the women's narratives. They threatened the flow and order of chronological time. It was in these moments that I experienced the durational force of the political and state violence on the women's lives. In these moments, they remained baffled by the lack of language at their disposal to convey the enduring persistence of their traumatic memories.

Lorenza gave me her oral testimony about the day in 1973 when her daughter Laura was killed by a car bomb that exploded as she was leaving the university where she was studying. At one point in a lighter moment of her testimony, Lorenza was telling me about the laughs she and Laura shared over the sorts of clothes Laura wore in the 1970s: "It was a time when you wore everything very short", she said, smiling (Ferrari 2009). But then Lorenza's facial expression suddenly changed. When I asked her what had happened to her in that moment, she told me:

> You see when I speak of this I'm smiling, because they're beautiful things, beautiful memories but then the other part [memories of daughter Laura's death] taps me on the shoulder. (Ferrari 2009)

The grief Lorenza felt on remembering her life without her daughter at that moment during her oral testimony physically tapped her on the shoulder and again asserted its influence over her life. In exploring Lorenza's testimonial experience, we can see the way in which her deep memories of trauma can arise unexpectedly, and can puncture her "reconstructured universe" (Grunebaum and Henri 2003, p. 107). In Lorenza's narrative, I saw how deep memory "disrupts chronology, where we are safely situated, and drags us into the menacing realm of duration" (Langer 1995, p. 18).

Delbo (1995) believes that something integral to remembering traumatic events is lost when a temporal frame is superimposed on processes of remembering, and when deep memories are confined to history's pages. I believe it is important to explore Delbo's concept of how deep memory works in the context of the women's narratives, as a way of understanding the vital role it plays in producing real-time somatic experiences for survivors of violence. In her major work, *Auschwitz and After*(Delbo 1995), Delbo suggests that what makes deep memory so valuable is its resistance to historicisation and its preservation within memory of the affective experience itself (Bennett 2002). What Delbo's notion implies is that deep memory resists being recalled within the framework of a narrative of the past, but instead is re-triggered and felt as a "real-time" embodied experience (Bennett 2002, p. 339). We can see the way in which the deep memory of her daughter's death makes Lorenza's experience of trauma ever-present. Lorenza explained how her deep memories have a way of overruling any happy memories she might have:

> These are experiences that have marked my life and they [the experiences] turn you into a different person, for the rest of your life. Because you have to learn to live with this [memory], but it's not easy; it's not easy because you don't know how to get over it.... (Ferrari 2009)

How do people live with the disruptive impact of trauma in which certain memories become obstacles that prevent individuals from continuing on with their lives? Caruth (1995, p. 151) suggests that trauma "does not simply serve as record of the past but precisely registers the force of an experience that is not yet fully owned". In listening to Lorenza's words, her deep memories of trauma tell us that the violence that pervaded Argentine society in the 1970s and 1980s "is an abyss that we cannot pass over with equanimity into the future" (Langer, cited in Delbo 1995, p. xiii). In bearing witness to another's traumatic memories, one is reminded that we are in the presence of a past that cannot be effaced (Langer, cited in Delbo 1995). After hearing her testimony, I asked Lorenza to describe how she saw herself in the present day compared with the moment in time when she learned of her daughter's death. Lorenza became distracted and talked for a few minutes, repeating over and over the same thoughts, until she stopped suddenly and said:

> I see myself…I see myself…I'm sorry that I keep repeating myself but I see myself without Laura…I see myself without Laura. (Ferrari 2009)

Lorenza's narrative is shot through with a tension between the conflicting nature of the two modes of remembering—common and deep memory. One produces a narration, while the other collapses it (Grunebaum and Henri 2003). Her narrative shows how the duration of deep memory works, that it "is a constantly re-experienced time [that] threatens the chronology of experienced time. It leaps out of chronology, establishing its own momentum, or fixation" (Langer 1995, p. 15). Despite her efforts to give testimony in a chronological and linear way, Lorenza's common memory would regularly be punctured by the shattering, disruptive moments of deep memory. During moments of her testimony, the two forms of remembering would overlap and would sometimes emerge as mutually indistinguishable. Lorenza appeared exasperated and troubled when her deep memories intruded on her common memory, interrupting the smooth flow of her narrative. Her deep memories refused to be tamed and integrated into chronological or historical time. Instead, the raw psychic material of her deep memories "bear witness to something *real,* something out of time but yet transmitted in the time of speech as unconscious testimony" (Faye 2003, p. 164). Lorenza's deep memories represent an embodied, "perpetual present time" of lived trauma, and have the potential to keep the initial wounding of trauma open (Faye 2003, p. 107).

In listening to the women's narratives, the extent to which they were compelled to live alongside deeply traumatic memories that continue to be unintegrated into their conscious life became clear. Their testimonies were full of examples of how the initial trauma they experienced defied simple comprehension, despite their best attempts at assimilating the past through psychoanalysis and a commitment to giving public testimony. The deep memories that emerged in the women's oral testimonies were as Caruth (1995, p. 151) describes: "while the images of traumatic re-enactment remain absolutely accurate and precise, they are largely inaccessible to conscious recall and control." Lorenza's testimony showed the way in which she could become split between the chronological current of her common memories and the durational persistence of her deep memories. Her deep memories would bear witness to the truth of their traumatic experiences, which—though having come from another time and another place—were nonetheless re-evoked and kept unconsciously alive in the present.

5.6 Living Long Term with Deep Memory

The Argentine women's oral testimonies tell us much about what continues to dominate their lives as survivors of violence. To call oneself a survivor, according to Elizabeth Lira (1997, p. 227), is to recognise that there was a risk of or closeness to death, often leaving those who survived with the "taste of death". The experience of watching a loved one being violently kidnapped or disappeared has had long-lasting effects for many of the women I spoke with. For example, Silvia explained how she has lived with being a victim of violence:

> I feel like I was also kidnapped, as if I also couldn't speak, I couldn't say anything…I was young but for so many years I dealt with other things that in reality I didn't feel like I was living on earth. (Ibarzábal 2009)

Silvia's comment attests to the way the victims of political and state violence in Argentina have become "a symptom of history that they cannot entirely possess" (Caruth 1995, p. 4–5). Silvia's body has become a site and focus for her memories of trauma, which remain ever-vulnerable to revival. This raises an important issue about the long-term consequences of living with deep memories that are too painful to acknowledge in a person's everyday reality and identity. In particular, for the women I spoke with, who had to cope with raising young children on their own after the disappearance of a partner or husband, the annihilation of the family unit has been one of the most painful and anxiety-inducing aspects of their internal worlds, a painful wounding that has stamped itself on how they now live their lives. Noemi, whose partner was disappeared, begins by remembering how difficult it was to teach her young children to protect themselves during the military dictatorship:

> To protect the children, a lot of the time you had to lie, say whatever; I had to teach my children to lie. I used to tell them, "you can't say this"; this was terrible for the kids also. Or, "If someone asks you, you have to tell them…", and for example, if I hadn't returned home,

> later [after partner's abduction] I rented an apartment, on the ground floor and my oldest daughter made friends with the doorman and sometimes the doorman knew everything that was going on. So I told my daughter, "You have to say that dad is on holidays", because my daughter had seen her father being kidnapped. And all of these things to protect them, to help them appear invisible. (Ciollaro 2009)

Noemi told me that both of her children have been through deep crises in their lives as a result of what they lived through and that the disappearance of their father, her partner Eduardo, has left a profound and deep hole in their lives. Noemi explains how shame, rejection and other affects altered her and her children's understanding of their selves and their relation with the past:

> It wasn't easy. It was not at all easy. It was painful and…and on top of that I had to adjust [the story of what happened to their father] depending on the age of the kids because there were things that were really difficult [to understand] and I had to respond to their questions…when we returned to democracy and we were bombarded with all sorts of very perverse information in one way or another; they showed bones in a way that was very…that provoked rejection (by society). It wasn't by chance. To have to explain all of this was very difficult, so…Everything was difficult because we were rejected…the talk of delinquent subversives…it was difficult to go on. (Ciollaro 2009)

In *Beyond the Pleasure Principle,* Freud argued that the repetition of trauma defines the shape of an individual's life (cited in Caruth 1996). Living through such a traumatic experience has radically disturbed Noemi's relationship with herself and the past. Her story is a powerful example of how identity can be altered by an encounter with extremely traumatic loss; the radical disruption of her life goals and plans has had an enduring and destructive impact on her identity, family unit and social relations (Lira 1997). Noemi described to me how her deep memories of the dictatorship play out in her present life: she finds herself still constantly "on the run" and "on the lookout" when in the company of her grown children. She tells me that she can never sit still, and is constantly on the move. She also told me that she always has to have a future plan to give her hope. She feels this is a direct result of the many years she spent in hiding in internal exile in Argentina, and that these deep memories of movement and flight have stayed with her into the present day. This she credits to a need to feel alive. She told me:

> I believe that the action and the necessity to…to have an object, a horizon, something that motivates you, is something fairly…is very related to all of this. I don't know…there's like…also like a need to feel an adrenaline rush, something like that…that has a lot to do with me wanting to feel alive…or…it's like this, how sometimes it's necessary to know that one is alive, because to be a survivor, you have a survivor mentality…. (Ciollaro 2009)

What I understand from Noemi's testimony is the extent to which her experiences of the dictatorship have radically altered and shaped, in new and defining ways, her sense of self. As such, Noemi finds herself needing to encounter ways of feeling alive in the present. In her testimony, I can hear the "locus" of her deep memory—her feeling that it was actually she herself who had died. The women all spoke to me of the deep pain they felt in their bodies when both consciously and unconsciously remembering their traumatic pasts. Many described the pain as "always there". For others, the deep pain they felt was not necessarily a complete disruption to their lives, but rather a pain that they felt in the background of their daily lives that could rise up unexpectedly. Sara Ahmed suggests that pain:

> is not simply a function of the amount of bodily damage alone. Rather, the amount and quality of pain we feel are also determined by our previous experiences and how well we remember them, by our ability to understand the cause of the pain and to grasp its consequences. (2004b, p. 23)

For example, Mercedes, whose husband, Miguel Angel, was killed by the armed guerrilla movement in 1974, told me that the pain in her heart comes and goes in rhythm with times of public commemoration for her husband:

> It's like…Here I feel something [pointing to her heart]…as if someone is pushing on my sternum. It's…it's something I feel when I'm tense, when I'm afraid, um, when there's a commemorative ceremony for Miguel Angel such as this year when they placed a plaque in honour of the 35th anniversary of his death. Um…you see, here, like as if someone was pushing on me. I don't know if it's the heart, diaphragm, I don't know. Just here. (Castrofini 2009)

Many of the women told me of the heart pain they had continuously felt since the time of the traumatic event. Nenina described a particular feeling of pain in her heart that has stayed with her in the present:

> After the disappearance of my partner I had a problem of…I don't know what it was, I had a pain here [pointing to her heart] for a long time, and I still have it and I know it's not duodenum or the gallbladder or the liver. I used to describe it like a bullet wound…. (Boulliet 2009)

The pain that Nenina feels is all too familiar; she has felt it many times before. Elaine Scarry (1985) suggests that pain can be felt as if something from the outside is pressing upon the body, or even managing to get inside the body. Each time Nenina remembers her partner's disappearance, she feels the pain anew, and this deep pain manifests itself as a real bullet wound, making an impression on the surface of her body. And the deep pain, in the form of an imaginary bullet wound, demands that Nenina attends to her embodied existence and again propels her into the re-experienced time of deep memory.

Ahmed (2004b, p. 25) suggests that it "is not just that we interpret our pain as a sign of something, but that how pain feels in the first place is an effect of past impressions, which are often hidden from view". In other words, as Nenina's experience of living with a bullet-like wound in her heart shows, pain is not just a biological response but something already known (Philipose 2007). The amount and nature of pain Nenina feels have been determined by her past experiences and the degree to which she remembers them (Ahmed 2004b). They are also determined by her "ability to understand the cause of the pain and to grasp its consequences" (Melzack and Wall in Ahmed 2004b, p. 23). It is her interpretation of this physical experience that bestows upon it meaning as pain (Philipose 2007). Her recall of such an experience and her ability to contextualise the pain she feels is what allows Nenina to communicate her experience to others in a way that can be understood (Philipose 2007). Philipose (2007, p. 62, 63) suggests further that: "The interpretation of pain helps constitute the self—or, more precisely, the history, experience and meanings of pain contribute toward a person's sense of selfhood."

In seeking to understand the root of the women's deep memories of pain, I turn to social anthropologist, Fiona Ross's work in relation to South Africa's Truth and Reconciliation Commission (2003). Ross (2003, p. 147) recommends discovering the "locus of pain", or its original source. This, she believes, does not only offer new interpretations on the veracity of the intimate individual experience but can also "unleash" it from its original moorings (Ross 2003, p. 144). Ross's idea of discovering the locus of pain is similar to that of artist Sandra Johnston who, in her filmic work, attempts to "excavate" the moment of pain of trauma sufferers as a way of giving "pain a home in the body" (cited in Bennett 2002, p. 336). Identifying the locus of the women's pain within their oral testimonies can help understand that, which acts as an affective trigger within their deep memories, and makes the experience of trauma ever-present.

Silvia gave me her testimony about her father's abduction and her own traumatic involvement, at just 18 years of age, in the circumstances around her father's kidnapping. She began:

> So, it was 1974 and already there were more and more attacks by armed terrorist organisations in this country, and my family suffered a very important attack. My father was a military man and head of an army unit. We lived in front of this unit and one Saturday night, while he was eating with friends in another apartment, we—my brothers, sisters and I—were in our apartment also with friends who were visiting [and] were attacked. This was really very traumatic because they killed a lot of people, and many people were wounded. We had to try to…well…we had to hit the floor and stay all night like that because of the gunfire that was coming into our apartment…this attack lasted practically all night, with very intense gunfire, grenades, tanks, helicopters that arrived to evacuate the wounded, so finally…they killed another [military] leader, they killed a lady in front of her kids, they killed a soldier so they could enter the room, they wounded other people and they kidnapped my father. (Ibarzábal 2009)

Silvia then began to repeat and fill out some of the story she had just told me:

> The first feeling I had was fear, a lot of fear. We started to hear the gunfire and my father came home very quickly because we lived right in front of the [military] unit. My father came home really quickly and my brother, who at this time was ten years old, was sleeping…it was night-time. And I remember him [her father] lifting him out of bed and putting him on the floor and he began to lower the blinds quickly…and he told us to hit the floor. And so, he crossed the street to talk with other officials who were there and the soldiers, who were few because many were on vacation. This was my first feeling—fear… terrible…terrible. And as the gunfire was getting worse, you could hear the machine gun fire, and later you could hear the grenades, and later we heard the noise of the helicopters that came to evacuate the wounded. And one didn't know who they were taking away, or… we were left all night wondering where my father was…and later the tanks…The next day my mother went to visit a lady who was very badly wounded at the hospital in the area and to give blood. Before she went, she gave us each a sedative. So, at that moment I thought the worse because she was giving us a sedative…I thought they had killed him [her father]. But this wasn't the worst of it…When she came back from the hospital she told us that the lady had died, and that they had kidnapped him [her father]. And this is the worst, or… the impact [of the kidnapping] is worse. The uncertainty and lack of power was so heavy because you could do nothing, nothing more than wait…wait…wait…This was the worst,

> and clearly, now looking back, I would have really preferred that yes…that they had killed him [her father] that night and that he would never had to have then lived through what he did. (Ibarzábal 2009)

Silvia told me that while kidnapped and in detention, her father had written her and her two other siblings a letter each. These letters were found in the pocket of her father's trousers after he was shot. After 35 years, though having read both her brother's and sister's letters, Silvia has never been able to bring herself to read the letter her father wrote for her because of the deep pain she knows doing so will bring. She told me:

> No, no, no…My brother and sister can read those sorts of things but I can't…Out of the three of us [siblings], I'm more able to speak publicly than them, give an interview, write something that gets published…But always waiting at the bottom of things is a profound pain. (Ibarzábal 2009)

Silvia told me that after she saw where her father was held while in captivity, she slept for two straight days because she was in so much pain and shock. She told me there was no way to avoid remembering what had happened to her father and her family. She said that she was constantly and unexpectedly faced with feeling deep pain in the most subtle of ways:

> You know what happened? This last week, I was working on my computer and my husband was looking for some papers beside me, and there are places in the house where everything is disorganised, and so we have to put everything in its place. He was looking for some papers and he was opening boxes and at that moment a photo fell from one of the boxes right next to my computer. And it was a photo of my father. And so, I looked at the photo of my father, well, it was of my mother and father's wedding; it was a photo that was taken of them kissing, with the cake beside them…a typical wedding photo. And I was filled with so much sadness because I thought about the fact that he missed out on raising his kids…he didn't know his own children, he didn't get to know his grandchildren…. (Ibarzábal 2009)

When Silvia talks about the effects of the father's disappearance on her life, and that she has never been able to read the letter her father wrote to her, one hears a deep pain caused by grief, the "locus" of her pain; and within the locus there are no words (Ross 2003). Silvia tried to explain for me the inexplicable. Her attempt to describe the way these painful memories affected her in the present brings to mind the words of Argentine scholar Luisa Valenzuela (cited in Gordon 2008, p. 83), best known for her work in response to the dictatorship: "What goes unsaid, that which is implied and omitted and censured and suggested, acquires the importance of a scream." When I asked her how she feels when remembering, Silvia told me:

> Abominable. Even though I'm not a person of faith [in religion], I have never felt hatred…it's a feeling I've never experienced, but instead I feel a deep pain…So you ask me how I feel…abominable…I feel bad, in this moment I feel so much pain, so much anxiety and here I am sitting here telling you this 35 years later. (Ibarzábal 2009)

Judith Butler offers a poignant description of how deep memories can resist and undermine the efforts of those attempting to recover from trauma to lead a normal, daily life:

> I think one is hit by waves, and that one starts out the day with an aim, a project, a plan, and finds oneself foiled. One finds oneself fallen. One is exhausted but does not know why. Something is larger than one's own deliberate plan, one's own project, one's own knowing and choosing. (2004, p. 21)

Silvia's story shows just how difficult it is for the women interviewed to cope on a daily basis, when their existence has been so disfigured by the violent wrenching away of a loved one. "Memory must work between the figure of the one who has died and the life disfigured by death", argues artist Doris Salcedo (cited in Bennett 2002, p. 347). The grief felt by the women who have survived the disappearance and death of loved ones is heartbreakingly explained in Delbo's *Days and Memories* (2001, p. 5) when she tells the story of one women's grief on surviving her sister: "One doesn't die from grief…You go on living." Delbo further expands on what the woman must endure in the aftermath of losing a loved one:

> You go on living, yes. It's worse. She lives in her grief, lives with her sorrow, that unfaltering double of herself. She bears her grief ever since she bore in her arms that sister of hers, who died in the night…Softly she blew her breath upon her sister's face to warm the lips that were turning blue, to impart her own breath to them, and when her sister's heart stopped, she was filled with anger at her own which continued to beat. Which yet beats today, after all these years she has spent on the borders of life. And when she says that you don't die from grief, she's apologizing for being alive. Barely alive. (2001, p. 5)

In witnessing the recall of such deep memory, it becomes clear that no amount of public truth-telling, including oral testimony, can ease the pain of the women's deep memories that persist outside the parameters of closure (Langer 1995). Silvia told me that even when she saw on television that the man held responsible for the killing of her father had died, it did nothing to ease her painful memories:

> Clearly the pain and the traumatic experience I lived through, or, the awful memories—this never changes. So, he [her father's murderer] was imprisoned for three years, was pardoned and was freed. This man had the opportunity to form a political party, which never amounted to anything because he became sick and died. And even then I didn't feel anything when he died, not happiness or sadness, not even the feeling that he deserved it… no, nothing. And I believe that it's because of this, that nothing changes [of feeling painful memories]. (Ibarzábal 2009)

Silvia's deep memories, and the physical and psychic pain with which they leave her, prevent her from transcending the deep pain associated with her past. Though the object of Silvia's pain (her father's murderer) is no longer alive, she feels that despite his death, nothing has changed. Her narrative shows us how the locus of pain remains with the individual long after experiencing the original trauma. Her deep memories are a clear sign that her life will not be one of renewal, but will continue to be one of endurance. Her pain does not just magically dissipate with this man's death. Though she perhaps would have thought she would feel a sense of peace or relief, or perhaps even justice, if such a thing were to happen, she admits that she feels nothing. Some of the other women with whom I spoke also conceded a similar experience. For example, Cristina told me:

> Looking back, it occurs to me that if I could have…if they could have allowed me to…who knows, know the truth of what happened to my husband, over these last thirty-two years,

> I could have gotten over the hurt so much sooner…who knows maybe, maybe not. I can't see that which didn't happen…I don't know…I only know that which happened. (Muro 2009)

While Cristina thinks she would have overcome the deep pain she now feels had she known the truth about what really happened to her husband following his disappearance much earlier, she cannot be certain that this would have been the case. The women's testimonies reveal how deep memory can inhibit the sense of relief and finality that the concepts of truth and justice are supposed to deliver. Their deep memories will never leave them, will never fade with time, and will never cease to be a burden on their lives. While we, as listeners, might wish to intrude on the women's memories, hoping that closure and certainty is possible amidst such devastation, it is revealing how deep memory defies closure or indeed any type of certainty.[2] To those who tell her that surely time has healed her wounds, Eliana tells them:

> I believe that even if they returned the bodies, even if we found the remains and held ceremonies with their ashes and everything, the pain would still be there…because those who give their DNA, [in order] to have a chance of greater certainty can never take away [the pain] of disappearance…I don't know. You need to ask the people who have found the remains [of loved ones] if it has brought them any relief. And on the other hand, you think, "What would I do if they gave me them [the remains] back? What would I do if I found the remains?" (Carreira 2009)

Eliana finds herself contemplating an unbearable future predicament. While she goes forward with the process of submitting her DNA in the hope of finding the remains of her sister, she asks whether her actions will really deliver her what she is seeking. Though she wants to feel relief from knowing with certainty where the remains of her sister are, Eliana admits that this knowledge may not in fact provide her with the relief she seeks. Though Eliana hopes to feel relief one day, she knows that she could also continue to be stalked by the durational time of deep memory. Langer (1995, p. 22) tells us how duration "relentlessly stalks the memory of the witness, imprinting there moments immune to the ebb and flow of chronological time". What Eliana is saying is that: "No public ritual can ease the sting of such private recall, which persists outside the frame of consolation or closure" (Langer 1995, p. 22).

This exploration into how deep memories work tells us that, in bearing witness to the women's testimonies, we cannot disable the potency and persistence of deep memories. We cannot ignore their disruptive force or sweep them under the carpet altogether to achieve a "tidier", more seamless version of history. Instead, we need to honour what deep memories have to tell us so they may be a source of

[2] Grunebaum and Henri (2003) highlight how survivors of traumatic violence can experience further disembodiment when their personal memories of violence are silenced and edited out of public memory in the name of nation-building. Their discussion reveals how commissioners of South Africa's Truth and Reconciliation Commission (TRC) would interrupt survivors' oral testimonies in response to their own feelings of personal discomfort at hearing the details of extreme violence especially that inflicted on women. They investigate how the narrative structure of the TRC process covered over "problematised" personal memory by constructing a public memory based on heroism, sacrifice and redemption (Grunebaum and Henri 2003).

a different kind of understanding of Argentina's violent past. In critically analysing the way in which deep memory plays out in survivors' everyday lives, we are given insight into why oft-repeated statements such as a "past that refuses to go away" or "an unmastered past" remain relevant to the Argentine context today. The women's embodiment of their traumatic memories points to that which is residual and indigestible, and "against which historical knowledge seems to falter and break" (Faye 2003, p. 163). Exploring deep memory exposes the unconscious ways in which the women remain attached to this violent period of history. It shows us that even when survivors of violence successfully manage to seek justice, the psychical and physical pain provoked by deep memory will continue to be a part of their lives, insofar as memories of torture, disappearance and murder continue to exist (Perera, 2001).

In deep memory, time itself divides and splits in such a way that individuals unconsciously relive and re-enact the violence they originally experienced (Langer 1995). Engaging with women's deep memories of trauma clearly shows how "disruptive memories come to bear out the powerful consequences of trauma on an individual who narrates the memory of that trauma" (Grunebaum and Henri 2003, p. 103). The women live in two different worlds: the world of trauma and the world of their everyday life. The women exist in a parallel existence, switching from one to the other simultaneously. Though they are not incomparable worlds, it can be impossible to bridge the two existences at times and the women, as Delbo eloquently describes it, "live in a double existence" (cited in Langer 1991, p. 6). Exploring deep memory allows us to engage with the various complex layers of memory through which a traumatic experience is viscerally experienced by survivors, so we can enter the realms of the traumatic experience on its own terms (Langer 1995). Only then can we acknowledge just how histories live on undiminished, their substance unaltered, in the present day and beyond.

Chapter 6
Social Forces Shaping Memory Transmission

6.1 Trauma and Group Identity

> And so, after my father's death, all of a sudden I was the one who had to pick up the pieces of my family because my family wasn't coping, so I had to try to move forward with this, this … When one is a survivor it's a difficult thing to carry. Because even though my brothers and sisters are here, and they have their families, they have children, they're stigmatised for this [father's history]. And that makes me sad because we are good people … but we have holes in our hearts that prevent us from feeling free [enough] to confront [the challenges] that life brings every day (Paz 2009).

Victoria's traumatic memory of the kidnapping and murder of her father captures the essence of the period of political terror leading up to the 1976 military coup, and the rupture of her and her family's history. Victoria draws on her experiences of trauma to shape her life narrative; in turn, her identity is shaped by this narrative (Antze and Lambek 1996). Victoria's story marks "an intersection of personal and societal histories and becomes a *benchmark*" that allows her to say "I was there" at a significant point of Argentina's history (Gaskell and Wright 1997, p. 179). Gaskell and Wright talk about the way in which traumatic memories play an important role in the organisation of an individual's own identity: "Selected memories become the props or pillars of a person's self-definition" (1997, p. 177). Since her father's murder, Victoria has identified very strongly as the official keeper of her father's memory, and regularly gives oral testimony in the public sphere as a way of remembering her father. She told me:

> Even though people tell me that I am [a victim], I don't like being seen as a victim. I prefer … the victim is my father, and yes, in a certain way so am I even though I don't like identifying as such (Paz 2009).

Though Victoria does not want to see herself as a victim, because her father was a victim of political violence, it is an identity she also agrees to assume. In remembering this violent period of Argentina's past through the lens of her own private history, Victoria's memories of trauma not only locate her as an individual but also serve to identify her as a member of the group El Centro de Estudios Legales Sobre El Terrorismo Y sus Victimas (Centre for Legal Studies of Terrorism and its Victims) (CELTYV). As Victoria discusses the significance of the traumatic events she lived through with others, her memories become the shared property and part of the identity of the group;

J. Stockwell, *Reframing the Transitional Justice Paradigm*,
Springer Series in Transitional Justice 10, DOI 10.1007/978-3-319-03853-7_6,

they "map" the significance of the violence she experienced onto the group's history (Gaskell and Wright 1997). While Victoria may not wish to see herself as a victim, the group with which she is associated employs its members' experiences of trauma and victimisation as the group's justification and legitimisation. CELTYV adopts the discourse of human rights to legitimise its claims for political, legal and social recognition of its painful past, and hence the equal treatment and support of its members.

In Argentina, different memory groups place trauma at the heart of memory; what is remembered gains in moral weight (Mistzal 2004). The core meaning of the different groups' identities is sustained by their own unique interpretation of the traumatic past, and as such develops into a strong duty to remember (Mistzal 2004). With the decline of national memory as a stable source of group identity, traumatic memory has been assigned an increasingly greater role in Argentina; it provides the identity of a group and supports identities that might otherwise remain on the margins of memorial culture (Mistzal 2004). The politicisation of the traumatic memories of memory groups, which establish their memories of the past as not only a source of a sense of inheritance but also as their identities' sole justification and legitimisation, has its consequences (Mistzal 2004). As remembering becomes overshadowed by what is remembered, traumatic memories have acquired a new status; they are employed by the politics of identity movements as a way of empowering groups to legitimise their claims and to address past injustices (Mistzal 2004).

While the use of memories of victimisation to restore a sense of moral community is not new, Jeffrey Prager believes that the "visibility of traumatic memory of collective injustice has surfaced in connection with the politics of identity, and these two factors, by working together, make the group's reason for being, and the individual's identification with it self-evident" (cited in Misztal 2004, p. 75). When a common past becomes more about the duty to remember than about real memories, memory groups are inclined to transform individuals' past sufferings into an "icon of identity" and an instrument of community power and cohesion (Mistzal 2003, p. 75).

Powerful collective memories about the period of state and political violence of the 1970s and 1980s have heightened political and social tensions in contemporary Argentina. In turn, strong bonds have been formed between individuals from within adversarial memorial cultures, resulting in highly specific collective memories. Much of the power of these collective memories, I argue, has in part been derived from the strong emotions that they provoke. For memory belongs in the "intermediary realm" between individuals; it develops and grows out of the interplay of interpersonal relations, and as such the emotions play an important role in this process (Assmann 2006b, p. 3).

6.2 Social Sharing of Emotions

The women's emotional investment in the recalling and retelling of their traumatic experiences is strong. However, this investment can reinforce their fixation on a past that keeps in place, and possibly deepens, their already traumatised state (Jelin 2003). As Dori Laub explains:

> [T]here is so much destruction recounted, so much death, so much loss, so much hopelessness, that there has to be an abundance of holding and of emotional investment in the encounter, to keep alive the witnessing narration: otherwise the whole experience of the testimony can end up in silence, in complete withholding (cited in Yaeger 2006, p. 415).

Cristina reflected on what motivated her personally to emotionally invest in the retelling of her traumatic past:

> I'm not so sure that everything is finished with; it could happen again. We always thought that it would never happen again and …First of all I was anxious, I was very anxious … now it gives me a feeling of … a feeling of terror that come back to worry me, like I used to have [during the dictatorship]. There are moments when that feeling comes, for example with what happened to Jorge Julio López,[1] is like [the feeling] I had in the very beginning, in the middle of my stomach. I think of my kids, grandkids, of what could happen to other kids (Muro 2009).

Cristina is prompted by events, such as further disappearances during the trials of the military, including that of Jorge Julio López, an eye-witness of human rights abuses and survivor of one of the military's clandestine detention centres, to evaluate the probability of a repeat of the terror she experienced, and is filled with fear as a result. Contemporary theories of emotions indicate that they function in a way that prepares an individual to cope with his/her environment (Finkenauer et al. 1997). Scherer (1984) proposes that individuals continuously perform appraisals of their environment, and the outcome of this process can lead to different emotional states (in Finkenauer et al. 1997). In turn, these varied states can prepare the individual for an interaction with the environment (in Finkenauer et al. 1997). As explored in the previous chapter, Cristina can be plunged into deep memories of terror with the same intensity that she experienced in the past. She experiences embodied memories of fear whenever she is confronted with the perceived instability of present realities. As a result, she feels motivated to protect the future for her children and grandchildren, and is compelled to continue relating her own traumatic story with others as a way of preventing a return to this violent past.

As Cristina repeatedly and openly relates her emotional story, and her feelings and reactions to others, her private emotional experience "feeds" into collective memory through an important social psychological process called the "social sharing of emotions" (Rimé and Christophe 1997, p. 133). There is a good deal of empirical evidence suggesting that emotions tend to be socially shared (Rimé and Christophe 1997). While researchers previously considered emotions as merely a short-lived and intrapersonal phenomenon, more recent theories and evidence on emotions reveal strong evidence that emotions are essentially interpersonal communicative acts, which instead involve long-term social processes: The more individuals are upset, the more likely they are to share their story with others and to elicit vivid, precise and long-lasting memories of the event (Rimé and Christophe 1997).

[1] Jorge Julio López is a survivor of one of the military's clandestine detention centres. He was forcefully abducted and disappeared between 1976 and 1979. He was again kidnapped in September 2006 on his way to court to testify against renowned perpetrator of human rights abuses, Miguel Etchecolatz, the ex-director general of police investigations for Buenos Aires province. He has remained disappeared ever since.

This process can influence the way a historical experience is organised in memory and perhaps recalled in the future (Pennebaker and Banasik 1997).

Pennebaker and Banasik suggest that, "for societies to exist at all, the societal members must share a very high percentage of their experiences to increase the cohesiveness of their memories" (1997, p. 7).[2] The creation and continuance of a group's collective memory is a dynamic social and psychological process that encourages a societal or cultural group's members to talk, rehearse and reflect about the circumstances in which they were involved (Pennebaker and Banasik 1997). This interpersonal interaction is a critical process for an individual's and group's organisation and assimilation of an event into the form of a collective narrative (Pennebaker and Banasik 1997).

An emotional experience often provokes verbal rehearsal and social sharing with others in a group because of the affected individual's need to understand, process and learn about what they experienced (Finkenauer et al. 1997). Indeed, sharing their narratives with others has been an important vehicle for individuals in Argentina to cognitively process and make meaning following the experience of emotional trauma. This was particularly true for Eliana, who told me that she could not bring herself to look at a photo of her disappeared sister for 10 years, so consumed was she with the guilt of both having survived her, and of her own actions during the dictatorship. She still grapples with the fact that while her sister was disappeared, Eliana was out celebrating the Football World Cup with her young son. She told me:

> There are things that are incomprehensible. For example, I remember with a terrible feeling of guilt that I celebrated the World Cup but in reality later, to make peace with myself… in reality, at this time, my son was little; he was 4 years old and we went out into the plaza in Lomas to celebrate the World Cup … But later, I thought how could I have … how could I have gone out and celebrated? … (Carreira 2009).

Eliana said she lived in denial about the fate of her sister until as recently as 2000, when she finally decided to find out more and joined the organisation Las Familiares. She said she was so fearful about finding out the truth about her sister that she had lived in a fantasy world until only recently. She preferred to believe that her sister was in exile somewhere or was in a psychiatric institution (Carreira 2009). Even after joining Las Familiares, Eliana said she continued to deny many things,

[2] Maurice Halbwachs (1992) originally asserted that, rather than residing within the individual, memories are formed and organised within a collective context, and that as a result various groups of people have different collective memories, which in turn give rise to different modes of behaviour. In other words, Halbwachs (1992) believes that the memory of individuals is influenced by the social context in which they function and that virtually all experiences and perceptions are shaped by one individual's interaction with another. Halbwachs makes the important observation that collective memory deals with "memory *in* the group, and not memory *of* the group" (Bartlett, cited in Wertsch 2002, p. 22). He writes: "While the collective memory endures and draws strength from its base in a coherent body of people, it is individuals as group members who remember" (Bartlett, cited in Wertsch 2002, p. 48). Collective memories thus emerge as members of a group, who have all participated in an event being remembered, share and discuss memories based on their individual experiences—although some may remember events differently from others (Wertsch 2002). Memory is thus an intersubjective process, derived from people remembering and sharing memories together (Halbwachs 1992).

including details told to her by Maria Del Soccoro, who was imprisoned with her sister during the dictatorship. She told me:

> I tell you I have a grand ability to deny what is happening around me, but what I did do was listen to what Maria had to tell me, tranquilly, because Maria told me a lot of things. So much so that at times I would say, "Maria I'd prefer you shut up rather than tell me …." (Carreira 2009).

Committing to give oral testimony in the public sphere was one way for Eliana to open up to learning more about her sister from those who knew her. However, delving into what happened to her sister following her disappearance by the military forces only began once Eliana felt ready to approach the organisation Las Familiares. Once she became part of the group, Eliana began the process of remembering her sister with others within the context of the group. For example, Maria del Socorro's memories radically shaped Eliana's own memories of her sister. Eliana's experience shows the back-and-forth interplay between individual and collective remembering. The dynamics of the group not only transform and shape the memories of the group itself, but also impact on the individuals who form part of it.

Becoming part of the organisation Las Familiares and giving her oral testimony in the public sphere has also been a way for Eliana to confront internal demons in relation to her own actions during the dictatorship. Eliana feels guilty about her own denial of her sister's disappearance for so many years. The guilt she feels compels her to invest emotionally in the repeated public sharing of her personal, truthful, and painful story. She told me that she will never rest, but will continue to give oral testimony because of, among other things, a moral obligation she feels towards her sister's memory:

> I'm ticked off. And yes, on top of that I have a moral obligation; I'll never find any peace unless I do something (Carreira 2009).

Oral testimony has played a crucial role in how events have collectively been assimilated and remembered in Argentina. The significance of the political and state violence of the 1970s and 1980s has been orally transmitted within Argentina's memorial cultures, and individuals' perceptions and understanding of the event have been shaped by those giving oral testimony. In continuously speaking publicly about their traumatic memories and relating their emotional experiences in the form of oral testimony, the women I interviewed have thus played a significant role in socially sharing their emotions. However, I suggest that this process has contributed significantly to the ongoing polarisation between the Right and Left. I argue that the process of telling and retelling of individuals' memories never "exhausts" the violence that was inflicted during the period of political and state violence, but instead symbolises and even evokes it. The fear and terror associated with past violence are strongly communicated by the women in their narratives, and this in turn can engender strong feelings in those listening.

There is a good deal of empirical evidence—particularly as demonstrated in a study by Pennebaker et al. (1987)—of Holocaust survivors talking about their traumatic experiences, to suggest that exposure to the emotional narrative of another can induce considerable emotional changes in the individual listening (Rimé and Christophe 1997). In fact, Rimé and Christophe's study showed that the more the survivors revealed their in-depth emotions when talking about their experiences, the more emotionally affected were the listeners (1997). This process is important for the transmission of private emotional experiences into the wider community because:

> If exposure to the social sharing of an emotion elicits in its turn an emotional state in the listening persons, then it should be predicted that these listeners would later be inclined to socially share with some third persons the narrative to which they were exposed (Rimé and Christophe 1997, p. 137).

While the "primary" social sharing of emotion involves the affected individuals narrating their experiences on several different occasions, "secondary" social sharing involves a different process whereby the recalled information is transmitted through a chain of individuals (Rimé and Christophe 1997). Studies have found that rather than recalling stories verbatim, listeners are more likely to reconstruct the story and process the received emotional information through a filter of pre-existing "schemata" of emotions (Rimé and Christophe 1997). Rimé and Christophe conclude that this combination of repeated telling of a strong emotional experience and the related number of serial reproductions serves collective interests; secondary social sharing "contributes to the spreading of emotional knowledge within a community" (1997, p. 144). We can see this process clearly at work when Gladys, whose military husband was killed by the armed guerrilla movement in 1976, reiterated information that she had received through others about the "real" fate of the *desaparecidos:*

> The children that they [human rights organisations/families of the disappeared] say are disappeared … you can't believe that it's true. Some friends of mine went to see the names listed on the posters [of Las Madres] in the Plaza de Mayo and they know for a fact that they are alive. So it's not certain … it's not certain (Echegoyen 2009).

Gladys is visibly angry as she reconstructs and shares with me "information" that she has received from others within her memorial group. It is information that serves to create a doubt about the fate of the *desaparecidos*. As Gladys circulates the information, her emotional experience also circulates and spreads throughout her social group. Harber originally developed the idea that communicated emotional experiences can "feed" social knowledge of emotion, using the term "the human broadcaster" (cited in Rimé and Christophe 1997, p. 143). Harber proposed that individuals' inclination to communicate an emotional experience served both an intrapersonal need, in the sense of gaining perspective, as well as an interpersonal need for news (cited in Rimé and Christophe 1997). Therefore, as individuals repeatedly relate their emotional experiences to others, the social group gradually assimilates those experiences and, as a result, is furnished with new emotional knowledge (cited in Rimé and Christophe 1997). And as we can see from Gladys' narrative, as the two groups of women share memories about their traumatic life events in the public sphere, the attitudes of those listening can become more extreme towards past collective issues and the current society (Paez et al.1997).

In going beyond the women's standard narratives of trauma and violence, and in exploring the transmission of their emotions, we can see how the women have "an ability to affect and be affected" when they talk about their shared pasts (Massumi 1987, p. xvi). I argue that the women's emotions are a social force that remains and is at work in the public sphere long after they have shared their experiences with others. I suggest that the women's emotions leave an affective residue, or what Gregg and Seigworth (2010, p. 9) call a "bloom-space". These emotions are a central part of unseen forces that mark the "passages of intensities" between individuals, and determine the relationship between ourselves and others (Gregg and Seigworth 2010, p. 13). This residue has what Anna Gibbs (2010, p. 187) describes as an "energetic dimension" or "capacity". I suggest that it is this capacity which contributes towards a sense of the continuance or "on-goingness" of animosity and resentment over time. The affective residue helps to sustain and preserve the connections between those ideas, thoughts, values and habits that act as an affective charge within a politics of remembering in contemporary Argentine society.

6.3 Transmission of Affects

Though not always visible or noticed, powerful affects are also released in the process of individuals remembering and sharing their traumatic pasts. Like the emotions, affect is another social force that structures group identities, and the traffic between the individual and collective forms of remembrance. Affect also plays a role in what Stern calls "the interpersonal traffic of feeling" (cited in Watkins 2010, p. 278). Affect is not momentary or transient in quality, but accumulates over time and predisposes individuals to act and react in particular ways (Watkins 2010). Affect is the name we give to those forces that can serve as a kind of "raw psychic material" to drive us towards movement and thought, and influence our conscious and unconscious habits, behaviours and attitudes (Tumarkin 2009, p. 8). Indeed, the vital forces of affect go beyond the emotions, argue Gregg and Seigworth (2010, p. 2), and can transpire "within and across the subtlest of shuttling intensities: all the minuscule or molecular events of the unnoticed."

When the body is in the grip of experiencing affects, stimuli overwhelm the body, and the body responds by registering them as intensity (Gregg and Seigworth 2010). Affect is this intensity. Silvan Tomkins explains that affect has the power to influence consciousness by amplifying our bodily awareness:

> The affect mechanism is like the pain mechanism in this respect. If we cut our hand, saw it bleeding, but had no innate pain receptors, we would know we had done something which needed repair, but there would be no urgency to it. Like our automobile which needs a tune-up, we might well let it go until next week when we had more time. But the pain mechanism, like the affect mechanism, so amplifies our awareness of the injury which activates it that we are forced to be concerned, and concerned immediately (in Tomkins et al.1995, p. 88).

Sigmund Freud claims that affect does not so much think but act, and that it "persists in immediate adjacency to the movements of thought" (cited in Gregg and Seigworth 2010, p. 2). Affect cannot be fully realised in language, as it is always prior to or in excess of conscious states of perception (Massumi 2002). It has a grammar of its own, and is the body's way of preparing it for action and reaction in a given environment at a certain level of intensity (Massumi 2002). Massumi defines affect in terms of its autonomy from conscious perception, emotion and language; it is about the body opening up to the indeterminacy of its automatic responses (Deleuze and Guattari 1987). Affect plays a huge role in how attachments are formed and what keeps those attachments in place (Ahmed 2004b). It can be both intimate and impersonal, and

> accumulates across both relatedness and interruptions in relatedness, becoming a palimpsest of force-encounters traversing the ebbs and swells of intensities that pass between "bodies" (bodies defined not by an outer skin-envelope or other surface boundary but by their potential to reciprocate or co-participate in the passages of affect) (Gregg and Seigworth 2010, p. 2).

It is within this ever-gathering growth of force relations that the inherent power and potential of affect lie—in the body's ability to affect and to be affected (Gregg and Seigworth 2010). Gilles Deleuze's work on corporeality suggests the ways in which affect is mediated through the dynamic interaction between different bodies: "A body affects other bodies, or is affected by other bodies; it is this capacity for affecting and being affected that also defines a body in its individuality" (1988, p. 123). Deleuze's theory challenges assumptions about the boundaries and the boundedness of bodies, or "what we take to be our own and how one body relates to others" in its vicinity (Probyn 2010, p. 76). In Deleuze's model, affect does not encroach on the body from the outside, and it does not emerge from the inside (Probyn 2010). Instead, the body is "always already wholly implicated in its milieu" (Gatens 2004, p. 115).

We can apply Delueze's model of bodily affect to contemporary Argentina as a way of understanding how the fear lodged deep inside the mental space of Argentine civilians by the military government persists and circulates in non-verbal and non-representational ways among individuals and throughout the society today. In our interview, Abuela Buscarita and Abuela Raquel told me that a well-known secret detention centre used by the military to torture the *desaparecidos* was located around the corner from the Abuelas head office. They avoid walking or driving past the centre because it induces so much fear and anxiety within them—so much so that it can raise the hair on their skin. The women know that, historically, the building holds within it a level of danger; they already have an impression of the risks associated with the building and this impression is felt on the surface of their skin (Ahmed 2004a). The fear and anxiety is exacerbated as the Abuelas pass by the building because they are physically reminded of their deep losses, and this anxiety is displaced on to the object of their fear (Ahmed 2004a): the detention centre. As a result, fear shapes the borders between the Abuelas and the building, as they affectively grasp that it is a danger that should be avoided.

Deleuze's idea about the ability of bodies to affect and to be affected provides a powerful way of understanding how the women's feelings of loss, melancholy, and anger when remembering their traumatic pasts can accumulate, seep into and reside within other bodies in the public sphere, altering individuals' understanding of their selves as well as their relation with the past (Probyn 2010). Going public with their narratives ensures that testimony occupies a public sphere, which can include both identifiable witnesses as well as potential addressees (Rothberg 2008). In this way, the circulation of the women's narratives and the accompanying affects result in the shaping of the contours of the public space they inhabit (Rothberg 2008). Their public testimonies fill this space with "the psychic and physical losses that cannot be transcended" (Rothberg 2008, p. 219).

If we think about Deleuze's explanation of how affect works, then we are able to consider what this process of remembering may produce in the context of post-dictatorship Argentina. Looking to affect to understand what is really being remembered in Argentina and the frequently and consequentially intangible ways in which it is being remembered means we can move away from the total reliance on declarational forms of remembering towards engaging with pre-cognitive and non-representational mnemonic processes. Exploring how affect is retained and accumulated, and the way in which it can circulate between bodies and shape subjectivities, is crucial to our understanding of how it can form and mobilise individuals or groups in different ways over a period of time. If we come to understand how affect works to align individuals with communities, we can also explore the crucial role it plays in the materialisation of collective bodies, including the "body of a nation" (Ahmed 2004a).

6.4 Affect and Perception

A number of scholars (e.g. Brennan 2004; Gibbs 2001; Probyn 2005; Sedgwick 2003) suggest that affects can be contagious. Anna Gibbs describes this process:

> Bodies can catch feelings as easily as catch fire: affect leaps from one body to another, evoking tenderness, inciting shame, igniting rage, exciting fear—in short, communicable affect can inflame nerves and muscles in a conflagration of every conceivable kind of passion (2001, p. 1).

Teresa Brennan's work on the transmission of affect (2004) develops this idea in her model of connectedness and transmission of affects. In *The Transmission of Affect* (2004), Brennan asks (2004, p. 1): "is there anyone who has not, at least once, walked into a room and 'felt the atmosphere?'" Brennan's idea also forms part of the intellectual history of crowd psychology and the sociology of emotion, and explains that we are not self-contained in terms of our energies; there is no clear boundary separating individuals and their environment. She suggests that it is primarily a modern and western approach to assume that the individual is energetically self-contained, and that affects and feelings are an individual's alone (Brennan 2004).

Brennan's study of the transmission of affect in crowd settings and gatherings indicates that the affects of one individual can enter another.

Brennan hypothesises that the origin of transmitted affects is social, since affects can arise from within an individual but can also occur as a result of an interaction between an individual and his/her environment: "By the transmission of affect, I mean simply that the emotions or affects of one person, and the enhancing or depressing energies these affects entail, can enter into another" (2004, p. 3). This, she asserts, does not mean that an individual's particular emotional experience is irrelevant. Instead, Brennan points out that if one picks up on another's feelings or emotions, the thoughts one attaches to that affect remain one's own: "they remain the product of the particular historical conjunction of worlds and experiences I represent. The thoughts are not necessarily tied to the affects they appear to evoke. One may as well say that the affects evoke the thoughts" (Brennan 2004, p. 7). We can see in Gladys' example how the doubt spread among other members of her memorial group leads her to openly and publicly doubt the claims of Las Madres and the human rights movement in her narrative.

I suggest that we look to theories of affect contagion as a way of understanding the role affects may play in the constitution of a relationship between individuals, groups and communities (Ahmed 2004a). In her model of the sociality of emotions, Sara Ahmed (2004a) suggests that emotions create "surfaces and boundaries" that assist individuals to discern between what is inside and outside in the first place. She believes that surfaces and boundaries are made precisely through the emotions, or through how individuals respond to objects, situations or others (Ahmed 2004a). Ahmed (2004b) uses the term "object" to refer to objects, situations or individuals.

Rather than the emotions themselves circulating, Ahmed (2004a) argues that it is the objects of emotion that move and circulate, and that are the sites of personal and social tension. Her thinking stems from Descartes' critique of the idea that emotions are reducible to sensations insofar as they are caused by objects (Ahmed 2004b). Descartes suggests that we do not have feelings for objects because of their very nature but because of the "shape" of the contact we have with them (Ahmed 2004b, p. 5).[3] The example of what physically happens to the Abuelas as they come into contact with a former clandestine detention centre is an example of Descartes' theory.

In exploring the sociality of affects, we can begin to understand how affects work to align some individuals with some and against others (Ahmed 2004a). Ahmed's theory of affective attachment in particular gives us a way of understanding how

[3] Ahmed (2004b) argues that emotions are about objects that shape, but are at the same time also shaped by, contact with these objects themselves. The object need not have a material existence to work in this way but can also be something imagined. For example, an individual can have a memory of something, and that memory can trigger a feeling (Pugmire, cited in Ahmed 2004b, p. 7): "The memory can be the object of my feeling in both senses: the feeling is shaped by contact with the memory, and also involves an orientation towards what is remembered." An individual might feel pain when they remember an event, and in remembering the event they might attribute pain to what is remembered (Ahmed 2004b).

emotions play a crucial role in the "surfacing of individual and collective bodies" (2004a, p. 25). How we feel about others is what aligns us with a collective (Ahmed 2004a). A collective body only "takes shape" as an effect of such alignments, through the impressions made by others (Ahmed 2004a). While Ahmed's theory relates to the circulation of the emotions, her argument seems pertinent when it is also extended to affect. I suggest that her theory offers a way to talk about both emotions and affect, and the ways in which both of them can shape individual and group perception.

Emotions and affects align individuals with communities through an intensity of attachment—or in other words, those ideas/thoughts/ties that connects us to one thing or another: that which makes us feel; or that which holds us in place (Ahmed 2000). In this way, the forming of the individual and the nation arises partly by viewing the "other" as the cause of one's emotional duress (Ahmed 2004a). It is through being moved by the proximity of another that affective attachments take place, affecting some differently from others (Ahmed 2004a). So, for example, when the group Las Abuelas de la Plaza de Mayo was nominated to receive the Nobel Peace Prize, an email petition was circulated by El Centro de Estudios Legales Sobre El Terrorismo Y sus Victimas (Centre for Legal Studies of Terrorism and its Victims) (CELTYV) asking for signatures in protest at the nomination of Las Abuelas. The petition stated that Las Abuelas had never spoken out in support of the victims of the armed guerrilla movement, and was in fact associated with those guerrillas who had killed their family members (the Right routinely refers to the mothers and grandmothers of the disappeared as "mothers of terrorists"). The petition, to date with nearly 22,000 signatures, was sent to the Nobel Prize committee citing opposition based on the following rationale:

> This association [Las Abuelas], made up of mothers of combatants of illegal armed organisations, does not bring a message of peace to Argentina, nor does it recognise since its creation, the criminal actions committed by its family members involved in terrorist organisations that are responsible for attacks on more than 18,000 innocent victims.
>
> The families of the victims of terror have never heard, in 26 years of democratic rule, one word of consolation or empathy from members of an organisation which supports the impunity of terrorists, a unilateral version of history, and the actions and disappearance of the collective memory of thousands of innocent victims of bomb attacks, kidnappings, torture, assassinations, and robberies, all left unpunished (www.petitiononline.com/celtyv1a/petition).

Such a narrative produces a polarisation between the two groups of victims, and sets up an "us" versus "them" dichotomy that blames Las Abuelas for destroying any future possibility for peace and reconciliation in Argentina. The online petition reveals the existence of a perceived injury: the refusal of Las Abuelas to negate the violence committed by the armed guerrilla movement is constituted as the cause of CELTYV members' ongoing feelings of pain. CELTYV feels it is the injured party—the one that is hurt by the silence of Las Abuelas. It perceives this wall of silence as a direct provocation, and holds Las Abuelas accountable for putting the well-being of the nation at risk.

One's perception of another involves a form of "contact" between the individual and the "other" that is shaped by longer histories of contact (Ahmed 2004b, p. 194): "These histories have already impressed upon the surface of the bodies at the same time as they create new impressions." It is the "moment of contact", shaped and informed by past histories, that allows the proximity of the "other" to thus be perceived as threatening (Ahmed 2004a). In this way, we can see how affects work to secure collectives through the way they align some individuals together, but are against others (Ahmed 2004a). In the example of the online petition, hatred plays a role in shaping collectives by way of generating and sustaining injured parties that adopt defensive approaches against those whose proximity is perceived as threatening. CELTYV feels threatened and victimised by Las Abuelas in the present because the organisation is seen as fighting for the memory of those "subversives" who killed their family members.

The intensity of attachment the women feel for the "other" has been shaped by the changing political approaches to collective remembering in Argentina over the last three decades. As a result, the affective responses the women have towards their traumatic memories are partly triggered by the collective political approach to memorialisation in Argentina (Traverso 2010, p. 182). This point was clearly articulated by Gladys, who expressed her despair with what she perceived as the current government's "protection" of human rights groups within Argentina. Gladys believes, these groups shelter those who committed crimes within the armed guerrilla movement, including those who killed her husband.

Trust has been shown to be essential for effective social and political systems (Dunn and Schweitzer 2005). However, because Gladys feels excluded from current political discourse, and perceives the government's inaction over trials for guilty individuals formerly associated with the armed guerrilla movement, she is unable to trust the current political arrangement or any groups that she perceives are associated with it. Trust can also be influenced by one's past experiences or by information given by another about the trustee's reputation (Dunn and Schweitzer 2005). For example, Gladys told me that her husband was killed prior to the military dictatorship by one of her work colleagues with whom she had shared confidences about her husband's political views. Unbeknown to Gladys, her colleague was part of an armed guerrilla group (Echegoyen 2009). Gladys found it very difficult to trust claims made by the families of the *desaparecidos* as a result of her past experience. She told me:

> I've never met them [Las Madres de la Plaza de Mayo], but it makes me mad because they appear with their posters, they are totally protected by this government, they are subsidised by this government, they have initiated countless schools that teach classes, like I've told you, that are Chavista.[4] And so, it's like they've started a cult that is really … I don't know if they know or if they are completely mistaken, but the other day I received an email where there was a list that included the children of Carlotto (president of Las Abuelas) and Bonafini (president of Las Madres) so that they could … It was a voting list, so they could

[4] *Chavista* is a term used to describe the political ideology based on the ideas and programs associated with the president of Venezuela, Hugo Chavez.

> vote ... They're [the disappeared children] alive. So, all those who they say are disappeared, it's not certain ... (Echegoyen 2009).

Paloma Aguilar Fernandez (cited in Jelin 2003, p. 147) suggests that: "One tends to see one's contemporary adversaries through the prism of the adversary that one had in the past." She further argues that "the probabilities of erroneously perceiving present problems increase when an actor had directly experienced similar situations in the past" (Aguilar Fernandez, cited in Jelin 2003, p. 147). Gladys was very confused by the different messages she had received, and mistrustful of some of the claims made by the families of the *desaparecidos* because of her association with them as mothers of "subversives" in the past. In Gladys' narrative, she would often refer to anyone connected to the *desaparecidos* as *subversivos* or "subversives". This term, used by the military government to describe the *desaparecidos* during the dictatorship, is still used by those affiliated with the political Right to describe those involved in human rights organisations today.

Gladys' example illustrates the vexed relationship in Argentina between the changing politics of remembrance and affect. How the women assimilate this difficult relationship can also be seen at a more personal level. Lita told me that she has found herself in very difficult circumstances—circumstances, she admits, that not many of the families of the *desaparecidos* have had to deal with. Lita's cousin served during the military dictatorship and is currently being investigated in connection with crimes against humanity. Lita told me just how compromised she has felt when others within the human rights movement have questioned her because of her continuing association with her cousin. "How can you even say hello to your cousin?" she has been asked. "This mix is not easy", Lita told me (Boitano 2009). She continued with some trepidation:

> He [her cousin] knows very well what I have been doing and has always treated me with respect. On top of that, we grew up together ... he's someone I played with as a kid (Boitano 2009).

The hostility Lita encounters from others within her memorial group because of her connection with her cousin can be explained by Marcus (2000). He suggests that a common application of emotion as information has been the linkage between social category and affective information (Marcus 2000). He draws on studies by Fiske and Pavelchak (1986) to explain that: "If someone is a member of group A, a group I like (or dislike), then I can quickly assess him by applying to him the affective tag of group A" (cited in Marcus 2000, p. 230). Group affect, Marcus (2000) suggests, becomes a reliable gauge of wide political application. In other words, inherent in such a process, individuals do not feel the need to obtain further details or understand an individual in his/her contemporary circumstances, since they can just refer to the group affect tag (Marcus 2000). Marcus's group affect tag theory is further explained by Ahmed (2004a): It is not just how we feel for the collective, but also how we feel about others outside the group that is what aligns us with a collective; the collective only "takes shape" as an effect of such alignments. The emergence of "feelings-in-common" is traceable through how we perceive these impressions that are left by others (Ahmed 2004a, p. 27).

As individuals, we become aware of ourselves through our contact with others (Merleau-Ponty 1962). This contact can generate both positive and negative affects. Power relations have a particular impact on the alignment between individuals when soliciting the recognition of others becomes a measure for the acknowledgement and confirmation of an individual's self-worth. When recognition functions in a negative way and carries with it the resultant force of negative affects, it can have a detrimental effect on an individual's self-worth. The ability of affect to accumulate and its relationship to recognition—and the ways in which this interconnected process may obliterate the possibility for empathic alignment with others—can be seen in the following example of the adversarial nature of interactions between different memorial cultures in Argentina.

In our interview, Barbara told me that to talk about her father is to recuperate his memory. As she was only very young when her father was killed, Barbara has relied on newspaper cuttings and anecdotes from her father's colleagues to paint a picture of who her father really was. The role her journalist father played in the violence of the 1970s before his death—unsolved in her mind—can be a source of intense frustration. "He never killed anyone, I'm sure of it", Barbara told me. She continued:

> Where is the proof? Something … Yes he worked for El Claudillo, a magazine of the extreme Right. He wrote for it yes … for me he wasn't a member of the AAA just because he wrote for this magazine (Tarquini 2009).

She explained further:

> The situation was very violent. He [her father] had a weekly television program where … Tarquini [her father's name] was an easy target. Everyone in the world knew it because he was a very straightforward type, very energetic, and he talked very … he said some very heavy things and in a strong way. My mother said that she knew that he was going to be killed … I don't know … because he was very honest, spontaneous … there were times … he was an exhibitionist (Tarquini 2009).

Barbara describes her internal anguish at the lack of evidence provided by those attempting to vilify her father as a member of a right-wing paramilitary group, and the frustration she has suffered when her efforts to clear her father's name have been thwarted. She often dreams of her father when she is facing great inner turmoil in her life, and she sees him as her protector, not someone who was violent. She tells me that reading his poetry helped her know that her father was not a monster, but that he was killed for speaking publicly about his beliefs. Barbara does not know who killed her father, and tells me of her efforts to leave the past behind are to no avail. She said:

> I never knew that I would be able to dedicate so much of myself to investigating this and it has taken up a large part of my life. I never knew that it would cost me so much emotionally … They [her family] tell me to leave the topic alone; that Papa is dead; that we know who he was; that it's futile to keep searching … I went to the human rights organisations to demand my rights as a victim of the military government because my father was a victim. They told me no, that my father was a fascist, that he didn't belong [to human rights organisations]. I went with witnesses, a lawyer, and friends. How could they say this to me? … They said that [my father] was an activist of the extreme Right and that he had to have fought. But I said that my father wasn't a bad person … What a disaster. The truth is that the human rights organisations here don't exist for me (Tarquini 2009).

When I interview Barbara, she is full of gratitude that I am talking with her at all. She tells me she feels alienated within Argentine society and is forced to dwell on its margins due to what she feels is the public misrepresentation of her father. What is happening in Barbara's case is explained by Brison, who writes:

> How (and even whether) traumatic events are remembered depends on not only how they are initially experienced but also how (whether) they are perceived by others, directly or indirectly, and the extent to which others are able to listen empathically to the survivor's testimony. The traumatic event is experienced as culturally embedded (or framed), is remembered as such (in both traumatic and narrative memory), and is shaped and reshaped in memory over time according, at least in part, to how others in the survivor's culture respond (1999, p. 42).

Barbara struggles with feelings of stigmatisation and public shame because of the presumed role her father played in the terror inflicted by the military. Shame is about appearance, suggests Ahmed (2004b), insofar as it is about how the individual appears to others. The individuality of shame can thus be linked to the sociality of shame since individuals can experience a sense of separateness or "apartness" in the moment of their exposure to another (Ahmed 2004b). Barbara's story illustrates the way in which our perception of something as beneficial or harmful depends on how it affects us (Ahmed 2004b). It is this dependence that opens up a gap in the determination of feeling: "whether something is beneficial or harmful involves thought and evaluation, at the same time that it is 'felt' by the body" (Ahmed 2004b, p. 6). Because of her interface with political and social judgements about the actions of her father in the past, Barbara feels ashamed that she herself has done something wrong; she feels that she is to blame in some way for her father's actions. Current political and social conditions produce within Barbara an ambiguous coexistence between feelings of shame and pride. She carries these contradictory emotions within herself, experiencing great anxiety at being unable to restore her father's memory in the public sphere and attain a sense of pride about who she is.

In Barbara's case, she has failed to elicit for herself a sense of social recognition. As Honneth (1995, p. 95) explains: "Recognition itself must possess the character of affective approval or encouragement." These affects, suggests Watkins (2010, p. 273), "are the corporeal instantiation of recognition, the sensations one may feel in being recognized, which accumulate over time, fostering a sense of self-worth." Moments of recognition therefore function as an affective force (Watkins 2010). Barbara's perception that political, social and cultural recognition is withheld from her when she remembers her father creates feelings of having failed in the eyes of the "ideal other" (Ahmed 2004b).

In Barbara's example, recognition functions in a negative way, and carries with it the resultant force of negative affects. Barbara's sense of shame and her shattered sense of self-worth bind her negatively to others in her failure to "live up to" others (Ahmed 2004b, p. 107). Not only does Barbara have the impression that the government and human rights organisations are marginalising her personal memories of her father; these groups also leave her with the impression that she has something to feel shameful about. She feels that she cannot be a legitimate and recognised player in Argentina's collective memorial culture.

6.5 Damaged Social Bonds

When considering the physical, emotional and psychological damage that the women I interviewed have endured, it is not just the effects of trauma on an individual's bodily or "skin" surface that we need to think about, but the ways in which the "skin" of the community has been also affected (Ahmed 2004a). For example, the violence experienced during the 1970s and 1980s was not just inflicted on the bodies of those individuals who personally lived through the terror, but was also inflicted on the body of Argentine society; society itself was torn apart by the disappearance and murder of thousands of its citizens. The Argentine community was damaged insofar as attachments with loved ones were severed. This has resulted in a collective trauma that has involved "a blow to the basic tissues of social life that damages the bonds attaching people together and impairs the prevailing sense of communality" (Erikson 1995, p. 187).

Kai Erikson (1995) suggests that trauma has a social dimension, and can create community. Erikson argues that the tissues of a traumatised community, as something distinct from a group of traumatised individuals, can be damaged by trauma in the same way as the tissues of the mind and body. In other words, she suggests that traumatic wounds inflicted on individuals can combine to create a group culture that is "more" than the sum of the individuals' private wounds (Erikson 1995). Erikson writes:

> To describe people as traumatized is to say that they have withdrawn into a kind of protective envelope, a place of mute, aching loneliness, in which the traumatic experience is treated as a solitary burden that needs to be expunged by acts of denial and resistance. What could be less "social" than that? (1995, p. 186).

However, while trauma can move to the centre of one's being and make an individual feel as if he/she has been set apart from others, it is also possible to feel that trauma is shared with hundreds of others (Erikson 1995). For many survivors of Argentina's clandestine detention centres, and the families of disappeared and murdered individuals, feeling different from others after experiencing a trauma has become a kind of calling, and has drawn individuals together who are similarly affected (Erikson 1995). While the numbness and dislocation shared by traumatised individuals mean that relating to each other can be painful and difficult, they can still be shared as a source of communality and shared identity (Erikson 1995). The force of trauma can be both centripetal and centrifugal (Erikson 1995, p. 186): "It draws one away from the centre of group space while at the same time drawing one back." In this way, estrangement can become the basis for communality (Erikson 1995). The community can offer "a cushion for pain" and a "context for intimacy" as it serves as "a repository for binding traditions" (Erikson 1995, p. 188).

While trauma can engender a sense of community between individuals and groups, it can also damage the texture of a community (Erikson 1995). Dori Laub and Nanette Auerhahn (1989) write that the link between individuals is predicated on the possibility and expectation of empathy. However, when individuals' vital needs either go unheeded or are ignored by others, those individuals lose the expectation that their needs will in some way be met (Laub and Auerhahn 1989). Laub and Auerhahn write that when this occurs:

> Faith in the possibility of communication dies and intrapsychically there may no longer be a matrix of two people—self and resonating other. Accordingly, we propose that an essential feature of the trauma suffered by a survivor of genocide is the victim's feeling of inability to affect the environment interpersonally so as to elicit a sense of mutuality (1989, p. 379).

In other words, the victim no longer feels they have anyone on whom they can count, as the link between the self and the "other" is obliterated by a failure of empathy (Laub and Auerhahn 1989). A failure of empathy indicates a failure in an individual's interpersonal environment: The message one sends out is not responded to or mediated by another (Laub and Auerhahn 1989). Though of a different political persuasion, Barbara was told by the government agencies that she did not have the right to claim assistance as a victim of the military dictatorship because her father was deemed a fascist. Barbara told me:

> I went to speak with forensic psychologists who were reconstructing cases. I wanted to know how they operated, how they worked out to which group the murdered belonged. And they told me, no, your father was a fascist. A lot of doors closed for me because of the ideology of my father (Tarquini 2009).

The lack of receptivity for her grief and trauma has made Barbara feel as if she is not regarded as a citizen with equal rights within Argentine society. Barbara feels there is no understanding or empathy for her experience of loss, and feels desperately alone as a result. "Being discriminated against for the ideology of my father doesn't give me the motivation to keep fighting [for his memory]", Barbara told me (Tarquini 2009). Barbara does not feel she is able to engage within her environment interpersonally, and as such is unable to elicit a sense of mutuality (Laub and Auerhahn 1989). She is left feeling that she has nobody within the government or human rights organisations on whom she can count.

In the current climate, empathy for those on the other side of the ideological divide in Argentina is difficult to fathom. Rare was the occasion when one of the women was able and willing to find within herself genuine empathy for another. However, Victoria told me:

> The military government committed very grave human rights violations and I feel the pain of these families very profoundly, and of the people who were killed because of the actions of the military. As a human being, I feel the pain of victims of whatever political affiliation. Because of what I've lived through, I can't remain indifferent to the pain of other Argentines. I quietly approached some families [of the disappeared] that I could trust so that they could explain to me and teach me about the violence they suffered; so they could help me to see what the families of terrorists also went through. For my pain and the injustice that happened to my father to take its rightful place [in Argentina's collective memorial record], I had to find out the other side of the story. If not, then my story is partial and subjective (Paz 2009).

While affective resonances in remembering practices can create borders between the self and others, they can also "give" these others meaning or value in their moment of separation; this is a giving that can temporarily transform the other through the movement engendered by the affective response itself (Ahmed 2004a). Victoria looks for ways to be moved by emotions and affects into a different relationship with the pain she suffers. In doing so, she attempts to create a different kind of attachment to those in adversarial memory groups (Ahmed 2004b). Victoria resists remaining trapped in restrictive ways of thinking. She actively fights against the theory that one forever remains who one was in the past. Instead, Victoria engages with some willing families of the *desaparecidos* as a way of understanding another viewpoint, and ultimately finding within herself empathy for those individuals affected by state terror.

In Argentina, considerable social damage has been produced by the significant absence of empathy for the grief of others. This has denied both groups of women what they desire: The acknowledgement and empathic engagement with their suffering by those individuals instrumental and directly responsible in causing their emotional pain (Ross 2003). When the women believe their memories have not been given the moral, social, cultural and legal recognition they feel they deserve within the public sphere of collective remembrance, affective alignment fails; this failure of affective alignment perpetuates the stalemate between members of the different communities (Ahmed 2004a).

What this means for the women I interviewed is that the failure of empathy for the other group's grief destroys the possibility for communication between adversarial memorial cultures. LaCapra (2001, p. 213) proposes a concept of traumatic empathy that "should be understood in terms of an affective relation, rapport, or bond with the other" that yields an "affirmation of otherness within the self". The women's ideologically charged projections result in certain fixations "that project onto others or deposit into others negative affects"; in turn, these can create the illusion of affects being "located" in other individuals of ideologically opposed groups (Schwab 2010, p. 112). The circulation of negative affects can radically disturb people's understanding of themselves, as well as their relations with others and the past (Probyn 2010). What is then produced is a lack of what Ahmed (2004a, p. 36) calls "fellow feeling": The women's pain cannot be shared through empathy with others in different memory groups.

What are the implications of this failure of alignment for the intergenerational transmission of individuals' traditions and beliefs, and their accompanying affects? Ahmed (2004a) suggests that our response to affects may be dependent on past associations and interpretations that are made by the group of which we form a part, including our ancestors. In what follows, I turn to exploring how the affective registration of memories of an individual's past in one generation can be experienced as a traumatic memory "at a later time and place" in another (Faye 2008, p. 162). It is vital that we incorporate the notion of affect and what it produces—as it passes "from body to body, from skin to skin, in those resonances that circulate about, between, and sometimes stick to bodies and words" (Gregg and Seigworth 2010, p. 1)—into our understandings of how to remember the past. In particular, this notion allows us to account for how children born after a traumatic event can embody their parents' and ancestors' unconscious memories of trauma (Faye 2003). Exploring the intergenerational transmission of affective memory is crucial to grasping how the political and state terror that was experienced in Argentina in the 1970s and

1980s will continue—beyond the lives of its survivors—to "leave traces of a deep memory beyond individual recall, which will defy any attempt to give it meaning" (Friedlander 1993, p. 254).

6.6 Intergenerational Transmission of Affective Memory

Jill Bennett believes that the affective transmission of traumatic memories may flow not only between bodies but across generations (2003). In *The Shell and the Kernel* (1994), Abraham and Torok discuss the "phantom effects" that plague the children of parents who have lived through a traumatic experience (cited in Schwab 2010, p. 55). Abraham suggests that, assuming that the individuals can inherit the "secret psychic substance of their ancestor's lives", those individuals can potentially manifest symptoms that are not directly linked to their own life experiences but are linked instead to a parent's or ancestor's psychic traumas (cited in Schwab 2010, p. 78). Susana Kaiser (2005b) has conducted research on how the experience of living under terror has been transmitted to following generations, and how the psychic remains of fear have manifested themselves in Argentina's post-dictatorship generation. In her interviews with Argentine youth who were born during or following the period of military dictatorship, Kaiser (2005b) illustrates how fear has persisted throughout the years; it has been transmitted by those who were directly affected by the violence to those who were mostly too young to remember.

Kaiser (2005b) believes the "witness generation's" transmission of memories has influenced and shaped the post-dictatorship generation's ways of thinking and acting. Kaiser (2005) applies the term "witness generation" to refer to those who lived through and witnessed the period of political and state violence. For example, most parents of those interviewed had told their children to avoid activities that had been targeted for repression in the past (Kaiser 2005b). One young woman, mimicking her father's voice and gestures, told Kaiser (2005b, p. 56) that her father can put her in a state of paranoia on passing a police station as he says, "Let's cross the street." "He always does that", she tells Kaiser (2005b, p. 56). By witnessing her father's embodied reaction, the daughter understands the embodiment of terror associated with the police station in the past (Kaiser 2005b).

In another example, another young girl, Laura, talks about her father hiding books that were forbidden during the dictatorship:

> Books like [Marx's] *Capital* ... my father has all the books by Marx and Lenin. But they're all hidden, even now. They were always hidden. We have a large bookshelf that [my father] built during the dictatorship. The shelves have room for one book in the back and one book in the front hiding the back row. Those books were always hidden. There are several revolutionary, "evil" books (cited in Kaiser 2005b, p. 56).

In discussing the intergenerational transmission of fear, Laura talks about how the attitudes and experiences of the parents have been crucial in shaping the fear of the next generation:

> [Some kids] were breastfed with fear. If a kid lives in a home where her parents are terrified and don't go out at night, she feels those things. There were parents who were always afraid during the military regime. They couldn't live a quiet life, scared that "[the military] would come and take us away". When you live in fear, you transmit this to your children (cited in Kaiser 2005b, p. 56).

While the children of the witnessing generation that Kaiser interviewed did not think the political conditions were comparable to those that brought about the dictatorship, many discussed being afraid of being tortured, and could not discard the possibility of a repeat of the violence in the future (Kaiser 2005b). As long as the torturers' identities are still unknown and they continue to roam freely within society, it stands to reason that "if they did it once they could do it again" (Kaiser 2005b, p. 56).

Those in the next generation of Argentines have become witnesses not to the original trauma, but to the affective traces that trauma has left on their ancestors. For the children of the witnessing generation and for those who were very young during the dictatorship period, recognising and acknowledging the psychic life of their parents and relatives in their own psychic life means uncovering and deciphering their ancestors' unspoken suffering and painful history as well as their guilt, shame and crimes (Schwab 2010). Marianne Hirsch remarks: "For survivors of trauma, the gap between generations is the breach between a traumatic memory located in the body and the mediated knowledge of those who were born after." (in Miller and Tougaw 2002, p. 71–72). Taking up Hirsch's idea, Esther Faye suggests that a repressed, mnemic registration of an individual's traumatic past in one generation can be experienced as a traumatic memory "at a later time and place" in another generation (2008, p. 162).

In her autobiography, *My Name is Victoria: The Extraordinary Story of one Woman's Struggle to Reclaim her True Identity* (2010), Victoria Donda recounts her life growing up with people who were not her real parents, under a name that was not her own. She was kidnapped from her mother as a baby by the military security forces in the ESMA detention centre. Victoria, whose name for 27 years was Analía, lived a fairly normal childhood and adolescence in the southern suburbs of Buenos Aires, in a typical middle-class family (Donda 2010). Victoria's mother, Cori, was 5 months pregnant when she was disappeared. From testimonies of survivors of the ESMA, it was established that Cori gave birth to a girl in 1977 when her brother-in-law was the head of the intelligence service. A survivor of ESMA, Lidia Vieyra, testified that when Cori gave birth to a baby girl, she called her "Victoria" and threaded a blue thread through her earlobe in the hope that someone would recognise her daughter (Donda 2010).

Victoria's political activism during her university days brought her into stark conflict with the values and ideals of her family (Donda 2010). Already feeling like the black sheep of the family, Victoria writes: "As I continued to oppose the right-wing discourse of my family, an ideological rift opened up between us that grew even wider as my political commitment became an essential part of me" (Donda 2010, p. 112). It was not until she discovered the truth about her real origins and the shocking revelation of her uncle's involvement in her parents' murder, as well as her own kidnapping and adoption, that Victoria was able to fully embrace her legacy.

It was then that she contacted Las Abuelas and found out about her real heritage. Victoria's life has been portrayed in the Argentine film *Eva y Lola* (2010, Argentina, Sabrina Farji). Featuring at various film festivals in Europe, the USA and Latin America, the film is the first of its kind to convey the complex reality of young Argentine individuals who recover their identities. With the full support of Las Abuelas, the director, Sabrina Farji, powerfully addresses the issue of recovery of stolen identities. The film is based on the true stories of Victoria Donda and another young woman, Victoria Griguera Dupuy, who recovered their identities through Las Abuelas early in 2000. Donda met Griguera at the Faculty of Law (Donda 2010). When they met, they had no idea that they shared a common history—the mother of Donda and the father of Griguera were both imprisoned in the ESMA. Representing, according to the director, a "patchwork" of different individuals' experiences of identity retrieval, the film portrays a very convincing account of the struggles faced by hundreds of young people dealing with issues of identity and loss (Farji in Ranzani 2010). It received strong reviews within Argentina; even the conservative daily newspaper *La Nación* suggested that the director had convincingly captured many of the difficult issues facing the children of the disappeared (San Honorio 2010).

Eva y Lola is a film about two young women who find out, in different ways, that they are both children of *desaparecidos*. In the film, best friends Eva (based on Griguera) and Lola (based on Donda) are performing on stage together in a punk rock cabaret between Christmas and New Year in Buenos Aires. During this time, Eva finds out that Lola is a child of the *desaparecidos* when she reads a newspaper article that Lola's "father", who tried to commit suicide, was implicated in the kidnapping of newborn babies of illegally incarcerated women. Lola is in denial about the truth of her own kidnapping as a baby when she tells Eva that "no one has the right to remove me from my family." Lola continues to argue that the couple have lovingly raised her and have shaped her as the person she is today. When she adds that there is nothing wrong with "adoption", Eva becomes frustrated and reminds her of the glaring difference between adoption and appropriation, implying that her "parents" stole her from her biological family. In reply, Lola says she does not want to argue about the truth. For Lola, as for many of the appropriated individuals who have recovered their identity, accepting the truth is extremely confronting—particularly if the individual perceives a loving relationship with the raising parents. For Lola, it is too confronting to accept the prospect of having no real parents and no real family. As a result, she initially rejects the notion of investigating her identity because why would she do so if she is happy with the "parents" who raised her?

Lola begins to feel confusion in her life, not only as a result of her raising father's attempted suicide but also because she is beginning to realise that the man she thought was a loving father is actually a former torturer and not her real father. The character of Lola portrays what it is like for those individuals who live through a phase of initial shock followed by an identity crisis, in which they perceive themselves being torn in two. Donda (2010) herself explains how she had to divide this new awakening into little pieces because it was too overwhelming to consider all at once. At first, she had to establish who she was. She had to work out a way to combine the new "I" with the old "I", particularly when she felt that the old "I" was based on a series of lies. Donda writes about how she eventually came to combine her new and old identities:

> But Analía was not condemned to disappear—I am Analía. What would vanish, or in fact come crashing down, were the structures that had supported her—her place of birth, her parents, even her true age. But Analía would live on in Victoria. Her essence would be redefined, but she would never stop being me (2010, p. 136).

In the film, Lola also finally begins to establish that her two personalities are actually of the same person. Once she has overcome the initial shock of no longer having any parents and questioning her identity, Lola has to consider what to do next. She becomes increasingly uneasy that her biological family might be looking for her. She also has a growing curiosity about her biological family. Though she is fearful of the consequences that finding out her real identity could have for her raising parents, Lola becomes increasingly angry that her raising parents have withheld the truth about her real identity and her appropriation as a baby. For Donda, not only was her real identity withheld from her but also her real birthdate. For years, she had felt "out of sync" and ahead of many of her peers both academically and in terms of physical maturity (Donda 2010, p. 50). It was only once she discovered her true identity that she was able to explain why this was so: Though she estimates her date of birth to have been between the months of July and September 1977, her date of birth was registered as 17 September 1979. Two years later. Donda wrote about the pain associated with feeling as if 2 years of her life were erased:

> The most violent effect, and the weight I still find most difficult to bear, is that even today I feel that the price I had to pay in order to have access to my real identity was to lose two years along the way, two years that no one, ever, can restore to me. For some reason, that loss is more painful for me to face than the lie of the people who called themselves my parents (2010, p. 51).

In the movie, when she watches an advertisement from Las Abuelas and sees the face of a grandmother who is looking for her grandchild, Lola realises she is one of the missing children and, following a difficult period of uncertainty, submits to undergoing a DNA test. She eventually meets her grandmother in the final scene. In the film, Eva also has no parents—her father is a *desaparecido* and her biological mother died a number of years previously. Eva embodies the traumatic memory of her disappeared father and the loneliness of a life without him by making daily imaginary phone calls with him to discuss her problems. The loneliness affects her life very deeply as she realises that she no longer has any parents. Like Lola, Eva has to deal with a lost life in which she has ended up all alone. At first, in watching Eva make the imaginary phone calls to her father, we get the feeling that by pretending she has a father, her life is made less lonely. However, as the film progresses, it becomes clear that the more often she calls her imaginary father, the more she begins to realise how alone she really is.

The film demonstrates different expressions of the processes of melancholy and mourning in the lives of the girls and those around them. Loneliness and silence play key roles as the two girls express the legacy of violence imposed by the military regime through their performances. Eva does everything she can to help her friend accept the truth about her family. However, in doing so, Eva must also confront her own past. After the two girls visit the *Parque de la Memoria* (Memorial Park located on the River Plata in Buenos Aires), they locate the name of Eva's father on the list of the missing engraved on the wall of one of the monuments. Opened in 2007, La Parque de la Memoria is Argentina's first state-funded monument dedicated to the disappeared victims of the military dictatorship (1976–1983). A jagged path dotted by sculptures winds past a stone wall engraved with a list of nearly 9,000 names of "victims of state terror" beside the River Plata, where many were thought to have drowned after being thrown off planes (http://memoryandjustice.org/site/parque-de-la-memoria).

In finding her father's name listed, Eva finally learns to accept that her father has disappeared and will never return. The story shows the ways in which the two girls, like many of the children of the *desaparecidos,* attempt to recreate bonds with their disappeared parents. For some, this can become an obsession as they attempt to join the embodied traumas of their own history with that of their parents. They endeavour to feel what their parents must have felt, try to understand some of the difficult choices they made, and work to restore the lives of their kidnapped parents as well as their own. Victoria Donda (2010) also describes recognising the psychic life of her mother in her own psychic life. She explains how she felt her mother come alive inside of her as her passion for political activism grew (Donda 2010). She felt her mother's genes and blood were as formative to the person she was to become as those external elements that eventually changed her life. Donda explains the extent to which she embodies the trauma of her parents and grandparents when she writes:

> The suffering of my paternal grandparents during all those years is mine now, and for the rest of my life I'll bear an irrational guilt for not having been able to meet them (2010, p. 41).

Once they find out they belong to the *generación robada* (stolen generation), the children of the *desaparecidos* undergo a difficult re-evaluation of their lives. The shock of realising that they are a completely other person to what they thought they were can catapult these individuals into a world of sudden pain. Buscarita's granddaughter, Claudia Poblete, said of being reunited with her biological family after 22 years: "Getting to know my [birth] family was like stumbling into a story full of pain in which I found it difficult to play a part" (cited in Qassim 2007). Claudia recounts the dilemmas she has faced in coming to terms with having "two" families. While her adoptive father was eventually sentenced to 7 years prison for appropriating her, for a number of years Claudia continued to live with her adoptive mother, who was spared house arrest. In the early years, she would not consider leaving the couple, who had been her "parents" for all of her life. She said:

> To begin with, I wanted to protect them, I was afraid of what could happen to them. Later on, I managed to make them feel responsible for their actions and to make them understand that they could face a trial for the decision to keep me the way they did (cited in Qassim 2007).

Claudia further explains the thinking around her decision to continue living with the couple who she now refers to as her "appropriators":

> I can't separate the 21 years I spent with them from my [present] life. Yes, the relationship has changed. My decisions and theirs have meant that we no longer see each other in the same way. And when we talk about the past, we always end up arguing. But they are part of my identity and my memories, the good and the bad (cited in Qassim 2007).

Eventually, Claudia decides to change her name from the one (Mercedes) that the couple had given her and reverts to her real birthdate. This decision marks a significant break with her appropriators and the past. She explains how she coped with making this decision:

> It took me six months to take the decision to change my name. For a while, it was like having a split personality. I behaved in one way at home and in another way outside, maintaining Claudia and Mercedes as two separate people. It was only with time—and I continue to struggle with this even now—that I felt that I was only one person and could accept myself as such (cited in Qassim 2007).

Claudia and other young individuals not only suffer shock on finding out the truth about their real identities, but are also forced to deal with difficult choices and their consequences with regard to themselves and their families. In particular, many of these young individuals are faced with a heartbreaking situation when ordered to testify in trials to prosecute their "adoptive" parents. Inevitably, when Claudia was called on to testify in the trial of her raising parents, the couple who appropriated her felt betrayed (cited in Qassim 2007). Claudia is constantly called upon to straddle the two worlds of her present and her past, and to deal with the inevitable confrontations between the two. Her wedding has proved to be a very contentious issue. Though Claudia wishes to celebrate this happy occasion with both her birth and adoptive families, Buscarita remains adamant that she will not meet Claudia's appropriators. This greatly upsets Claudia, who explains:

> Getting married is what has most helped me put into perspective both my relationship with my appropriators and with my biological family. I don't think I will ever reach an equilibrium with what has happened to me, but every step I take in my life provides me with new perspectives. My marriage was one, a change in my career was another, the day I have my own child will be another. Forming my own "family" has helped me to construct my own identity and allowed me to look towards the future, not the past (cited in Qassim 2007).

As we have seen from these stories, the generation of Argentine individuals who have recovered their identity has been forced to cope with exceedingly difficult dilemmas, including the decision to condemn the persons they have for decades called their parents. They have had to cope with extreme confusion and powerlessness as their identities have been turned upside down and they have been made to feel as if they have been torn into parts. They have also had to open up to whole new families as well as grapple with new categories to define those who had previously been family. Many individuals who have managed to recover their true identity have had to deal with anger, loneliness and grief on learning that they have been lied to for decades. And many channel this deep pain into social movements that raise awareness of the theme of the deceased, the *desaparecidos* and the *generación robada*. Raising awareness has a price, however. Donda recounts the threats she, Las Abuelas and others received due to their association with the film *Eva y Lola*. She writes:

> The offices of the Grandmothers and HIJOS received not only letters but also phone threats to half the project. In my own house, I even found a note telling me to shut up, which as if by some creepy twist in time was signed by the Triple A and accompanied by a cute little bow tied with a blue ribbon.[5] Minutes after I phoned the Grandmothers to discuss how we could join forces to defend ourselves, my phone rang. When I picked up, I heard a tape recording of the conversation I had just finished having with Estela de Carlotto [head of Las Abuelas organisation] (Donda 2010, p. 177).

Despite also being forced to deal with hostility and threats of further violence, these individuals form part of a generation of young people who continue work to ensure that their deep memories of trauma are kept alive for decades to come, as they seek to recover their real identities as well as recuperate the "unspoken suffering and secret histories" of their disappeared and deceased parents (Schwab 2010, p. 80). Though they may have never known their parents, the children of the disappeared have nonetheless received and assimilated the effects of their parents' traumatic histories belatedly, through the narratives and actions of the previous generation (Hirsch, in Miller and Tougaw 2002). In this way, trauma both solidifies and blurs generational differences (Hirsch, in Miller and Tougaw 2002). What does this mean for Argentina now and in the future?

It becomes clear that we cannot possibly understand Argentine social or public life without understanding the transmission of affective memory; we cannot hope to understand the forces that are at play to keep such deep animosities in place decades after the end of the dictatorship. Affect is created as the women repeatedly share their narratives of violence and loss in the public sphere. Affect is that which is said and which remains unsaid in the oral testimony encounter. It is that which can communicate and motivate overtly and publicly; but it is also an excess that remains unprocessed and misrecognised, evading consciousness yet provoking behaviour all the same. In the same way that Laura feels fear and paranoia on passing by a police station because her father would regularly tell her to cross the road away from it, or in the way that Victoria Donda feels she must imbibe the suffering of her grandparents, we can see that the migration of affect between bodies carries ideas along with it (Probyn 2005). The next generation of Argentines' histories of family trauma and suffering will continue to flare as the transmission of affect ignites the memory of their ancestors' fate. Traumatic memory will always be, in this regard, an issue of the present (Bennett 2003).

[5] At the time of her birth in the ESMA, Donda's mother, with the help of the attending nurse, threaded little pieces of blue cotton through her daughter's ear lobes so that she could be recognised (Donda 2010).

Chapter 7
Haunting

7.1 Legacies of Historical Violence

While the period of political and state violence of the 1970s and 1980s may have ended, the historical legacy of trauma lives on. Dealing with the unfinished business of trauma in Argentina means engaging with the tangible and expansive significance of haunting. The notion of traumatic repetition, of endings that are not over, is what haunting is about, suggests Avery Gordon (2008). According to Gordon:

> Haunting is a constituent element of modern social life. It is neither pre-modern superstition nor individual psychosis; it is a generalizable social phenomenon of great import. To study social life one must confront the ghostly aspects of it. (2008, p. 7)

In the case of Argentina, haunting is undoubtedly "a generalizable social phenomenon" made explicit through the absence/presence of the *desaparecidos*. The *desaparecidos* are not simply missing individuals, but social figures who open the door to understanding haunting in Argentina (Gordon 2008). They make us confront the "ghostly aspects" of the military's systematic use of disappearance and force a reckoning within society: They make those who attempted to erase them from memory confront the violent actions of the past. "Haunting is a part of our social world", writes Gordon (2008, p. 27), "and understanding it is essential to grasping the nature of our society and for changing it."

To look for lessons about haunting, we need only to turn to those social structures such as language, streetscapes and buildings that keep Argentina's ghosts vital. Language that was used by the military junta during the military dictatorship in particular makes explicit the presence of the ghosts of the *desaparecidos*. The military dictatorship gave rise to a new era of distorted meanings of words, which then entered into popular Argentine discourse. This distortion has left a legacy of violence at the heart of everyday language in Argentina. These words were not new to the Argentine vocabulary; however, in 1976 they began to be used with substantially altered meanings that were marked by the experience of terror. For example, the word *perejil,* meaning parsley, took on a whole new significance during the years of the dictatorship. The mother of a disappeared child, Mathilde Mellibovsky, says she can never again bring herself to say the word:

J. Stockwell, *Reframing the Transitional Justice Paradigm,*
Springer Series in Transitional Justice 10, DOI 10.1007/978-3-319-03853-7_7,

> Parsley. That's what they called our children. Parsley is so abundant here, so cheap, greengrocers traditionally give it away. No, I always tell them, no. I won't say it, I won't have it. That's how they thought of our children—cheap little leaves made for throwing away. (cited in Feitlowitz 1998, p. 49)

I hear the word *perejil* used ubiquitously in Argentina. People say it to each other in every day conversation as an endearing way of saying "idiot", or yell it as abuse on the streets to passing motorists who nearly run them over. *Perejil* was one of many words appropriated from the Argentine language that were perverted by repressors in the clandestine detention centres. The slang that was developed among those who tortured the *desaparecidos* in the clandestine detention centres was, as Marguerite Feitlowitz describes it (1998, p. 49), "an amalgam of borrowings and home-grown inventions." Used as a name for those they tortured, *perejil* was most likely translated from the French *persil,* a term used against agitators for Algerian independence (Feitlowitz 1998). Many of the other expressions that were used by repressors had their roots in Nazi rhetoric (Feitlowitz 1998). Used to ritualise torture, *perejil* and other words carried an "extra psychological twist" for detainees (Feitlowitz 1998, p. 50). The word *parrilla* describes the traditional Argentine grill for cooking meat, which is the centrepiece of any Argentine social occasion. It was also used to name the metal table on which detainees were tortured. Restaurants serving grilled meat can be seen on just about any street corner in Buenos Aires: "Parrilla, parrilla, parrilla—sustenance, pleasure and annihilation, all present in a single quotidian word" (Feitlowitz 1998, p. 49). These sorts of words, which once offered comforting associations for detainees, were instead translated into acts of pain and degradation (Feitlowitz 1998).

Asado (n. barbecue), a popular social ritual within Argentine culture, was another word that saw its usage changed during the military dictatorship. Its meaning was described in the testimony of Jorge Carlos Torres, a seaman who was stationed at the ESMA:

> I knew that the bodies of the dead prisoners were taken away from the school in green trucks to the sports field at the far end, the other side of the Avenida Lugones, on the river bank. Two people were in charge of each truck and I once heard them say to the NCO on guard duty that they had come "to have a barbecue", which was a way of describing the job…At night the bonfires of burning bodies could be seen…. (cited in CONADEP 1986, p. 130)

We also know from the testimonies of survivors and perpetrators of the clandestine detention centres that those prisoners who were told they would be *traslado* (v. transferred) were actually being taken away to be killed (CONADEP 1986).

> In a transfer in February–March 1977 they took a man called "Tincho". They took him down to the basement, gave him an injection and soon afterwards he began to feel weak and dizzy. He heard the others vomiting and then pass out and be dragged away. Once before after a transfer some of my companions had noticed the marks made by rubber soles dragged across the basement floor. They took Tincho out with the rest through a door on the right of the main entrance to the basement. They put him in a lorry and took him to a place which he thinks may have been Buenos Aires Municipal Airport. He was made to climb the steps of an aeroplane and asked for his name and number at the top. They had obviously

> got the wrong person because he was taken down again and returned to the third floor of the Navy Mechanics School. (Norma Susana Burgos, cited in CONADEP 1986, p. 129)

Words such as *traslado* and *desaparecido* came to define an age, and some of the words' pre-dictatorship meanings have fallen almost entirely away (Feitlowitz 1998). For survivors of the clandestine centres, the word *traslado/a* carries more grief and terror than any other (Feitlowitz 1998):

> Tension reached untold heights for most of the prisoners. It produced a strange mixture of fear and relief, given that one both dreaded and longed for the transfer that on the one hand spelt certain death, and on the other meant the end of torture and agony. One [also] felt… fear of death, though not the fear of any death—which most of them could have faced with dignity—but of that particular death which is dying without disappearing, or disappearing without dying. A death in which the person dying had no part whatsoever…as though dying being already dead, or like never dying at all. (File no. 3821 in CONADEP 1986, p. 167)

At the 1985 trial of the ex-commanders of the junta, one survivor told the judge:

> Sir it is very hard for me to use the word "transfer", because it was employed when they took someone we would never see again. So I will use the word only to refer to those persons, and in all other cases, must use the word "move". (cited in Feitlowitz 1998, p. 53)

Following the 1985 trial of the ex-commanders in which the country learned first-hand details of the military's previously clandestine activity, a flood of new terminology was ushered into the Argentine language (Feitlowitz 1998). This had an extraordinary effect on the common usage of many words (Feitlowitz 1998). For example, young people started to say "*vos no existe*" ("you don't exist!"), a saying with two extremes of meaning: either that someone was the greatest or that someone was nothing (Feitlowitz 1998). Torturers commonly used this terminology as they taunted prisoners in the clandestine detention centres (Feitlowitz 1998). Before the trial, such an expression was not in general use (Feitlowitz 1998). Likewise, a commonly heard phrase, *darese máquina*—meaning "to give someone the machine"—was a reference to the *picana* (electric prod) that was used to torture prisoners. Today, it can mean "don't bother me" or "you're getting on my nerves" (Feitlowitz 1998).

From the dictatorship era also sprang new phrases such as *estoy fusilado* (I'm shot) to convey tiredness, or *no hay drama* (there's no drama) to reassure normality. When Nenina returned from her Spanish exile post-dictatorship, she was incredulous that such phrases were being bandied about among the general population. Nenina told me:

> I returned in October 1984. The fashion during much of this time was to say "there's no drama", as if to say, "everything's alright". They would say "come to my house, there's no drama", and I would think to myself, how can you say "there's no drama"…30,000 disappeared…bones that are being uncovered everywhere, because at that time there were excavations and excavations and excavations. 10,000 political prisoners and there was no drama? (Boulliet 2009)

Born out of extreme situations of violence inflicted on the general population, these words and phrases have now been assimilated into everyday language in Argentina, and their perversions have contributed to the sinister undertones and surreal quality of life in Buenos Aires: "The repression lives on in such aberrations of the language, in the scars it left on the language" (Feitlowitz 1998, p. 62). The inclusion of slang associated with the dictatorship in common contemporary parlance is indicative of how this violent period continues to be subliminally remembered, ever-present and kept historically alive. Yet it is also indicative of how quickly violence can be skirted over and normalised within a society. The novelist Julio Cortázar has said: "Under authoritarian regimes language is the first system that suffers, that gets degraded" (cited in Feitlowitz 1998, p. 61). Feitlowitz (1998) takes Cortázar's observation one-step further when she suggests that language is also the last system to recover once a violent regime has ended. Feitlowitz writes:

> When a people's very words have been wounded, the society cannot fully recover until the language has been healed. Words mark the paths of our experience, separate what we can name from ineffable terror and chaos. At once public and intimate, language is a boundary between our vulnerable inner selves and the outside world. When, like skin, the language is bruised, punctured, or mutilated, that boundary breaks down. We have then no defense, no way to protect ourselves. What we knew, we no longer know; names born of the truth of shared experience ring false. *On a mal dans sa peau*—we are uneasy in our own skin. (1998, p. 62)

Feitlowitz (1998) wonders whether the continued usage of words such as *parrilla* and *asado* as part of everyday language in Argentina is a deliberate effort to salvage earlier untainted meanings or a sign of societal denial. It could also, she suggests, be a sign that life moves on. Perhaps, however, it is a sign of the will of those individuals who suffered at the hands of torturers and who were disappeared, to ensure the memory of terror does not fade. Nenina told me that she and her friends, who are mostly survivors of the clandestine detention centres, satirise phrases from the period when they talk with each other. She told me:

> I have a lot of friends, most of who were prisoners [in the clandestine detention centres]. So in the prison, when they were going to let you go free, they would call your surname and say, for example, "González! With everything!" "With everything" meant with all of his/her things because they were either going to set you free or send you to your death. So with many of my friends, I'll call them on the phone and say "López! With everything!", and we kill ourselves laughing….(Boulliet 2009)

Nenina told me that laughter was certainly an act of defiance used by the *desaparecidos* in the detention centres. She believes that she and her friends also use this type of black humour with each other as a way of remembering the violence of the period without having to recall the actual violence. In the words of Avery Gordon (2008, p. 64), "the ghost is alive, so to speak", and while it may not be visible to the naked eye, it nonetheless has a seething presence and makes itself known in its own way. While the changes in the Argentine language may have originated in the secret detention centres, those changes did not only happen to those imprisoned there (Gordon 2008). These new manifestations of language continue to ravage the living language. Words and phrases that were born out of the extreme violence of the dictatorship have been absorbed into everyday language, suggesting that many people have internalised that part of Argentine history with which the words are associated (Gordon 2008).

Other powerful examples of how the traces and marks of this violent past remain part of the present public sphere and built environment in Argentina include the appearance of green Ford Falcon cars. The Ford Falcon was the car of choice for the police and paramilitary groups who forcibly kidnapped thousands of individuals off the streets and whisked them away in the dark of night to the clandestine detention centres. They are still seen everywhere. Nenina described for me the level of anxiety then felt by the general population on seeing these ominous green Ford Falcons on the street:

> In this time, at least in Buenos Aires and Rosario…the streets were empty, the neighbourhoods as well. You didn't just walk along Corrientes Street like you can now and see people walking about. No. What you could see were the Ford Falcons, [the kidnappers] pointing their weapons…pointing their weapons like this outside the cars…making displays of terror. (Boulliet 2009)

On the day she returned to Argentina, Nenina Bouillet took a taxi home. It was a green Ford Falcon. She told me how incredulous she was on seeing green Ford Falcons lined up in the Ezeiza airport taxi rank, waiting to take fare-paying passengers home:

> When I saw a Ford Falcon I jokingly asked, "And where do I have to go? In the boot?" Later I found out that the taxis at Ezeiza were driven by what they called "unemployed labourers", [who were] the groups of…those who formed part of the grupos de tareas [those responsible for carrying out kidnappings]…they were the taxi drivers at Ezeiza. (Boulliet 2009)

While green Ford Falcons were one of the reigning symbols of the military's terror, today, eerily, they are part of a normal everyday Argentine street scene. In a symbolic gesture of leaving the past behind and as a way of raising government funds, in March 1990, President Carlos Menem, coordinated a public auction of a group of 146 green Ford Falcons that were used to kidnap thousands of individuals and to haul dead bodies to mass graves (Feitlowitz 1998). These were cars that had "sucked up" thousands of individuals off the street (Feitlowitz 1998). They were also the cars that had hauled away dead bodies (Feitlowitz 1998). One of the police officers who had been in possession of one of the cars had reportedly complained at the time that they smelled of vomit, faeces and urine, and "the stink of fear" (Feitlowitz 1998, p. 172). Nevertheless, each car fetched some US$ 10,000 (Feitlowitz 1998). The identity of the bidders who would buy one of these cars has remained difficult to establish (Feitlowitz 1998).

The Ford Falcons evoke a vivid association with the military dictatorship, and Argentine artists consistently depict the cars in film and photography as a physical embodiment of the terror enacted on Argentine society. The Ford Falcon image can also be seen on building walls all over Argentina as a reminder of state terror. These images also evoke the memory of the *desaparecidos,* most of whom were last seen by their families being taken away in these cars. Still circulating within the public sphere, the Ford Falcon remains entrenched in the public imagery as the embodiment of kidnappings, disappearance and torture of thousands of individuals.[1] It has, without a doubt, become "the single most recognisable icon of repression" (Robert 2005, p. 12). As a result, some drivers of the Ford Falcons have felt compelled to place a sticker in the back window, which reads, "My Falcon was not to blame. *Nunca más*." One member of the "Friends of the Falcon" club defended the Ford Falcon's seedier connection with violence and terror during the military dictatorship: "It's not the Falcon's fault. The police probably just needed a car that didn't break down, so they got Falcons" (Alejandro Hernandez cited in Ortiz 2007).

Gordon (2008, p. 66) suggests that: "There is a certain routineness to shocking associations in Argentina." While there may no longer be terror and oppression like there was on the streets during the dictatorship, the streets nonetheless still testify to the history of this violence. The past and the present are intimately intermeshed on a daily basis in contemporary Argentina. The story of Susana Barros's abduction exemplifies this eerie normality. On 21 August 1979, Susana Barros boarded the #128 bus to go home. The bus was stopped and a soldier in civilian clothes leapt on to the bus, waved a gun about and pulled Susana violently off the bus by her hair (Feitlowitz 1998). Susana remembers one woman saying, "*Por el pelo, no*" (Not by the hair) (Feitlowitz 1998, p. 149). Susana was then dragged to the sidewalk, where she was violently kicked and punched by a group of men, who then kidnapped her and took her to a secret detention centre (Feitlowitz 1998).

While the passengers of the #128 were disembarking at the terminal, explains Feitlowitz (1998), Susana was being stripped, blindfolded and tortured. Because she survived her ordeal, we know what happened to Susana, writes Feitlowitz (1998), but we do not know any more about the other passengers on that bus, including the woman who was the only one to have uttered a word. No witness has ever come forward to report what they saw (Feitlowitz 1998). The #128 bus is still in circulation today, following the same route as it did back in 1979. One wonders whether the bus is frequented by any of those passengers who, though they most probably knew what they were seeing at that moment in 1979, made the decision to remain silent.

The fear that was spread by the military was designed to make "all the Argentineans disappear as persons and as citizens" (Bouvard 1994, p. 43). Philipe Sollers explains what possibly happened to the passengers of the #128 bus as a result of what they experienced when he says:

> Who is called on to disappear? A little bit of everyone, and, by extension, those who will dare to ask what became of you. The social fabric is thus held in suspension…Fear, agony, guilt, anxiety, trouble, pervasive malaise: the living become virtually disappeared, potential spectres…It is a question of slow poisoning, a delayed psychic bomb. Identity is changed, it becomes hypnotized. (cited in Gordon 2008, p. 124)

The passengers of the #128 bus were—to use Avery Gordon's (2008, p. 124) term—"haunted into submission". It is likely the passengers remained silent that day because seeing such a spectacle produced a fear that "exterminate[s] all social life in

[1] Argentine investigators unearthed 43 Ford Falcons that may have been used to kidnap individuals during the military dictatorship in a warehouse at the Puerto Belgrano naval base, located near the city of Bahia Blanca in Buenos Aires province. The cars were searched for traces of blood, hair and other evidence that could be used in investigations of crimes against humanity (Henao 2001).

the public realm" (Gordon 2008, p. 124). The passengers chose to remain silent in the face of the terror they experienced, and perhaps they live with the haunting memory of what they saw that day. Perhaps they too are experiencing "the gray shades of an everyday life charged with a phantom reality" (Gordon 2008). If any of the #128 passengers are still riding that bus, perhaps even in the same seats, one wonders whether they remember Susana each time they reach that fateful stop where her life and theirs was violently and abruptly marked from that moment on.

Argentina is home to many such legacies of terror, incarnating this violent past. A bricks-and-mortar testament to human rights abuses committed by the military regime, La Escuela de Mecánica de la Armada, the ESMA is one of the most renowned secret detention centres in Buenos Aires. The ESMA is one of the many sites at which the human rights movement is working to ensure that the violent repression of the military dictatorship is not forgotten. The real purpose of this building was only made public following the transition to democratic rule, and it stands as a stark reminder of the thousands of individuals who were disappeared by the military regime. Labelled the "Argentine Auschwitz" (Feitlowitz 1998, p. 25), and located on one of Buenos Aires busiest thoroughfares on Avenida Libertador, the ESMA achieved notoriety as the largest of the 560 clandestine detention centres used by the military junta during its reign. The building was used to detain more than 5,000 Argentine citizens during the dictatorship, of which just 150 individuals survived to provide invaluable insight as to what went on inside its walls.

However, throughout the dictatorship the junta repeatedly denied the existence of these *chupaderos* (literally, places that "sucked" their victims out of thin air). The head of the junta in 1976, General Videla, could often be heard telling foreign governments and journalists: "In Argentina, political prisoners don't exist. No one is persecuted or constrained on account of his political ideas" (cited in Feitlowitz 1998, p. 28). However, the walls of the ESMA, along with those of other macabrely named sites such as El Olimpo (Olympus), El Vesubio (Vesuvius), Club Atlético (Athletic Club), and La Escuelita (the Little School), were witness to physical and psychological torture, forced separation of families and the degradation of thousands of men, women and children. As such, these buildings remain part of the dictatorship's haunting legacy.

The Kirchner government opened the door of the ESMA to the public in 2004. For the survivors and families of the *desaparecidos,* it was a deeply affecting experience to enter into the terror, horror, loneliness and repression that were still contained within its walls. The families could walk through the darkened rooms of the *Capucha* (hood) in the attic of the building where individuals were kept blindfolded; stand in the small "maternity ward where female political prisoners gave birth to babies who were then taken permanently away from them"; enter the basement, otherwise known as the *Huevera* (egg box), where egg cartons once lined the walls to muffle the screams of individuals undergoing torture; or stand in the ground floor corridor of the *Dorado* (golden room) where prisoners were lined up and given a sedative before being transferred to the death flights. Nenina, who now works with the *Instituto Espacio para la Memoria,* described the feeling of the *desaparecidos* being all around her, and told me just how incredulous she was on being given the keys to the ESMA:

> It seems [now] so crazy, so [crazy] that I can't…sometimes I can't understand it. I was…I work in the Institute for Memory and we look after ESMA and other clandestine detention centres. And once, I was opening the door to a section [of ESMA], with a key to go and see…to see something and there I was, and I looked at my hand that held the key and I said to myself, "what am I doing with a key to ESMA?" Really crazy…that's for certain, if someone would have ever told me [that I would be holding the key to ESMA]…I would have said, impossible. (Boulliet 2009)

The recuperation of the ESMA—now a museum—by the families of the *desaparecidos* is yet another example of how the legacies of the past allow us to better comprehend haunting in Argentina.

7.2 Disappearance as Haunting

The emblematic figure of the *desaparecidos* embodies the most traumatic and haunting legacy of the military dictatorship. Soon after the fall of the military regime, many of those who had been living in exile during the dictatorship returned home. Nenina's recount of her arrival back in Argentina gives a firmer understanding of what it felt like to live with the social reality of the *desaparecidos* after the return to democratic rule in 1983. Having been exiled in Spain during the dictatorship, Nenina arrived at Ezeiza Airport in Buenos Aires, feeling the emotional and chaotic energy of the place and the people. She describes the confusion in the arrivals lounge as she searched for her family:

> They [family who were waiting] were shouting out our names, and I exited through the door…I saw through the door that was open, they were all shouting "Where are they?" And when I heard them say this [later on reflection] I said to myself, "This is the catch-cry [of the families looking for the disappeared]." I was shouting, as you do when you arrive on a plane, "Where are they?" [By this] I meant where were the people who were waiting for us? But later I always remembered that I entered back into the country shouting "Where are they? [referring to the disappeared]". (Boulliet 2009)

What began as a catch-cry of Las Madres de la Plaza de Mayo during the dictatorship period—"*Donde estan*? Where are they?"—continues to be called out by thousands of people in their ongoing search for disappeared family members. At rallies and marches organised by human rights organisations in the Argentine capital of Buenos Aires, the phrase *Donde estan*? is chanted in unison by tens of thousands of people searching for the *desaparecidos*. At these marches, one is faced with a jigsaw puzzle of giant black and white photographs mounted on placards, depicting the young faces of the *desaparecidos*. There is also a long banner picturing life-sized photos of the *desaparecidos,* which is carried by family members above their heads. Deprived of their family member's final remains and unable to conduct a proper burial, being a family member of a *desaparecido* is one of the most anxiety-filled existences an individual can have, believes mother of four disappeared daughters Elsa Sánchez de Oesterheld:

> I believe that the disappearance is one of the most brutal things that can exist in today's war. It is the inhumane of the inhumane. I don't know how to express it. It's one of the most horrendous things because from one moment to the next a child disappears, a loved one, son, father, brother, whatever, husband, and this person has vanished into thin air without ever knowing what happened to him. It's very difficult to come to terms with. That's the anxiety, the despair that in my personal case will obviously die with me. (cited in Robben 2005a, p. 261)

Disappearance is a complex system of repression that extracts people from their familiar world and takes them, silently yet visibly, into "an unfamiliar place where certain principles of social reality are absent" (Gordon 2008, p. 112).[2] For example, the police station where survivor Ana Maria Careaga was held captive was in a populated area in the neighbourhood of La Boca, a working class suburb in Buenos Aires (Feitlowitz 1998). What frustrated Ana most was hearing buses passing and people walking by while she was in her cell (Feitlowitz 1998). While she was enduring torture, the world was passing by just a few metres above her head; life was going on as usual (Feitlowitz 1998). She told Feitlowitz:

> In the afternoon, when the sun was at a certain angle, I could see on the floor the shadows of the people passing by, getting in and out of their cars. Yes, that I think was the worst. To be so close to them, for them to be so close to us, and yet so far away. It was surreal. We were in the world but not part of it, alive in the realm of death. (1998, p. 166)

Prisoners of the clandestine detention centres were forced to endure torture, and were sometimes made to witness the torture of family members, friends or other prisoners (CONADEP 1986). The *desaparecidos* existed in what Taussig (1987, p. 4) terms a "death space", and they were constantly reminded by their torturers that they were disappeared, forgotten about, without any hope of being set free. The feeling of being in this death space was explained by one survivor:

> The most vivid and terrifying memory I have of all that time was of always living with death. I felt it was impossible to think. I desperately tried to summon up a thought in order to convince myself I wasn't dead. That I wasn't mad. At the same time, I wished with all my heart that they would kill me as soon as possible…The normal attitude of the torturers and guards towards us was to consider us less than slaves. We were objects. And useless, troublesome objects at that. They would say: "You're dirt." "Since we 'disappeared' you, you're nothing. Anyway, nobody remembers you." "You don't exist." "If anyone were looking for you (which they aren't), do you imagine they'd look for you here?" "We are everything for you." "We are justice." "We are God."…Repeated endlessly. By all of them. All the time. (cited in Gordon 2008, p. 78)

---

[2] Disappearance as a form of repression has been used in many countries and in many political situations. The term has been used to describe political repression in Guatemala from 1966, in Chile from 1973 and in Argentina from 1976 (Gordon 2008). Amnesty International traces the origins of the term back to the 1941 Night and Fog Decree enacted by the German High Command, which "ordered that, with the exception of those cases where guilt could be established beyond a doubt, everyone arrested for suspicion of 'endangering German security' was to be transferred [secretly] to Germany under 'cover of night'" (Amnesty International, cited in Gordon 2008, p. 72). Disappearance in Argentina remains a significant case not only because it was systematically practised (as it was in Guatemala), but also because of the powerful mode of collective resistance to state terror it produced, in the actions of Las Madres de la Plaza de Mayo (Gordon 2008).

The disappeared individuals became impossible to trace because they were kidnapped in unmarked cars and the authorities denied any knowledge of their existence or of the clandestine detention centres where they were held (Robben 2005a). Because of the nature of disappearance, incriminating evidence was destroyed; bodies were thrown into the ocean, burned or buried in mass graves (Gordon 2008). The nature of disappearance, as it was used by the military in Argentina (and also in Uruguay and Chile), constructs those individuals whose remains cannot be recovered or found as ghosts who "refuse to have their presence erased but insist on returning to demand that their name be honoured" (Labanyi, in Resina 2000, p. 66). The thousands of individuals who were disappeared under the auspices of the military terror in Argentina cannot, according to sociologist Avery Gordon (2008), be considered as a grand historical fact or simply as a mass of data about an event. Gordon (2008, p. 126) believes that contemplating the disappearance of thousands of individuals can only be experienced as haunting, for "disappearance is a state-sponsored method for producing ghosts, whose haunting effects trace the borders of a society's unconscious."

By making the disappearance of individuals a "public secret", the authoritarian regime scared "a little bit of everyone into shadows of themselves, into submission" (Gordon 2008, p. 126). Disappearance, as it was used in the Argentine context, was not only about death; it was a state of being repressed, and was a systematic procedure used by the military regime to produce ghosts to haunt a whole society into submission (Gordon 2008). However, though the leaders of the military junta believed they could physically control what happened to the *desaparecidos* during their time in power, they have been unable to control the ghostly impact that their violent actions have produced ever since: "The *desaparecido* always bears the ghost of the state whose very power is the defining force of the field of disappearance" (Gordon 2008, p. 127). In other words, the military regime created an identity that continues to haunt all those who had a hand in its creation (Gordon 2008). A virtually breathing presence in Argentine society, the ghostly aspect of the *desaparecidos* will continue to sustain the clamour of legal and moral claims that await recognition and justice.

7.3 Haunting Recognition

Jacque Derrida proposed the term "hauntology"—or in its French form, *hautologi*—in his *Spectres of Marx* (1994), when he reintroduced the idea of ghosts as having agency, and attending to the ghost as being a subject worthy of inquiry. Hauntology replaces the act of being and presence with the figure of the ghost: that which is neither present nor absent, neither dead nor alive (Davis 2005). Further, there is a strongly ethical dimension to this notion:

> Attending to the ghost is an ethical injunction insofar as it occupies the place of the Levinasian Other: a wholly irrecuperable intrusion in our world, which is not comprehensible within our available intellectual frameworks, but whose otherness we are responsible for preserving. (Davis 2005, p. 373)

Both Gordon (2008) and Derrida (1995) believe that ghosts are not just psychic projections, as suggested by Freud, but a form in which the past lives on in the present. Gordon (2008, p. 7) insists that haunting is "neither pre-modern superstition nor individual psychosis", but is "a constituent element of modern social life."

As Fredric Jameson makes clear, hauntology has little to do with whether or not one believes in ghosts:

> Spectrality does not involve the conviction that ghosts exist or that the past (and maybe even the future they offer to prophesy) is still very much alive and at work, within the living present: all it says, if it can be thought to speak, is that the living present is scarcely as self-sufficient as it claims to be; that we would do well not to count on its density and solidity, which might under exceptional circumstances betray us. (cited in Sprinker 1999, p. 39)

Haunting, or what Jameson terms "spectrality", challenges one's belief in the "stability of reality"; it causes us to waver (cited in Sprinker 1999, p. 38). Jameson suggests that: "Spectrality is not difficult to circumscribe, as what makes the present waver: like the vibrations of a heat wave through which the massiveness of the object world—indeed of matter itself—now shimmers like a mirage" (cited in Sprinker 1999, p. 38). Disappearance is a prime example of that which "makes the present waver" in Argentina, as we are forced to deal with the ghostly presence of the *desaparecidos*. Ghosts are the "might have beens" of history that return as an embodied alternative reality and open up "a hole in reality as we like to think we know it" (Labanyi, in Resina 2000, p. 79).

The systematic use of disappearance in Argentina terrorised a nation's population through "the uncertainty that such a publicized secret harbours", but which the state and its various representatives claimed to know nothing about (Gordon 2008, p. 79). General Videla defined and summed up the status of a *desaparecidos* when he said "the disappeared does not exist; he is neither alive nor dead, he's disappeared" (cited in Kaufman 2007, p. 235). Disappearance is about when the boundaries of rational and irrational, subjectivity and objectivity, conscious and unconscious, knowing and not knowing, are found to be unstable:

> A haunted society is full of ghosts, and the ghost always carries the message that the gap between personal and social, public and private, objective and subjective is misleading in the first place. That is to say, it is leading you elsewhere, it is making you see things you did not see before, it is making an impact on you; your relation to things that seemed separate or invisible is changing. (Gordon 2008, p. 98)

Though they have achieved a level of moral and legal recognition from the state in recent years, the families of the *desaparecidos* struggle with what sociologist Avery Gordon terms a "haunting recognition" (2008, p. 63). She believes that the ghosts of the *desaparecidos* make themselves known to Argentine society through haunting, and work at pulling those remembering "affectively into the structure of feeling of a reality we come to experience as recognition" (Gordon 2008, p. 63). Haunting recognition is when the people you love are there one minute and gone the next; when familiar, everyday words are altered and used in the most sinister of ways; when a building you are used to passing by every day harbours the memories of torture and deprivation; and when a society is haunted by terrible deeds that were systematically occurring, but were denied by every public institution (Gordon 2008). These examples convey the complex ways in which the social reality of haunting plays out in Argentina (Gordon 2008).

Haunting, Gordon (2008, p. 134) suggests, is about reliving traumatic encounters in all their vividness and violence, "so as to overcome their pulsating and lingering effects." Families have relived their own traumatic encounters through oral testimony, but they have also borne witness in non-narrative or visual ways. Following the return to democratic rule, debate ensued within the human rights movement about how best to represent the *desaparecidos,* given they had not been counted in any historical or public record yet continued to "persist in a limbo *between* life and death—like spectres haunting the living, wanting to be heard, acknowledged and remembered" (Lazzara 2006, p. 102). The determination to draw attention to the issue of the *desaparecidos* in tangible and visible ways has been a crucial strategy for the families seeking to recreate and to repossess those who were violently taken away from them (Longoni et al. 2008). Among the different creative strategies developed by the families of the *desaparecidos* and others within the human rights movement, I will explore two: the uses of photographs and silhouettes.

7.4 Animating Photographs

Roland Bathes (cited in Gordon 2008, p. 110) tells us that photographs attest "that the object has been real, the photograph surreptitiously induces belief that it is alive…Photography's inimitable feature…is that someone has seen the referent *in flesh and blood,* or again *in person.*" Though no longer here in flesh and blood, those who were disappeared and murdered by political and state terror in the 1970s and 1980s continue to assume a highly visible presence in modern-day Argentina by virtue of photographs. When I met Lorenza, a tiny photograph of her daughter Laura's face on a ring worn on her finger takes on a life-sized presence. I was so drawn to Laura's young, happy face that it was difficult to focus my attention on what Lorenza was telling me. Laura's inability to speak for herself became a noisy silence in the room. We may not have talked about her photograph, but Laura's presence was magnetic. Its magnetism made me want to find out more about this young, vibrant girl, and more about the violent circumstances that took her away at such a young age. Nearly all of the women I interviewed wore photographs of their loved ones, as rings on their fingers, as badges pinned to their clothes, or as pendants around their necks. These photographs are powerful testaments to what was lost. The faces depicted are all young; many are smiling. And they are remembered as such. "I think of them as young people", explained Maria (del Socorro Alonso 2009). Though the individuals remembering get older, the faces of those they remember remain frozen in time. And this can be disconcerting for some. Graciela told me:

> And I look at him [her husband] in the photograph, and he is eternally young, and I look at myself in the mirror and I look like I could be his grandmother (Lois 2009)

Graciela continued:

> For a mother it is different because they can immortalise their young children but when it is one's husband it's horrible because I'm already old and he stays young like Dorian Gray.... (Lois 2009)[3]

In 1983, photographs became one answer to the question of how to permanently represent the absence of the *desaparecidos* and the atrocities of the military (Langland 2005). Photographs were first used by Las Madres, as a way of publicly drawing attention to their search. From early on in the dictatorship, members of Las Madres visited police stations, government offices and hospitals with photographs of their children in hand, searching for news of their sons and daughters (Longoni 2010). These private photographs offered undeniable proof of the existence of the *desaparecidos* (Langland 2005). Soon after its formation, Las Madres members made small posters with the photographs of their missing children, and wore them on their bodies, or held them up as they walked around La Plaza de Mayo (Longoni 2010). The shift in the photographs' usage from the private to the public sphere began with Las Madres' decision to wear the photographs of their loved ones on their bodies during demonstrations (Longoni 2010). This action denoted the strength of the familial bonds that linked the missing child with the mother who wore his/her portrait (Longoni 2010). The photograph, though a small image, communicated a reason for Las Madres to be in the Plaza de Mayo and became a powerful initiative that served to strengthen the bonds between all those who dared to demonstrate (Longoni 2010).

In 1983, some human rights activists enlarged photographs of the *desaparecidos* to a considerable size (70 × 50 cm), and mounted them on placards (Longoni 2010). From this moment on, the photographs were not just used as extensions of the mothers' intimate bodies but were now employed as part of a collective device (Longoni 2010). The photographs could now be raised to a height above a crowd, from which their visual power could reach an even greater number of people (Longoni 2010). The collective nature of such a strategy was, for the first time, able to extend the search for the *desaparecidos* from the missing individuals' intimate families to the larger public (Longoni 2010). Over time, as they moved towards mass exhibition in a public space, the photographs became ubiquitous symbols of the families' struggle for justice and recognition in the public sphere (Longoni 2010). Ana Longoni (2010) suggests this shift had two important consequences in the Argentine context. The first was an almost organic production of a centralised archive of the photographs of the *desaparecidos*. The second was the evolution of a visual politics, with the awareness of the impact that the faces of the *desaparecidos* could have on all those who saw them as their large images marched along with a crowd. In the early days after the return to democratic rule and beyond, the photos emerged as a collective symbol that could appeal to other families of the missing, as well as to the rest of Argentine society and the international community (Longoni 2010).

[3] In Oscar Wilde's 1890 novel, *The Picture of Dorian Gray*, a young man, Dorian Gray, is the subject of a painting by artist Basil Hallward. In the story, realising his beauty will one day fade, Dorian sells his soul to ensure the portrait would age rather than him (Wilde 2007).

The photographs furnish a kind of evidence (Gordon 2008). They reaffirm the existence of a "biography" that predated the kidnapping and disappearance of individuals and declare that "this was, this took place: this person existed" (Barthes, cited in Longoni 2010). The photograph's relationship to haunting is not simple, argues Gordon (2008, p. 103): "When photographs appear in contexts of haunting, they become part of the contest between familiarity and strangeness, between hurting and healing, that the ghost is registering." "To disappear", Gordon continues (2008, p. 104), "is to exist in a world where dispossession and unreality rule." The photographs assumed an enormous power to "give people an imaginary possession of" an "unreal past or present." The photographs were a powerful way of responding to feelings of dispossession and of countering the torturers' past taunts of "you are nothing" and "nobody cares about you." Stemming from feelings of dispossession, the photographs express a "longing to inhabit…neither oneiric…nor empirical…it is fantasmatic, deriving from a kind of second sight which seems to bear me forward to a utopian time, or to carry me back to somewhere in myself" (Barthes, cited in Gordon 2008, p. 109). The photographs personify the *desaparecidos,* and communicate that they have been here once and that they should be here now (Barthes, cited in Gordon 2008, p. 109). They silently emphasise that those missing were not "monsters but young men and women" whose absence must be accounted for (Franco 1992, p. 115). The young and smiling faces of men and women depicted in the photographs transport us to the middle of state terror. They make us wonder what kind of a future these young individuals may have been imagining for themselves before their disappearance.

Las Madres insists that disappearance is a state of being, and as such it "exists and is living with us, doing things to us, scaring us, driving us from our homes into exile, making us inconsolably lonely, or crazy, or unable to see what is right in front of our faces" (Gordon 2008, p. 113). In their weekly protests, with photographs of their missing children pinned over their hearts, the mothers of Las Madres silently and powerfully conjure the ghosts of their disappeared children and extend a hand to us, the spectators, to enter their world of collective grief and loss, where we have little choice but to be touched and altered by their search (Gordon 2008). Las Madres' photographs act as a spirit guide to the disappeared and to disappearance as an organised system of repression (Gordon 2008). The photographs—a token of absence and potent evidence of what is harrowingly present—are utilised by Las Madres to shatter the silence around the *desaparecidos* and to repossess what was taken away from them (Gordon 2008). The photographs say, "this face is mine… and I have a right to find it" (Agosin 1989, p. 94).

Las Madres did not consciously adopt the concept of "haunting". Nevertheless, as a consequence of knowing "what it means to be *connected* to the disappeared", they have helped us to gain a deeper understanding of haunting and its place in an Argentine society where state-sponsored disappearances occurred (Foss and Domenici 2001, p. 240). In the absence of human remains, the photographs have assumed a materiality in the mothers' articulation of loss and grief for their children. The photos have an emotional impact on all those who see them; they never wear out, never die and remain an important and enduring symbol (Foss and Domenici

2001). They ensure the continued ghostly presence of the *desaparecidos* within Argentine society, and are an enduring and potent weapon in the construction of the memory.

7.5 Life-Like Silhouettes

Originally conceived by three visual artists, the silhouettes made their first appearance on the Day of the Student, 21 September 1983 (Longoni 2010).[4] Otherwise known as "*el Siluetazo*", this event, which occurred at the end of the reign of the military, became an important moment in the history of this period. Supported by the human rights movement and by the friends and families of the disappeared, an artistic initiative coincided with the growing momentum within the human rights movement (Longoni 2010). It succeeded in creating an impressive visual reminder of those individuals the military was attempting to negate (Longoni et al. 2008). Members of the human rights movement "stood in" for the *desaparecidos,* as the empty shapes of bodies were traced on giant pieces of paper in La Plaza de Mayo (Longoni et al. 2008). To overcome the issue of homogeneity, efforts were made to individualise the silhouettes (Longoni et al. 2008). On each silhouette was written the name of a disappeared individual and their date of disappearance, and some were inscribed with more identifiable markers such as moustaches and beards (Longoni et al. 2008). Silhouettes of children and pregnant women were also made (Longoni et al. 2008).

While the photographs of the *desaparecidos* emphasise the biographies and lives of the *desaparecidos* before their kidnapping, the silhouettes emphasise the circumstances of individuals' kidnapping and disappearance, and the emptiness and absence such history entails (Longoni 2010). The silhouettes are an attempt to give form to and quantify the victims of the military through the physical space that their absent bodies would otherwise occupy (Longoni 2010). The silhouettes and the photographs both speak of the mourning of the families and friends of the *desaparecidos* and their struggles against the oblivion of the memory of their loved ones (Longoni 2010). Both representations of the *desaparecidos* are two cultural idioms that represent and elaborate the haunting terminology in post-authoritarian Argentina (Foss and Domenici 2001).

As groups of people recreated the *desaparecidos,* it became a process of collective construction (Foss and Domenici 2001). The silhouette, explains Longoni (2010), became an "index" of two bodies—one belonging to the disappeared individual and the other to the person who lent his/her body to create the image. In

[4] It is not certain whether the families had heard rumours and therefore decided to organise the demonstration in response to what was to come the following day, when the military junta issued a self-declared amnesty that prevented any legal penalties for crimes committed during the years of the dictatorship (Lewis 2002). If this was the case, it was perhaps an attempt by the families and human rights movement to reclaim the *desaparecidos* before they were legislated out of existence.

this way, "the broken ties of solidarity are reconstructed in a powerfully moving symbolic act" (Cerisola, cited in Longoni et al. 2008, p. 32, own translation). As individuals stepped in on behalf of the *desaparecidos,* they accepted that it could have been them, that they could have suffered the same fate as the person they were in effect body doubling (Longoni et al. 2008). That the body of the person demonstrating took the place of a disappeared individual made it possible to think of the silhouette as leaving a "breathing trace" (Cortinas, cited in Longoni et al. 2008, p. 33, own translation). The making of the silhouettes involved a performative act that was at once both intimate (the body of the demonstrator stepped in for the body of the disappeared) and collective (the constructive procedure was held in a public space) (Longoni et al. 2008). The process involved the decision of the demonstrators to put themselves in the place of the missing and to lend him/her "a breath of life" (Longoni et al. 2008).

The silhouettes were posted throughout the city of Buenos Aires as a way of granting the *desaparecidos* another opportunity to be present, and for the families to recreate a physical form to remember them (Longoni et al. 2008). It was a way of presenting the *desaparecidos* within the context of the "presence of an absence" (Flores, cited in Longoni et al. 2008, p. 7, own translation). Las Madres rejected the artists' initial idea of glueing the silhouettes to the ground, all too aware of the association that would be made by the general public between the silhouettes and death (Longoni et al. 2008). Instead, Las Madres asked that they always be kept upright (Longoni et al. 2008). Mother of disappeared daughter Graciela, Matilde Mellibovsky captures the powerful presence the *desaparecidos* began to assume from that moment on and the sense that their loved ones were marching alongside them when she says: "It was the first time that our kids had come out in the streets with us to march since their disappearance" (Mellibovsky 1997, p. 133).

Mellibovsky (1997, p. 134) explains the "unquestionable existence" of the *desaparecidos* that had to be restored: "I believe that for the first time our children's strong presence—which we feel all the time—was shared by the rest of the people." As the silhouettes were left on the street walls after the demonstration had finished, the *desaparecidos* acquired a public presence for the first time (Mellibovsky 1997). One of the artists involved in the projects commented at the time that, "the silhouettes didn't fill the emptiness, they only gave it shape. And quantity. Thousands of people made thousands of silhouettes of thousands of people" (Mellibovsky 1997, p. 132). The effect achieved by staging the event was of the *desaparecidos* protesting:

> Thousands of women and men and kids and the newborn and those not yet born, stood fiercely upright, accusing the torturers, the assassins, the corrupt, those who today still spit in our faces, demanding, threatening, a shameful forgetfulness…
> The disappeared. Wherever they might be, they haven't stopped struggling for a minute. They are more alive than us. (Mellibovsky 1997, p. 131–32)

The silhouettes gave material form to the *desaparecidos,* making them manifest in very real ways (Foss and Domenici 2001). One Argentine journalist commented that the silhouettes seemed to point from the walls at those who were to blame for their absence (Foss and Domenici 2001). The silhouettes broke the military's imposed silence over the existence of the *desaparecidos,* and made evident that which the public would have preferred to ignore (Foss and Domenici 2001). The Argentine public could no longer claim that they did not know of the disappearances (Foss and Domenici 2001).

The silhouettes were understood to be the visual manifestation of Las Madres' slogan "*Aparición con vida*" ("Bring them back alive") (Longoni et al. 2008). The catch-cry, "*aparición con vida*" began to be used by La Asociación Madres de Plaza de Mayo as a way of demanding that their children be brought back alive. It was also a way of communicating the organisation's rejection of the closure that exhumations were supposed to bring them (Renshaw 2010). It was a way of telling the government of the day that the dead person was still absent and that the return of their remains would not resolve the absence (Renshaw 2010).

There has been some debate about what the silhouettes really represent (Longoni et al. 2008). Gustavo Buntinx (cited in Longoni et al. 2008) believes they were proof of the fact that Las Madres were originally hopeful of finding individuals alive. Conversely, Eduardo Gruner (cited in Longoni et al. 2008) conceives of the silhouettes as representative of not just that which was "absent" but also that which was made to disappear through violence. Gruner (cited in Longoni et al. 2008) notes that the image was used as a substitution for the missing body and reproduced the police procedure of drawing the outline of a dead body in chalk before it is taken away from a crime scene. He says that it could be read as a "political gesture that appropriates the investigative methods of the enemy—of the so-called forces of the law—generating a continuity as if they were saying: 'It was you'" (Gruner, cited in Longoni et al. 2008, p. 34, own translation). But Gruner suggests that, despite the wishes of Las Madres, the silhouettes also represent corpses (cited in Longoni et al. 2008).

Buntinx (cited in Longoni et al. 2008, p. 40, own translation) further argues that the silhouettes recouped a "magical-religious dimension" of art that "modernity had taken away". Longoni, Bruzzone and Aguerreberry (2008, p. 40, own translation) agree, claiming silhouettes restore an "auratic charge" to the image. This relates to Walter Benjamin's concept of auratic art, which is defined as "the expectation that what one is looking at is looking back at one" (cited in Longoni 2010, p. 6). Thus, the holding of *El Siluetazo* as an event did not just seek to raise public awareness; it was also an attempt to create "a ritual pact with the dead" by reversing what had been done by the military and reclaiming those loved ones who had been "trapped in the phantasmagorical borders of death for a new life" (Buntinx, cited in Longoni et al. 2008, p. 47, own translation).

Barthes (cited in Gordon 2008) also suggests that the power of these physical manifestations is to convey to those viewing the existence of something so profound that it comes to also mean something profound to the viewer. He uses the term *punctum* to refer to the power of such artistic forms to affectively move the viewer by arousing the image from its flat immobility and making it emerge and become alive (Bathes, cited in Gordon 2008). The photographs and silhouettes play a pivotal role in provoking Argentine society—particularly those not directly affected by the military violence—to create a relationship with the *desaparecidos* and to acknowledge, if not identify with, their trauma (Foss and Domenici 2001). The animation of the photographs and silhouettes summoned the "missing presence" of the *desaparecidos* but also gave rise to important issues for those looking on, including: "What does it mean to lose what one thought was secure?" and "What kind of society am I living in that not only sanctions but initiates these kinds of losses?" (Foss and Domenici 2001, p. 250).

Through these symbols, the ghost is not just a dead or missing person, but acts as a social figure (Gordon 2008). These social figures are used by Las Madres and the human rights movement to claim a public presence for the *desaparecidos* (Foss and Domenici 2001). They also communicate a continuing sense of the *desaparecidos* through the haunting of a nation's conscience (Foss and Domenici 2001). Seeing Las Madres walk along with the photographs and silhouettes of the *desaparecidos* makes public the hidden dimensions of the state apparatus's use of disappearance, the kind of public secret that haunted the population into submission through the widespread use of fear (Foss and Domenici 2001). The use of these two methods revealed that the ghosts of Argentina that remain as a result of the military's actions cannot be "completely managed" (Gordon 2008, p. 127), but "remain as living reminders of what has been and still is unresolved" (Foss and Domenici 2001, p. 251).

7.6 Haunting Attachments

The power of the photographs and silhouettes as symbols to convey the profound absence of loved ones makes them very difficult to relinquish (Foss and Domenici 2001). It could perhaps be said that the *desaparecidos* have become prisoners of their photographs as a result and/or that they have, with time, become venerated icons (Vezzetti 1996). For families to ever relinquish these symbols, argues Vezzetti (1996), would seem like giving up on their loved ones. The women with whom I spoke are "locked in" by these powerful symbols, "moving back and forth between the symbol and the devastating [sic] experience for which it stands with a persistence that many a ghost would envy" (Foss and Domenici 2001, p. 253).

If haunting demands a willingness to engage the ghost, then the female family members of the *desaparecidos* with whom I spoke have more than demonstrated their insistence to do so (Foss and Domenici 2001). The women all understand on a visceral level what it is to be connected to the *desaparecidos*. They understand this connection because of a "special contact" they have with the loss (Gordon 2008, p. 112). It is a contact that has emerged because of the responsibility the women take for the *desaparecidos,* and "their attempt to communicate with them and to locate them, showing their faces, eyes, and mouths in public", as well as the women's "extraordinary absence of fear of trafficking in and with the haunting remains of state terror…" (Gordon 2008, p. 112).

The absence of bodily remains and a lack of knowledge about the fate of loved ones are an open wound that constantly triggers the memories of family members. These markers characterise what Boss (2006, p. xvii) terms "ambiguous loss": "an unclear loss that defies closure", and the most stressful kind of loss. Boss (1999) assumes that ambiguous loss can traumatise. She argues that symptoms of unresolved grief are similar to post-traumatic stress disorder (PTSD) (Boss 1999). PTSD "is a disorder resulting from psychologically stressing events that were outside the realm of usual human experience. These events were never resolved and thus are continually re-experienced, even years after the original event" (Boss 1999, p. 23, 24). While ambiguous loss is also a psychologically distressing event that lies outside the parameters of a "normal" human experience, and lacks resolution, ambiguous loss continues to exist in the present (Boss 1999). "It is not post anything", argues Boss (1999, p. 24). Another psychoanalyst, Elizabeth Lira, who has written about PTSD among individuals who lived through state terror in Chile, similarly argues that the term PTSD cannot adequately capture the ongoing nature of state terror, "because there is nothing 'post' about it" (cited in Hollander 2010, p. 122). Lira prefers to use the term "culture of fear" to emphasise that an "individual subjective experience is shared simultaneously by millions of people, with dramatic repercussions for social and political behaviour" (cited in Hollander 2010, p. 122). Julia Braun suggests that while PTSD symptoms may occur among a population at large or in individual cases, in contexts that have experienced state terror, PTSD is a "repetitive trauma" whereby one trauma is layered upon another (cited in Hollander 2010, p. 122).

From a psychoanalytic perspective, ambiguous loss produces traumatic anxiety in individuals because of a combination of the known and the unknown (Boss 2006). Boss explains this further: "The intellectual and relational uncertainty of living with someone both here and not here produces a terrible anxiety of bizarre human experience" (Boss 2006, p. 5). The persistent ambiguity that arises for the families because of their inability to officially certify loved ones' bodily remains blocks "cognition, coping and meaning-making and freezes the grief process", argues Boss (Boss 2006, p. xvii). As a loss without end, ambiguous loss can become physically and emotionally exhausting for those enduring a life of relentless uncertainty (Boss 1999). Living with ambiguous loss has been inherently traumatic for the women I interviewed. They, in Boss's terms, are unable to come to terms with those memories that cause them a continuing sense of pain, confusion and distress (Boss 1999).

In particular, the partners and wives of the *desaparecidos* spoke to me about the difficulties they had encountered over the years to find their "place" in the remembrance of loved ones. In fact, Cristina told me that the wives and partners for many years were like the disappeared because nobody talked about them or about their loss. When human rights are spoken about in reference to Argentina, it is usually the mothers, grandmothers or children of the disappeared who are mentioned.[5] Being a partner of a *desaparecido* has been painful and distressing on a number of levels for Cristina. Transmitting the story about what happened to her partner, to

[5] Noemi Ciollaro, with whom I also spoke, has published a book of interviews she completed with wives and partners of the desaparecidos—Pajaros Sin Luz (2000)—and has raised awareness of their plight as a result.

her children and grandchildren is something she has done religiously. She told me about an epiphany that her granddaughter had at a Memory Day march on 24 March one year:

> She [Cristina's granddaughter] looked at me and said, "Grandma, so it's very sad to come to these marches"…because there were all these…for her it had been like a party and in that moment she realised…this [husband's/grandfather's absence] is with us every day, in one way or another, it's with us every day…(Muro 2009)

Graciela believes the uncertainty about what happened to the disappeared will never leave her. She told me that she cannot accept the grief that normally accompanies death because she has never seen a body. She has never been able to go fully through a process of grieving as a result:

> Now, what happens…you can't put the past behind you, you keep doing things, but you can't put the past behind you…the pain doesn't leave, it doesn't hurt because you've never seen a body…pain comes with death…different cultures [deal with burying the dead] in different ways, whether that's burning a body, I don't know…burying it. But we were never able to do this, so we live with this uncertainty until death …it's that we've never had the luck to identify remains. (Lois 2009)

The loss of loved ones, and the associated social and personal implications, have placed most of the female relatives of the *desaparecidos* in a state of limbo. The way that haunting plays out—the feeling of being in limbo—can make it difficult for the women to go a day without mourning their loved ones. When loss is converted into absence, argues LaCapra (1994, p. 698), "one faces the impasse of endless melancholy, impossible mourning, and interminable aporia in which any process of working through the past and its historical losses is foreclosed or prematurely aborted." The women with whom I spoke struggle to acknowledge or accept the loss of loved ones; instead, they embrace their absence. Another mother has said: "Let there be no healing of wounds…let them remain open. Because if the wounds still bleed, there will be no forgetting" (cited in Di-Paolantonio 2001, p. 463). In this instance, there is no breaking of an attachment with their loved one, but rather an "incorporation of the attachment as identification" so that the memory of the individual is preserved (Butler 1997, p. 167). And,

> insofar as identification is the psychic preserve of the object and such identifications come to form the ego, then the lost object continues to haunt and inhabit the ego as one of its constitutive identifications and is, in that sense, made coextensive with the ego itself. (Butler 1997, p. 167)

With the refusal to accept the loss of an individual, there is no abandonment of the object of love, but rather a transference of the "status of the object", whereby it becomes internalised (Butler 1997, p. 167). For example, the poet and activist Marjorie Agosin has written:

> Little by little I got used to talking about the disappeared, the political prisoners, and the jailers. To speak of them, to approach the vocabulary of the torn, of the unusual, of the ominous, became part of my everyday language. For years the presence of the disappeared inhabited my waking and sleeping hours until I was finally able to speak like them. I lost the feeling of objectively [objectivity]. I did not see them as beings occupying the uninhabited spaces of absence. In some way, they were everywhere. To speak of them did not become a

> way of re-conceptualizing the horror, neither was it a form of creating fiction from history. The transfer was complete. (1994, p. 217)

As Agosin refuses to abandon the disappeared, internalisation becomes one way in which her feelings of loss can be preserved within her psyche (Butler 1997). As Butler (1997, p. 167) explains, "the internalization of loss is part of the mechanism of its refusal." In continually mourning the *desaparecidos,* both publicly and privately, the women manage to maintain their suffering and loss as a fundamental part of who they are. Eliana told me that some relatives of the desaparecidos refused to give their DNA to the data bank, for fear that the remains of their loved ones should be found. She told me:

> We [her brother and herself] went to give DNA. There are some people who are part of the human rights organisations and don't want to go and give DNA. This is terrible. Because of fear, they don't want to do it…to find the remains and not know what to do. (Carreira 2009)

Eliana reveals the feelings of ambiguity that circulates among the families of the *desaparecidos* and the affective force that fear continues to have. For some, to be a family member of a *desaparecido* has meant also identifying as such. By refusing to give their DNA, these individuals are refusing the possibility of certainty and are instead choosing a never-ending mourning. In this way, they manage to preserve the legacy of their family's traumatic history; they keep loss as a part of what remains of themselves. When the female relatives of the *desaparecidos* think about what is lost, they also inevitably question what remains. Loss is inseparable from what is left, "for what is lost is known only by what remains of it" (Eng and Kazanjian 2003, p. 2). Cristina told me:

> This enormous absence that I have in my life won't allow things to close, like a pain; this loss, the uncertainty…the uncertainty and the guilt make me feel very bad. (Muro 2009)

Not just for Cristina but also for the other female relatives of the *desaparecidos,* what remains of their loss is an overpowering sense of uncertainty, vulnerability, survivor guilt and shame. It is these feelings that can make the women feel all the more fragile as a sense of anxiety rises up and stays with them. Raquel told me of her desperation and anxiety on not knowing the whereabouts of her children and grandchild:

> For those of us who got together, the majority [of us] would be crying; we couldn't stop crying. It was desperate. It's an anxiety that we still feel now…until now. For me, I feel this anxiety because I know nothing of my grandson and we don't know where the remains of our children are. (Marizcurrena 2009)

In their testimonials, the women recreate the lives of the *desaparecidos,* name their names, describe their personalities and call them back into being. When they tell their stories of the past, the women can hear how they themselves are in these stories; most feel as though they are trapped in old stories. While they do not necessarily want to be trapped, the women with whom I spoke are hesitant to let go of these stories because they do not feel that there is another place where they can belong (Gordon 2008). For some of the women, their compulsion to tell their painful story time and again—their need to be heard—indeed appeared to be how Felman describes this imperative (1992, p. 7): "The survivors did not only need to survive so that they could tell their story; they also needed to tell their story in order to survive". Raquel explained how being haunted by the memory of her missing children and grandchildren locks her into the state of being consumed by their absence:

> I am continuously thinking about them [her missing children and grandchild]. I can't think of anything else. (Marizcurrena 2009)

Raquel's feelings about her trauma are suggestive of what LaCapra (2001) describes as almost a "fidelity": Her trauma is a feeling with which she feels she must keep faith. "Part of this feeling", writes LaCapra:

> may be the melancholic sentiment that, in working through the past in a manner that enables survival or a reengagement in life, one is betraying those who were overwhelmed and consumed by that traumatic past. One's bond with the dead, especially with dead intimates, may invest trauma with value and make its reliving a painful but necessary commemoration or memorial to which one remains dedicated or at least bound. (2001, p. 22)

Raquel expresses her desire to remain with trauma, and as she does so, she expresses her resistance to any form of conceptual or narrative closure (LaCapra 2001). She made a decision a long time ago to be engaged with a process of endless bereavement (LaCapra 2001). As such, she remains tied to the historical and social effects she is recounting (Gordon 2008). Gordon writes:

> Haunting is an encounter in which you touch the ghost or the ghostly matter of things: the ambiguities, the complexities of power and personhood, the violence and the hope, the looming and receding actualities, the shadows of ourselves and our society. (2008, p. 134)

In being haunted, some of the women *touch the ghostly shadows* of themselves as the bond they embrace with the *desaparecidos* can make them feel like they too were disappeared. Graciela told me:

> I always dressed in black, black, black and at one moment I went to therapy and the therapist told me, you're not disappeared, your husband is…look at how you're dressed. (Lois 2009)

For Graciela, what is happening is that, in the words of LaCapra (1999, p. 699), "distinctions tend to collapse, including the crucial distinction between then and now wherein one is able to remember what happened to one in the past but realize one is living in the here and now with future possibilities". In identifying as one of the disappeared, Graciela could remain accountable to those individuals affected by the state terror. "The house has gone quiet", writes Avery Gordon (2008, p. 180), "not only because the ghost has come out of the shadows, but also because the women have closed themselves up inside it". The women find themselves bound to the *desaparecidos* in such an entangled way that loss will continue to be a part of their identity and mourning will never end. The need of the disappeared to be remembered has become inseparable from the needs of the women who remain without them (Gordon 2008). The past continues to take possession of the women's present lives and haunting remains a way of life (Gordon 2008). In this way, many of the women are unwilling and unable to let their loved ones go because that would mean they were, quite literally, "giving up their ghosts" (Foss and Domenici 2001, p. 255).

Most of the women are defined by the powerful, ever-present fear of their loved ones being forgotten. At times, their discourse can be such that it denies any other point of view apart from their own (Foss and Domenici 2001). This is more of a problem with Las Madres de la Plaza de Mayo than with other groups, including some within Las Madres de la Plaza de Mayo Linea Fundadora (Foss and Domenici 2001). For the women I interviewed, finding within themselves genuine empathy for another viewpoint is made extremely difficult because, as Avery Gordon (2008, p. 190) explains: "To be haunted is to experience the glue of the 'If you were me and I were you' logic come undone". The stasis of haunting is such that, rather than seek any sort of resolution or reconciliation, the women's identification with the *desaparecidos* and the deceased perpetuates their own ongoing internal repression, and with it dismissal of any dissonant discourse (Gordon 2008). While assuming a haunted state may have been an effective strategy for beginning a social movement, it has been less effective as time has gone on, argue Foss and Domenici (2001, p. 254), because "the 'betweeness' of the haunted state may keep transformative rhetorical possibilities from emerging".

The force of the ghosts' desire is not only negative, reasons Gordon (2008). The ghost is also pregnant with unfulfilled possibility, for the women to attend to that which the wavering present demands (Gordon 2008). The ghosts do not beckon a return to the past, but a reckoning with the women's own entrapment in loss and grief in the present. The ghost features the utopian dimension of haunting as it urges for "Someone, you or me" to come forward and say: "I would like to learn to live finally" (Derrida, cited in Gordon 2008, p. 184). The ghosts make the present waiver in Argentina as they urge the women to beware of forgetting that entrapment persists should they continually grieve them—an entrapment that can masquerade as emancipation (Derrida, cited in Gordon 2008, p. 184). In this way, the *desaparecidos* and the deceased continue to work in multiple ways, on multiple levels, in the here and now as they "structure the domain of the present and the prerogatives of the future" (Gordon 2008, p. 179).

Chapter 8
Considering Affect in Transitional Contexts

8.1 The Longevity of Deep Memory

The dominant human rights discourse on transitional justice constitutes a mix of mutually coherent and reinforcing aims that seek to "make peace with" and "find closure" on a violent past. These aims include preventing future violence, instituting accountability for human rights violations, achieving reconciliation and forgiveness, building and restoring societal trust and peace, and easing the psychological trauma of victims (Crocker 2003). While political violence has both human rights and health implications, current approaches to the national reconciliation scenario have focused on a therapeutic model, whereby victims rather than perpetrators "are made the evidence of past atrocities" as well as "the vehicle for re-establishing state legitimacy post-dictatorship through individual and social healing" (Humphrey 2005, p. 204). With their victim-oriented focus and their restorative and reconciliatory discourses, transitional justice initiatives have thus been concerned mainly with the mitigation of the effects of traumatic experiences of survivors of mass violence. Despite their relevance and centrality to addressing historical injustices and suffering, the fragmented and disruptive memories of individuals who have experienced violence and loss are all too often displaced by the nation-building discourse found in transitioning democracies (Grunnebaum and Henri 2003).

While the traumatisation of individuals and groups has been the central premise for national reconciliation projects, which seek to heal the wounds of the past and promote peace within fractured societies, the research findings in this book considerably complicate the notion that the process of enacting justice is automatically commensurate with the alleviation of individual trauma. When we drill down deeply underneath individuals' more formalised accounts, we are able to see how those mnemonic layers that are unconscious, inexpressible and uncontainable in language, can be lodged deeply within a survivor's body and are prone to involuntary eruptions. In this way, the deep memories of Argentine women I write about in this book assume a powerful presence in their lives, and prevent the women from envisioning a future for themselves in which their individual and their nation's past is safely left behind—contained and fixed in the past. Exploring deep memory exposes the unconscious ways in which the women remain attached to this violent

J. Stockwell, *Reframing the Transitional Justice Paradigm*,
Springer Series in Transitional Justice 10, DOI 10.1007/978-3-319-03853-7_8,

period of history. As I have shown, this attachment has serious and at times unpredictable implications for the politics of remembering in Argentina.

Of course, there have been many moments in contemporary Argentina when the instances of justice being achieved acted as a circuit-breaker of sorts, producing a sense of release from the condition of "stuckness", from the sense of being trapped in history. One such instance occurred in July 2012, when nine individuals—including two former Argentine military junta leaders, Jorge Videla and Reynaldo Bignone—were convicted for carrying out a systematic plan to steal babies from political prisoners during the 1976–1983 military dictatorship. The president of Las Abuelas, Estela de Carlotto, said of the verdict: "This is justice. It has arrived. Remember that we started in 1996, and at that time we didn't know whether or not we would ever see this moment" (Hernandez 2012). De Carlotto was also quoted as saying that the verdict will be "healing for the Argentine society". Others agree with her. Victoria Montenegro, who recovered her identity through Las Abuelas, said of the result: "With this verdict we can start repairing the damages caused by our history, even though this history still causes us pain" (Hernandez 2012). Yet it is important to remember that the pursuit and enactment of justice, in its myriad forms, can only go so far in healing individuals' deep pain. Affective memories, and their ongoing, relentless timings and rhythms, remind us that justice is not an endpoint but an important part of a survivor's ongoing journey through the wastelands of pain and vulnerability.

It becomes clear that we cannot have a discussion about justice and the remembering and forgetting of the violent past in transitional democracies without giving due consideration to those irreconcilable and disruptive embodied memories that resist being co-opted into the particular paradigms of dealing with the past. Deep memory defies closure—or indeed any type of certainty. While we may wish to imagine that justice is the answer in societies grappling with the traumatic past, we are well advised to consider that no amount of public truth telling, including the central place afforded in Argentina to narratives born of oral testimony, can diminish the women's deeply felt pain. Their narratives reveal that even when individuals affected by violence and loss manage to successfully seek justice as individuals and as part of various collectives, the psychical and physical pain provoked by deep memory will continue to be an irreducible part of their lives.

I believe that the focus on the role played by affective memories in shaping the Argentine women's narratives can further understand women's experience of memory, trauma and testimony in other historical and geographical contexts. Through articulations of their embodied memories of trauma, violence and loss, the women in this book reveal how reclaiming their own bodies as a site of memory "represents an important reclamation and recovery of survivors' bodies whose boundaries have been transgressed and humanity violated" (Grunebaum and Henri 2003). As illustrated in the Argentine context, exploring women's affective memories in the testimonial encounter can challenge historically silenced versions of remembering. However, what if we were to take affect seriously and explore what it has to tell us in other international contexts, where women's affective memories are all too often marginalised within formal testimonial discourse?

In many ways, remembering affectively is a process of remembering the tragic effects of trauma on individual lives; it is a form of remembering that allows the women to acknowledge and articulate the persistent physical and psychological impact of living with trauma, their moral ambivalence regarding survival and their ways of living with memories that will not—and cannot—be contained (Grunebaum and Henri 2003). Exploring women's affective memories in contexts re-emerging after conflict or authoritarian rule can challenge portrayals of women as selfless and passive victims; it can also foreground the embodied experiences of survivors and survival, and actively engender the transformation of pain into language. In this way, women are afforded a greater degree of control of their memories, their bodies and their language.

8.2 Affect and Empathy

"Historical truth, legal evidence and the moral high ground are on the side of the human rights movement", writes anthropologist Antonius Robben of present-day Argentina (2012, p. 314). Yet the considerable political and legal gains achieved by the human rights movement in recent years have not produced conditions necessary for a peaceful coexistence for Argentine society. The individuals and families affected by state violence continue to feel a sense of injustice over a number of unresolved legacies. With their loved ones thrown into the ocean by security forces, most of the families of the missing will never be able to bury their loved ones' bodies. The absence of bodies is often paralleled by the absence of truth. As those implicated in human rights abuses refuse to confess, the truth about what happened to each and every individual following their abduction by members of the security forces remains out of reach, becoming a source of eternal frustration and perceived injustice for tens of thousands of families.

At the same time, while Las Abuelas have challenged the endemic silence and denial over what happened to appropriated babies and children by zeroing in on the politics of memory and on the distortion of the historical record, many individuals remain unaware of the truth about their past. Though just over 100 young men and women have retrieved their real identities and have been reunited with their biological families since the return to democratic rule, this has come at a cost. The devastating impact the appropriation of a child can have on the level of family disintegration has been enormous for many families. We are still to see the repercussions that such a violent rupture within the family unit will have in the generations to come, according to Las Abuelas. Meanwhile, those young individuals who have recuperated their identities feel that they have lived a lie for decades. These are the years that can never be gained back.

While legal proceedings in relation to state terrorism are currently in process in Argentina, many of the women with whom I spoke voiced concerns that political and judicial gains to bring those accused of human rights abuses to trial could be lost with a change of government. Many also spoke about their lack of faith in a justice system that previously had failed them, and that continued to accommodate corrupt and biased judges. All of the women told me that they live in a constant state of uncertainty and fear, as a number of perpetrators have managed to keep their identities concealed and continue to live alongside them.

On the other side of the ideological divide, the current government's political approach to collective remembrance of the period of political violence during the 1970s is contributing to the social and cultural conditions that foster feelings of marginalisation, ostracism, resistance and anger, rather than playing a role in expanding social patterns of recognition among the families of victims of the armed guerrilla resistance. For these families, the truth about the armed guerrilla violence in the 1970s seems to be perennially out of reach as they await the political, social and legal recognition of the memories of their loved ones.

These unresolved legacies are part of what compels the women to give their oral testimony in the public sphere. As a result, oral testimony has played a crucial role in how events collectively have been assimilated and remembered in Argentina. As the significance of the political and state violence of the 1970s and 1980s have been socially shared within Argentina's memorial cultures, individuals' perceptions and understandings of the events have been shaped to a significant degree by those giving oral testimony. The telling and retelling of individuals' memories can never "exhaust" the violence that was inflicted during the period of political and state violence; instead, such testimony symbolises and even evokes it. As the women repetitively relate their emotional experiences to others, the social group gradually assimilates those experiences, and as a result is furnished with new emotional knowledge. As feelings and emotions are strongly communicated by the women in their narratives, this in turn engenders strong feelings in those listening.

By talking in the public sphere about their memories of violence and loss, I suggest that an affective residue is created, and it is this invisible but potent residue that contributes to a sense of the continuance of animosity and resentment over time. Looking back, there was one seemingly small encounter that led me towards the idea of looking to affective memory as a way of grasping why and how existing antagonisms continued to flourish in Argentine memorial culture. The encounter involved my 3-year-old daughter, Bonnie. This experience left a lasting impression because it revealed to me how the memory of the trauma of loss, which is an essentially alienating experience, could be mediated through the affective connections between bodies (Bennett 2002).

One afternoon, I took Bonnie to meet some of the women I had interviewed at the headquarters of one of the human rights organisations. There were five or six women in the room. One woman, Irma Morresi, had declined my invitation to be interviewed. Irma and her husband had found the remains of their son Noberto in June 1989. Noberto was "disappeared" by the military in April 1976. This was my first meeting with Irma. After a few minutes of being in the room, Bonnie went over to Irma, who was seated furthest away, and crawled up on to her lap, unprompted. As she cuddled up to Irma's chest, Bonnie proceeded to self-comfort and to suck her thumb for the next 20 min. To sit on the lap of a stranger was extremely out of character for Bonnie. Even if it was not, she could have chosen to sit on the laps of any of the other four women in the room. However, she chose the one woman I had not interviewed and who did not want to tell her story. I took a photograph of Irma with Bonnie on her lap. In the picture, Irma is smiling, hugging Bonnie tightly while Bonnie's face looks pained. As soon as we climbed into the taxi to go home, Bonnie burst into tears and said, "Mummy, I feel lonely."

This encounter offered me an important glimpse of the deep and unseen ways in which affect can work between individuals and groups. It showed me how affective memories can "pass from body to body, from skin to skin"; how they can "circulate about, between, and sometimes stick to bodies and worlds, and in the very passages or variations between these intensities and resonances themselves" (Gregg and Seigworth 2010, p. 1). It seemed to me that a feeling of loneliness passed between Irma and Bonnie. Did Bonnie catch Irma's loneliness or produce her own in the arms of an 'affected' individual? Regardless, it was a feeling that Bonnie continued to carry after their meeting. Though Irma may have chosen to remain silent about her deep pain, it was as if Bonnie still heard her on some level and tried to physically fill the void left by her disappeared son.

The affective dimensions of the oral testimonies that I was soliciting suddenly became very clear to me. The experience spoke very personally to me of just how illuminating the theory of affective transmission could be in not only explaining how nearly 30-year-old traumatic memories could be kept alive in the present through the circulation of affect, but also in how the lived experience of affect creates the surfaces of the individual and social body and renders these surfaces porous and open to being reanimated (Ahmed 2004a).

I contend that emotions and affects are social forces that remain and are at work in the public sphere long after the women have shared their experiences with others. For though not always visible or noticed, powerful affects are released in the process of individuals remembering and sharing their traumatic pasts. Both positive and negative affects persist and circulate in non-verbal and non-representational ways among individuals and throughout the society today. I argue that women's feelings of loss, melancholy and anger when remembering their traumatic pasts can accumulate, seep into and reside within other bodies in the public sphere, altering individuals' understanding of their selves as well as their relation with the past. As the women go public with their narratives, the circulation of their narratives and the accompanying affects they generate result in the shaping and reshaping of the contours of the public space they inhabit.

As this occurs, the women's emotions and affects align individuals with communities and play a crucial role in the materialisation of collective bodies, including the body of the Argentine nation. When considering the physical, emotional and psychological damage that the women I interviewed have endured, my book contends that it is not just the effects of trauma on an individual's bodily or "skin" surface that we need to think about, but the ways in which the "skin" of the community has also been affected. Though the link between individuals is predicated on the possibility and expectation of empathy, when individuals' vital needs go unheeded or are ignored by others, individuals lose the expectation that their needs will be met in some way. When this happens, affected individuals no longer feel they have anyone on whom they can count. The link between the self and the "other" is obliterated by a failure of empathy.

In Argentina, while I witnessed moments of recognition, empathy for the grief of those on the other ideological divide was generally difficult to fathom, and as a result considerable social damage has been produced. In particular, what both groups of women desire—the acknowledgement of and empathic engagement with their suffering by those individuals instrumental in and directly responsible for causing their emotional pain—has been continually denied. As the women believe their memories have not been given the moral, social, cultural and legal recognition they feel they deserve within the public sphere of collective remembrance, affective alignment has failed, and has left open the way for a continued stalemate between members of antagonistic memorial cultures.

For the family members of the *desaparecidos* I interviewed, finding within themselves genuine empathy for another viewpoint is also made extremely difficult because of another societal phenomenon: haunting. When there can be no burials and thousands of families find it difficult to properly mourn their loved ones, society remains in a stasis of haunting and tied to losses that never became real. Most of the women are defined by the powerful, ever-present fear of their loved ones being forgotten. Because they are unwilling and unable to let their loved ones go, the past continues to take possession of the women's present lives. The women find themselves bound to the *desaparecidos* in such an entangled way that loss will continue to be a part of their identity and mourning will never end. The need of the disappeared to be remembered has become inseparable from the needs of the women who remain without them. It can be argued that the stasis of haunting is such that, rather than seek any sort of resolution, the women's identification with the *desaparecidos* perpetuates the dismissal of any possibilities for empathic alignment with ideologically opposed others. While assuming a haunted state may have been an effective strategy at the start of the transition, it has been less effective as time has gone by. The notion of haunting as a fundamental part of modern-day Argentine society has kept transformative and discursive possibilities from emerging between antagonistic memorial cultures.

8.3 Affect and Vulnerability

An attention to affect, and particularly to the ways in which its rhythms, timings, shapes and contours come to mark the passages of intensities within and between individuals, compels us to rethink the impetus for survivors of violence and trauma to reconcile with their traumatic memories as quickly as possible—or even at all. Grief, Judith Butler tells us, is a slow process "by which we develop a point of identification with suffering itself" (2003, p. 30). In other words, it takes time for survivors' preoccupation with mourning and melancholia to move into new understandings and consideration of the vulnerability of others (Butler 2003). When we consider the time it could take for new understandings of the vulnerability of others to emerge between antagonistic memorial cultures, it may be fruitful to wonder what it would be like if we let go of the idea that history needed to be settled. What would it mean for transitioning democracies to let go of the mantras of "coming to terms with the past" and "moving on"? What if we shifted our attention to individuals' narratives, and really listened to what was being said, rather than skirting over the voices of individuals in the name of peace-building projects?

After all, affective memories can—and do—take their time to emerge into consciousness, both individual and collective. When so much pain and vulnerability exist, unready to be seen or narrated, and when we set limits on how long survivors can grieve because they become obstructions to our march towards reconciliation, are we not at risk of plunging them again, alone, back into the original trauma? Susan Brison (1999) reflects on the difficulties of living with her own traumatic memories of sexual violence while being part of a society that deals with the "unbearable" by pressuring those who have been traumatised to forget what happened to them. She argues that as individuals and as cultures, we impose "arbitrary term limits on memory and on recovery from trauma" (Brison 1999, p. 49). Telling survivors of violence to "put the past behind them" does not make their deep memories go away; however, it only makes memories more likely to be driven underground (Brison 1999). Brison's experience chimes with the words of cultural historian Maria Tumarkin, who asks: "How long will it take for experiences of violence and injustice to be lived through and absorbed, for the forgiveness to emerge, not to be forced out? We don't know. It will take *as long as it takes*" (2011, p. 143).

If we give due consideration to the workings of affect, we begin to realise that it could take quite some time for individuals' experiences of violence and injustice to be lived through in Argentina. After all, affect is not only transmitted between bodies but across generations. As individuals inherit the psychic substance of their ancestors, they can potentially manifest symptoms that are linked to a parent's or an ancestor's psychic traumas and losses, as well as to their resistance and strength.

Though they may have never known their parents, the children of the disappeared have nonetheless received and assimilated the effects of their parents' traumatic histories. They are inscribed not with the original trauma, but with its affective markings and multiple traces.

Family secrets and silenced traumatic history come back to haunt the children of survivors "like unknown ghosts of the past", argues Gabrielle Schwab (2010, p. 53), and condemn the next generation "to become the carriers of another person's or another generation's unconscious." Like Victoria Donda (2010, p. 111), who, in the process of recovering her stolen identity, felt the revolutionary commitment of her real parents in her blood "from the beginning", the next generation of Argentines may become the "war generation's political unconscious" (Schwab 2010, p. 53). In this way, their parents' political struggles for a better world, their parents' idealism and their parents' hostility may become part of their own psychic lives. The focus on affect and its transmission within and across generations makes visible the unseen yet powerful forces that are at play decades after the end of the political and state violence of the 1970s and 1980s.

Affect can provide "a motivating force for consciousness", as Megan Watkins tells us (2010, p. 279). In post-conflict and post-authoritarian contexts emerging out of periods of mass violence, the notion of affect is particularly relevant to raising our consciousness of how individuals carry the legacy of surviving violence and how they continue living with their heart-breaking loss. Most crucially, I believe, the notion of affect makes us conscious of the vulnerability of others. Judith Butler (2003) tells us that we need to critically evaluate and oppose such conditions that make some lives more vulnerable and more grievable than others: "From where might a principle emerge by which we vow to protect others from the kinds of violence we have suffered, if not from an apprehension of a common human vulnerability?" (Butler 2003, p. 30). We must acknowledge, however, what a mammoth task it is to recognise this "common human vulnerability" to which Butler refers—to ask individuals who have been pushed to the limits of humanity themselves to see the vulnerability of those who have pushed them. When I think about how some of the women I interviewed struggle to find a way to keep living with their memories, I question whether we can ask any more of them.

I believe we would be wise to follow Sara Ahmed's suggestion that we should respond to injustice in a way that highlights the complexity of the relation between violence, power and affect (2004). For Ahmed (2004), struggles against memories of injustice are not about "moving on"; rather, they are about how one is moved by feelings into a different relation to the norms that one is contesting and how this movement within an individual leads to the creation of different kinds of attachments to others, and thus to new kinds of interpersonal encounters and relationships. Of course, affect can—and does—result in negative attachment to others. Yet it is by following the trails of affect, with the "restlessness of its promise" and "the relief of its continued mobilization" (Stewart 2010, p. 353), that we can find new relational possibilities and new, non-reductive ways of thinking about memory in a society recovering from violence and trauma. It is my strong belief that it is in affect that we can find the promise of movement, of small shifts, of the "stuckness", slowly being eroded.

References

Abraham, N., & Torok, M. (1994). *The shell and the kernel: The renewals of psychoanalysis* (Vol. 1) (trans: N. T. Rand). Chicago: University of Chicago Press.

Agosin, M. (1989). *Women of smoke: Latin American women in literature and life*. Trenton: Red Sea Press.

Agosin, M. (1990). *Mothers of the Plaza de Mayo (Linea Fundadora): The story of Renee Epelbaum, 1976–1985* (trans: J. Malloy). Trenton: Red Sea Press.

Agosin, M. (1994). How to speak with the dead? A poet's notebook. *Human Rights Quarterly, 16*(1), 214–223.

Ahmed, S. (2000). *Transformations: Thinking through feminism*. New York: Routledge.

Ahmed, S. (2004a). Collective feelings: Or, the Impressions left by others. *Theory Culture Society, 21*(2), 25–42.

Ahmed, S. (2004b). *The cultural politics of emotion*. Edinburgh: Edinburgh University Press.

Antze, P., & Lambek, M. (Eds.). (1996). *Tense past: Cultural essays in trauma and memory*. New York: Routledge.

Arditti, R. (1999). *Searching for life: The grandmothers of the Plaza de Mayo and the disappeared children of Argentina*. Berkeley: University of California Press.

Asociación Madres de la Plaza de Mayo (n.d). http://www.madres.org. Accessed 27 Aug 2013.

Assmann, A. (2006a). History, memory, and the genre of testimony. *Poetics Today, 27*(2), 261–273.

Assmann, J. (2006b). *Religion and cultural memory: Ten studies*. (trans: R. Livingstone). Stanford: Stanford University Press.

Barahona de Brito, A. (2001). Truth, justice, memory, and democratization in the Southern Cone. In A. Barahona de Brito, C. González Enríquez, & P. Aguilar (Eds.), *The politics of memory: Transitional justice in democratizing societies* (pp. 119–160). Oxford: Oxford University Press.

Basile, T. (1989). Aproximaciones al "testimonios sobre la desaparición de personas" durante la dictadura military y la democracia argentina. *Cuadernos Angers, 2*(2), 45–63.

Bennett, J. (2002). Art, affect, and the "bad death": Strategies for communicating the sense memory of loss. *Signs, 28*(1), 333–351.

Bennett, J., & Kennedy, R. (Eds.). (2003). Introduction. In *World memory: Personal trajectories in global time* (pp. 1–15). New York: Palgrave Macmillan.

Booth, W. J. (2006). *Communities of memory: On witness, identity, and justice*. Ithaca: Cornell University Press.

Boss, P. (1999). *Ambiguous loss: Learning to live with unresolved grief*. Cambridge: Harvard University Press.

Boss, P. (2006). *Loss, trauma, and resilience: Therapeutic work with ambiguous loss*. New York: W.W. Norton.

Bousquet, J. P. (1983). *Las locas de la Plaza de Mayo*. Buenos Aires: El Cid Editor.

Bouvard, M. G. (1994). *Revolutionizing motherhood: The mothers of the Plaza de Mayo*. Wilmington: Scholarly Resources Inc.

J. Stockwell, *Reframing the Transitional Justice Paradigm*,
Springer Series in Transitional Justice 10, DOI 10.1007/978-3-319-03853-7,

Brennan, T. (2004). *The transmission of affect*. Ithaca: Cornell University Press.
Brison, S. J. (2003). *Aftermath: Violence and the remaking of a self*. Princeton: Princeton University Press.
Brison, S. (1999). Trauma narratives and the remaking of the self. In M. Bal, J. V. Crewe, & L. Spitzer (Eds.), *Acts of memory: Cultural recall in the present* (pp. 39–54). Hanover: University Press of New England.
Brysk, A. (1994). *The politics of human rights in Argentina: Protest, change, and democratization*. Stanford: Stanford University Press.
Butler, J. (2003). Violence, mourning, politics. *Studies in Gender and Sexuality, 4*(1), 9–37.
Butler, J. (2004). *Precarious life: The powers of mourning and violence*. London: Verso.
Butler, J. (2009). *Frames of war: When is life grievable*? London: Verso.
Calveiro, P. (2008). *Poder y desaparición: campos de concentración en Argentina*. Buenos Aires: Ediciones Colihue S.R.L.
Calveiro, P. (2005). *Política y/o violencia: una aproximación a la guerrilla de los años 70*. Buenos Aires: Grupo Editorial Norma.
Calveiro, P. (2007). Memoria, política y violencia. In S. Lorenzano & R. Buchenhorst (Eds.), *Políticas de la memoria: tensiones en la palabra y la imagen*. México: Universidad del Claustro de Sor Juana.
Caruth, C. (Ed.). (1995). Introduction. In *Trauma: Explorations in memory* (pp. 3–12). Baltimore: Johns Hopkins University Press.
Caruth, C. (1996). *Unclaimed experience: Trauma, narrative, and history*. Baltimore: Johns Hopkins University Press.
Catela da Silva, L. (2001). *No habrá flores en la tumba del pasado: la experiencia de reconstrucción del mundo de los familiares de desaparecidos*. La Plata: Ediciones Al Margen.
Centro de Estudios Legales Sobre el Terrorismo y Sus Víctimas (CELTYV). (2012). *Vísperas de guerra: Reclaman nulidad del indulto a Montoneros en causa que lleva a Graiver*. www.taringa.net/posts/apuntes-y-monografias/7617880/Argentina-a-un-paso-de-la-guerra_.html. Accessed 27 July 2012.
Centro de Estudios Legales y Sociales (CELS). (2012). *Causas*. http://www.cels.org.ar/wpblogs/. Accessed 29 Aug 2013.
Ciollaro, N. (1999). *Pajaros sin luz: testimonios de mujeres de desaparecidos*. Buenos Aires: Planeta.
Clough, P. T., & Halley, J. (2007). *The affective turn: Theorizing the social*. Durham: Duke University Press.
Comisión Nacional de Verdad y Reconciliación (CONADEP). (1986). *Nunca Más (Never Again). Informe de la Comisión Nacional sobre la Desaparición de Personas*. London: Faber.
Comisión Nacional de Verdad y Reconciliación (CONADEP). (2006). *Nunca Más. Informe de la Comisión Nacional sobre la Desaparición de Personas* (7th ed.). Buenos Aires: Editorial Universitaria de Buenos Aires.
Crenzel, E. (2008a). *La historia política del Nunca más: la memoria de las desapariciones en la Argentina*. Buenos Aires: Siglo Veintiuno Editores Argentina.
Crenzel, E. (2008b). Argentina's National Commission on the Disappearance of Persons: Contributions to transitional justice. *The International Journal of Transitional Justice, 2*(2), 173–191.
Crenzel, E. (2011). Between the voices of the state and the human rights movement: Never again and the memories of the disappeared in Argentina. *Journal of Social History, 44*(4), 1063–1076.
Crocker, D. A. (2003). Reckoning with past wrongs: A normative framework. In C. Prager & T. Govier (Eds.), *Dilemmas of reconciliation: Cases and concepts* (pp. 39–64). Waterloo: Wilfrid Laurier University Press.
Das, V. (1997). Langauge and body: Transactions in the construction of pain. In A. Kleinman, V. Das, & M. Lock (Eds.), *Social suffering* (pp. 67–92). Berkeley: University of California Press.
Das, V. (2001). Language and Body Transactions in the Construction of Pain. In V. Das, A. Kleinman, M. Lock, M. Ramphele, & P. Raynolds (Eds.), *Remaking a world: Violence, social suffering, and recovery* (pp. 157–200). Berkeley: University of California Press.
Davis, C. (2005). Hauntology, spectres and phantoms. *French Studies, 59*(3), 373–379.

Dawson, G. (2007). *Making peace with the past? Memory, trauma and the Irish Troubles*. Manchester: Manchester University Press.

Delbo, C. (1990). *Days and memory*. Evanston: Marlboro Press.

Delbo, C. (1995). *Auschwitz and after*. New Haven: Yale University Press.

Deleuze, G. (1988). *Spinoza, practical philosophy*. San Francisco: City Lights Books.

Deleuze, G., & Guattari, F. (1987). *A thousand plateaus: capitalism and schizophrenia*. (trans: B. Massumi). Minneapolis: University of Minnesota Press.

Derrida, J. (1994). *Specters of Marx: The state of the debt, the work of mourning, and the New international*. New York: Routledge.

Di-Paolantonio, M. (2001). Pedagogical law and abject rage in post-trauma society. *Cultural Values, 5*(4), 445–476.

Diana, M. (1997). *Mujeres guerrilleras: la militancia de los setenta en el testimonio de sus protagonistas femeninas*. Buenos Aires: Planeta.

Donda, V. (2010). *My name is Victoria: The extraordinary story of one woman's struggle to reclaim her true identity*. (trans: M. Bogin). New York: Other Press.

Donghi, T. (1988). Argentina's unmastered past. *Latin American Research Review, 23*(2), 3–24.

Dunn, J. R., & Schweitzer, M. E. (2005). Feeling and believing: The influence of emotion on trust. *Journal of Personality and Social Psychology, 88*(5), 736–748.

Eng, D. L., & Kazanjian, D. (Eds.). (2003). Introduction: Mourning remains. In *Loss: The politics of mourning* (pp. 1–28). Berkeley: University of California Press.

Erikson, K. (1995). Notes on trauma and community. In C. Caruth (Ed.), *Trauma: Explorations in memory* (pp. 183–199). Baltimore: Johns Hopkins University Press.

Farji, S. (2010). *Eva y Lola*. Argentina (Film).

Faye, E. (2003). Tenebrae after September 11: Art, empathy, and the global politics of belonging. In J. Bennett & R. Kennedy (Eds.), *World memory: Personal trajectories in global time* (pp. 160–176). New York: Palgrave Macmillan.

Feitlowitz, M. (1998). *A Lexicon of terror: Argentina and the legacies of torture*. New York: Oxford University Press.

Felman. S. (1992). Education and crisis, or the vicissitudes of teaching. In S. Felman & D. Laub (Eds.), *Testimony: Crises of witnessing in literature, psychoanalysis, and history* (pp. 57–74). New York: Routledge.

Finkenauer, C., Gisle, L., & Luminet, O. (1992). When individual memories are socially shaped: Flashbulb memories of sociopolitical events. In J. Pennebaker, D. Paez, & B. Rimé (Eds.), *Collective memory of political events: Social psychological perspectives* (pp. 191–208). Mahwah: Lawrence Erlbaum.

Fisher, J. (1989). *Mothers of the disappeared*. London: Zed Books.

Forgas, J. P. (2000). *Feelings and thinking: The role of affect in social cognition*. Cambridge: University of Cambridge Press.

Foss, K., & Domenici, K. L. (2001). Haunting Argentina: Synecdoche in the protests of the mothers of the Plaza de Mayo. *Quarterly Journal of Speech, 87*(3), 237–258.

Franco, J. (1992). Gender, death, and resistance: Facing the ethical vacuum. In J. E. Corradi, P. W. Fagen, & M. A. Garretón (Eds.), *Fear at the edge: State terror and resistance in Latin America* (pp. 104–120). Berkeley: University of California Press.

Fraser, N. (2009). *Scales of justice: Reimagining political space in a globalizing world*. New York: Columbia University Press.

Friedlander, S. (1993). *Memory, history, and the extermination of the Jews of Europe*. Bloomington: Indiana University Press.

Galak, O. (2006). Controversia por el prólogo agregado al informe "Nunca más". *La Nacion,* 19 May.

Gandsman, A. (2009). "Do you know who you are?" Radical existential doubt and scientific certainty in the search for the kidnapped children of the disappeared in Argentina. *Ethos, 37*(4), 441–465.

Gaskell, G. D., & Wright, D. B. (1992). Group differences in memory for a political event. In J. Pennebaker, D. Paez, & B. Rimé (Eds.), *Collective memory of political events: Social psychological perspectives* (pp. 175–190). Mahwah: Lawrence Erlbaum.

Gasparini, J. (2007). *David Graiver: el banquero de los Montoneros*. Buenos Aires: Grupo Editorial Norma.

Gatens, M. (2003). Privacy and the body: The publicity of affect. In B. Rossler (Ed.), *Privacies: Philosophical evaluations* (pp. 113–141). Stanford: Stanford University Press.

Gibbs, A. (2001). Contagious feelings: Pauline Hanson and the epidemiology of affect. *Australian Humanities Review,* 24.

Gibbs, A. (2010). After affect: Sympathy, synchrony, and mimetic communication. In M. Gregg & G. J. Seigworth (Eds.), *The affect theory reader* (pp. 186–205). Durham: Duke University Press.

Goni, U. (2010). Adoption scandal: Argentina hounds a high-profile mom. Time World, 5 July. www.time.com/time/world/article/0,8599,2001571,00.html. Accessed 20 June 2011.

Gordon, A. F. (2008). *Ghostly matters: Haunting and the sociological imagination*. Minneapolis: University of Minnesota Press.

Gorini, U. (2006). *La rebelión de las Madres: historia de las Madres de Plaza de Mayo*. Buenos Aires: Grupo Editorial Norma.

Gregg, M., & Seigworth, G. J. (Eds.). (2010). An Inventory of Shimmers. In *The affect theory reader* (pp. 1–28). Durham: Duke University Press.

Grunebaum, H., & Henri, Y. (2003). Re-membering bodies, producing histories: Holocaust survivor narrative and truth and reconciliation commission testimony. In J. Bennett & R. Kennedy (Eds.), *World memory: personal trajectories in global time* (pp. 101–118). New York: Palgrave Macmillan.

Halbwachs, M. (1992). *On collective memory*. (trans: L. A. Coser). Chicago: University of Chicago Press.

Hamilton, C. (2007). *Women and ETA: The gender politics of radical Basque nationalism*. Manchester: Manchester University Press.

Hartman, G. (1996). *The longest shadow: In the aftermath of the Holocaust*. New York: Palgrave Macmillan.

Hartman, G. (2006). The humanities of testimony: An introduction. *Poetics Today, 27*(2), 249–260.

Hayner, P. (1994). Fifteen truth commissions—1974 to 1994: A comparative study. *Human Rights Quarterly, 16,* 597–655.

Hayner, P. (2011). *Unspeakable truths: Facing the challenge of truth commissions* (2nd ed.). New York: Routledge.

Healy, C., & Tumarkin, M. (Eds.). (2011). Social memory and historical justice: Introduction. *Memory Studies, 4*(1), 3–12.

Henao, L. A. (2012). Suspected death squad cars found at Argentine base. Reuters, US Edition. www.reuters.com/article/2012/03/27/argentina-dictatorship-falcon-idUSL2E8QR0OQ20120327. Accessed 20 May 2012.

Hernandez, V. (2012). Stolen baby hails "liberating" verdict. BBC News. www.bbc.co.uk/news/world-latin-america-18733415. Accessed 23 Aug 2012.

Hirsch, M. (2002). Feminist reflections on trauma and transmission. In N. K. Miller & J. D. Tougaw (Eds.), *Extremities: Trauma, testimony, and community* (pp. 71–91). Urbana: University of Illinois Press.

Hollander, N. C. (1990). Buenos Aires: Latin mecca of psychoanalysis. *Social Research, 57*(4), 889–919.

Hollander, N. C. (2010). *Uprooted minds: Surviving the politics of terror in the Americas*. Hoboken: Taylor and Francis.

Honneth, A. (1995). *The struggle for recognition: The moral grammar of social conflicts*. Cambridge: Polity Press.

Humphrey, M. (2005). Reconciliation and the therapeutic state. *Journal of Intercultural Studies, 26*(3), 203–220.

Hutchison, E., & Bleiker, R. (2008). Emotional reconciliation: Reconstituting identity and community after trauma. *European Journal of Social Theory, 11*(3), 385–403.
International Center for Transitional Justice. (2012). http://www.memoryandjustice.org/site/parque-de-la-memoria. Accessed 20 Aug 2013.
Jaggar, A. M. (1989). Love and knowledge: Emotion in feminist epistemology. *Inquiry: An Interdisciplinary Journal of Philosophy, 32*(2), 151–176.
Jelin, E. (1990). *Women and social change in Latin America*. London: Zed Books.
Jelin, E. (1994). The politics of memory: The human rights movements and the construction of democracy in Argentina. *Latin American Perspectives, 21*(2), 38–58.
Jelin, E. (1998). The minefields of memory. *North American Congress on Latin America, 32*(2), 23–29.
Jelin, E. (2002). *Los trabajos de la memoria*. Madrid: Siglo XXI de España.
Jelin, E. (2003). *State repression and the labors of memory*. Minneapolis: University of Minnesota Press.
Jelin, E. (2008). Victims, relatives, and citizens in Argentina: Whose voice is legitimate enough? In R. A. Wilson & R. Brown (Eds.), *Humanitarianism and suffering: The mobilizations of empathy* (pp. 177–201). Cambridge: Cambridge University Press.
Jelin, E., & Kaufman S. (2002). Layers of memory: Twenty years after in Argentina. In D. E. Lorey & W. H. Beezley (Eds.), *Genocide, collective violence, and popular memory: The politics of remembrance in the twentieth century* (pp. 31–52). Wilmington: SR Books.
Kaiser, S. (2002). Escraches: demonstrations, communication and political memory in post-dictatorial Argentina. *Media Culture Society, 24*(4), 499–516.
Kaiser, S. (2005a). To punish or to forgive? Young citizens' attitudes on impunity and accountability in contemporary Argentina. *Journal of Human Rights, 4*(2), 171–196.
Kaiser, S. (2005b). *Postmemories of terror: A new generation copes with the legacy of the "Dirty War"*. New York: Palgrave Macmillan.
Kaplan, T. (1997). *Crazy for democracy: Women in grassroots movements*. New York: Routledge.
Kaplan, T. (2004). *Taking back the streets: Women, youth, and direct democracy*. Berkeley: University of California Press.
Van der Kolk, B. A., & Van der Hart, O. (1997). The intrusive past: The flexibility of memory and the engraving of trauma. In C. Caruth (Ed.), *Trauma: Explorations in memory* (pp. 158–182). Baltimore: Johns Hopkins University Press.
Kordon, D., Edelman, L., & equipo de asistencia psicológica de Madres de Plaza de Mayo. (2007). *Por-venires de la memoria: efectos psicológicos multigeneracionales de la represión de la dictadura: hijos de desaparecidos*. Buenos Aires: Ediciones Madres de Plaza de Mayo.
Kordon, D., Edelman, L., & equipo de asistencia psicológica de Madres de Plaza de Mayo. (1986). *Efectos psicológicos de la represión política*. Buenos Aires: Sudamericana – Planeta.
Kushner, T. (2006). Holocaust testimony, ethics, and the problem of representation. *Poetics Today, 27*(2), 275–295.
LaCapra, D. (1994). *Representing the Holocaust: history, theory, trauma*. Ithaca: Cornell University Press.
LaCapra, D. (2001). *Writing history, writing trauma*. Baltimore: Johns Hopkins University Press.
Langer, L. L. (1991). *Holocaust testimonies: The ruins of memory*. New Haven: Yale University Press.
Langer, L. L. (1995). *Admitting the Holocaust: Collected essays*. New York: Oxford University Press.
Langland, V. (2005). Fotografía y memoria. In E. Jelin & A. Longoni (Eds.), *Escrituras, imágenes y escenarios ante la represió*. Madrid: Siglo XXI de España.
Las Abuelas de la Plaza de Mayo. (n.d). http://www.abuelas.org.ar. Accessed 29 Aug 2013.
Las Familiares de Desaparecidos y Detenidos por Razones Politicas. (1988). http://www.desaparecidos.org/familiares/historia.html. Accessed 22 Feb 2013.
Las Madres de la Plaza de Mayo Linea Fundadora. (n.d). http://www.madresfundadoras.org.ar. Accessed 15 Jan 2013.

Laub, D. (1992). Bearing witness, or the vicissitudes of listening. In S. Felman & D. Laub (Eds.), *Testimony: crises of witnessing in literature, psychoanalysis, and history* (pp. 57–74). New York: Routledge.

Laub, D., & Auerhahn, N. C. (1989). Failed empathy—a central theme in the survivor's holocaust experience. *Psychoanalytic Psychology, 6*(4), 377–400.

Lazzara, M. J. (2006). *Chile in transition: The poetics and politics of memory*. Gainesville: University Press of Florida.

Lewis, P. H. (2002). *Guerrillas and generals: The "dirty war" in Argentina*. Westport: Praeger.

Leydesdorff, S., Passerini, L., & Thompson, P. (Eds.). (2005). Introduction. In *Gender and memory* (pp. 1–16). New Brunswick: Transaction.

Lira, E. (1997). Remembering: Passing back through the heart. In J. Pennebaker, D. Paez, & B. Rimé (Eds.), *Collective memory of political events: Social psychological perspectives* (pp. 223–236). Mahwah: Lawrence Erlbaum.

Longoni, A. (2005). Traiciones. La figura del traidor (y la traidora) en los relatos acerca de los sobrevivientes de la repression. In E. Jelin & A. Longoni (Eds.), *Escrituras, imágenes y escenarios ante la represió*. Madrid: Siglo XXI de España.

Longoni, A. (2010). Photographs and silhouettes: Visual politics in Argentina. *Afterall*, 25.

Longoni, A., Bruzzone, G., & Lebenglik, F. (2008). *El siluetazo*. Buenos Aires: Adriana Hidalgo Editora.

Lorenzano, S., & Buchenhorst, R. (2007). *Políticas de la memoria: tensiones en la palabra y la imagen*. México City: Universidad del Claustro de Sor Juana.

Mallinder, L. (2009). *The ongoing quest for truth and justice: Enacting and annulling Argentina's amnesty laws*. In Working Paper No. 5 from the Beyond Legalism: Amnesties, Transition and Conflict Transformation conference. Belfast: Queen's University.

Mannheim, K. (1972). *Essays on the sociology of knowledge*. London: Routledge and Kegan Paul.

Marcus, G. E. (2000). Emotions in politics. *Annual Review of Political Science, 3*, 221–250.

Martinez, D. (2010). Que te cuenten tu historia es un regalo de la vida. *Página, 12*, 28 February: n.p.

Massumi, B. (1987). "Notes on the Translation and Acknowledgements". In G. Deleuze & F. Guattari (Eds.), *A Thousand Plateaus* (pp. xvi-xvix). Minneapolis: University of Minnesota Press.

Massumi, B. (2002). *Parables for the virtual: Movement, affect, sensation*. Durham: Duke University Press.

Mellibovsky, M. (1997). *Circle of love over death: Testimonies of the mothers of the Plaza de Mayo*. Willimantic: Curbstone Press.

Merleau-Ponty, M. (1962). *Phenomenology of perception*. London: Routledge and Kegan Paul.

Middleton, D., & Brown, S. D. (2005). *The social psychology of experience: Studies in remembering and forgetting*. London: Sage.

Millar, G. (2010). Assessing local experiences of truth-telling in Sierra Leone: Getting to "why" through a qualitative case study analysis. *The international Journal of Transitional Justice, 4*(3), 477–496.

Misztal, B. A. (2003). *Theories of social remembering*. Maidenhead: Open University Press.

Misztal, B. A. (2004). The sacralization of memory. *European Journal of Social Theory, 7*(1), 67–84.

Navarro, M. (2001a). The personal is political: Las Madres de Plaza de Mayo. In S. Eckstein (Ed.), *Power and popular protest: Latin American social movements* (pp. 241–258). Berkeley: University of California Press.

Navarro, M (2001b). Argentina: The long road to women's rights. In L. Walter (Ed.), *Women's rights: A global view* (pp. 1–14). Westport: Greenwood Press.

Oliver, K. (2001). *Witnessing: Beyond recognition*. Minneapolis: University of Minnesota Press.

Ortiz, F. (2007). Argentine death squad cars try for new image. *Reuters*, 4 May. www.reuters.com/article/2007/05/04/us-argentina-falcons-idUSN0332251120070504. Accessed 11 July 2012.

Paez, D., Basabe, N., & Gonzalez, J. L. (1997). Social processes and collective memory: A cross-cultural approach to remembering political events. In J. Pennebaker, D. Paez, & B. Rimé (Eds.), *Collective memory of political events: Social psychological perspectives* (pp. 147–174). Mahwah: Lawrence Erlbaum.

Pagína 12. (2011). Un caso ya prescripto. 25 March, Buenos Aires: Argentina. www.pagina12.com.ar/diario/elpais/1-164888-2011-03-25.html. Accessed 11 July 2012.

Partnoy, A. (1988). *The little school: Tales of disappearance and survival in Argentina*. London: Virago.

Passerini, L. (1992). *Memory and totalitarianism*. Oxford: Oxford University Press.

Passerini, L. (2003). Memories between silence and oblivion. In K. Hodgkin & S. Radstone (Eds.), *Contested pasts: The politics of memory* (pp. 238–254). London: Routledge.

Patton, M. Q. (2002). *Qualitative research and evaluation methods*. Thousand Oaks: Sage.

Pennebaker, J. W., & Banasik, B. L. (1992). On the creation and maintenance of collective memories: History as social psychology. In J. Pennebaker, D. Paez, & B. Rimé (Eds.), *Collective memory of political events: Social psychological perspectives* (pp. 3–20). Mahwah: Lawrence Erlbaum.

Perera, S. (2001). Spirit possessions and avenging ghosts: Stories of supernatural activity as narratives of terror and mechanisms of coping and remembering. In V. Das, A. Kleinman, M. Lock, M. Ramphele, & P. Raynolds (Eds.), *Remaking a world: Violence, social suffering, and recovery* (pp. 157–200). Berkeley: University of California Press.

Philipose, L. (2007). The politics of pain and the end of empire. *International Feminist Journal of Politics, 9*(1), 60–81.

Pollak, M. (1989). Memória, esquecimento, silencio. *Estudos Históricos, 2*(3), 3–15.

Portelli, A. (1981). The peculiarities of oral history. *History Workshop Journal, 12,* 96–107.

Prager, J. (2008). Healing from history: Psychoanalytic considerations on traumatic pasts and social repair. *European Journal of Social Theory, 11*(3), 405–420.

Probyn, E. (2010). Writing shame. In M. Gregg & G. J. Seigworth (Eds.), *The affect theory reader* (pp. 71–92). Durham: Duke University Press.

Probyn, E. (2005). *Blush: Faces of shame*. Minneapolis: University of Minnesota Press.

Puget, J., & Kaes, R. (1991). *Violencia de Estado y Psicoanálisis*. Buenos Aires: Centro Editor.

Qassim, A. (2007). Broken bonds. *The Guardian,* 4 August. www.guardian.co.uk/lifeandstyle/2007/aug/04/familyandrelationships.family2. Accessed 20 Feb 2012.

Ranalletti, M. (2010). Denial of the reality of state terrorism in Argentina as narrative of the recent past: A new case of "negationism"? *Genocide Studies and Prevention, 5*(2), 160–173.

Ranzani, O. (2010). Son seres muy golpeados que siguen buscando la belleza. Página 12, 12 May. www.pagina12.com.ar/diario/suplementos/espectaculos/5-17919-2010-05-12.html. Accessed 23 July 2012.

Renshaw, L. (2010). Missing bodies near-at-hand: The dissonant memory and dormant graves of the Spanish civil war. In M. Bille, F. Hastrup, & S. F. Soerensen (Eds.), *An anthropology of absence: Materializations of transcendence and loss* (pp. 45-62). New York: Springer.

Resina, J. R. (2000). *Disremembering the dictatorship: The politics of memory in the Spanish transition to democracy*. Amsterdam: Rodopi.

Richard, N. (2001a). *Residuos y Metáforas: Ensayos de Crítica Cultural sobre el Chile de la Transición* (2nd ed.). Santiago: Editorial Cuarto Propio.

Richard, N. (2001b). Sitios de la memoria, vaciamiento del recuerdo. *Revista de Critica Cultural, 23,* 11–13.

Rigney, A. (2012). Reconciliation and remembering: (How) does it work? *Memory Studies, 5*(3), 251–258.

Rimé, B., & Christophe, V. (1992). How individual emotional episodes feed collective memory. In J. Pennebaker, D. Paez, & B. Rimé (Eds.), *Collective memory of political events: Social psychological perspectives* (pp. 131–146). Mahwah: Lawrence Erlbaum.

Robben, A. C. G. M. (2005a). *Political violence and trauma in Argentina*. Philadelphia: University of Pennsylvania Press.

Robben, A. C. G. M. (2005b). How traumatized societies remember: The aftermath of Argentina's dirty war. *Cultural Critique, 59,* 120–164.

Robben, A. C. G. M. (2012). From Dirty War to genocide: Argentina's resistance to national reconciliation. *Memory Studies, 5*(3), 305–315.

Robert, K. (2005). The Falcon remembered. NACLA Report on the Americas November-December: 12–15. www.mediaaccuracy.org/files/pdfs/SCone_Falcon.pdf. Accessed 20 Feb 2012.

Rohter, L. (2003a). Argentina revisits “dirty war”: Will General be tried? *The New York Times,* 1 September. www.nytimes.com/2003/09/01/world/argentina-revisits-dirty-war-will-general-be-tried.html?pagewanted=allandsrc=pm. Accessed 20 Feb 2012.

Rohter, L. (2003b). Now the dirtiest of wars won’t be forgotten. *The New York Times,* 18 June. www.nytimes.com/2003/06/18/international/americas/18LETT.html?pagewanted=all. Accessed 20 Feb 2012.

Romero, L. A. (2002). *A history of Argentina in the twentieth century*. University Park: Pennsylvania State University Press.

Roniger, L., & Sznajder, M. (1998). The politics of memory and oblivion in redemocratized Argentina and Uruguay. *History and Memory, 10*(1), 133–169.

Roniger, L., & Sznajder, M. (1999). *The legacy of human-rights violations in the Southern Cone: Argentina, Chile, and Uruguay*. New York: Oxford University Press.

Ross, F. (2003). Bearing witness to ripples of pain. In J. Bennett & R. Kennedy (Eds.), *World memory: Personal trajectories in global time* (pp. 143–159). New York: Palgrave Macmillan.

Rothberg, M. (2009). *Multidirectional memory: Remembering the holocaust in the age of decolonization*. Stanford: Stanford University Press.

San Honorio, R. (2010). EvaandLola blogspot. http://evaylola.blogspot.com.au/2010/05/la-nacion-buena-eva-lola-tiene-una-idea.html. Accessed 23 July 2012.

Sarlo, B. (2005). *Tiempo Pasado: Cultura de la Memoria y Giro Subjetivo: una Discusión*. Buenos Aires: Siglo Veintiuno Editores.

Scarry, E. (1985). *The body in pain: The making and unmaking of the world*. Oxford: Oxford University Press.

Scherer, K. (1984). Emotion as a multicomponent process: A model and some cross-cultural data. *Review of Personality and Social Psychology, 5,* 37–63.

Schwab, G. (2010). *Haunting legacies: Violent histories and transgenerational trauma*. New York: Columbia University Press.

Sedgwick, E. K. (2003). *Touching feeling: Affect, performativity, pedagogy*. Durham: Duke University Press.

Seri, G. (2008). Terror, reconciliation, redemption: The politics of memory in Argentina. *Radical Philosophy* 47. www.radicalphilosophy.com/issues/147. Accessed 20 June 2012.

Short, D. (2005). Reconciliation and the problem of internal colonialism. *Journal of Intercultural Studies, 26*(3), 267–282.

Shouse, E. (2005). Feeling, emotion, affect. *Media-Culture Journal, 8*(6). http://journal.media-culture.org.au/0512/03-shouse.php. Accessed 20 June 2012.

Soo-Jin Lee, S. (2003). Re-membering bodies, producing histories: Holocaust survivor narrative and truth and reconciliation commission testimony. In J. Bennett & R. Kennedy (Eds.), *World memory: Personal trajectories in global time* (pp. 87–100). New York: Palgrave Macmillan.

Sosa, C. (2009). A counter-narrative of Argentine mourning. *Theory, Culture and Society, 26*(7–8), 250–262.

Sosa, C. (2011). On mothers and spiders: A face-to-face encounter with Argentina’s mourning. *Memory Studies, 4*(1), 63–72.

Sprinker, M. (1999). *Ghostly demarcations: A symposium on Jacques Derrida’s Spectres of Marx*. London: Verso.

Stewart, K. (2010). Afterword: Worlding refrains. In M. Gregg & G. J. Seigworth (Eds.) *The affect theory reader* (pp. 339–354). Durham: Duke University Press.

Takemoto, T. (2001). Open wounds. In S. Ahmed & J. Stacey (Eds.), *Thinking through the skin* (pp. 104–123). New York: Routledge.

Taussig, M. (1987). *Shamanism, colonialism, and the wild man: A study in terror and healing*. Chicago: University of Chicago Press.

Taylor, D. (1997). *Disappearing acts: Spectacles of gender and nationalism in Argentina’s “Dirty War”*. Durham: Duke University Press.

Tello Weiss, M. (2006). *Vivimos al límite. Al límite entre la vida y la muerte, entre el bien y el mal”. El miedo en las memorias sobre la lucha armada en los “70. Miedos y Memorias en las sociedades contemporáneas*. Córdoba: Universidad Nacional de Córdoba.

Theidon, K. (2007). Gender in transition: Common sense, women, and war. *Journal of Human Rights, 6,* 453–478.
Timerman, J. (1981). *Prisoner without a name, cell without a number*. New York: Knopf.
Tomkins, S. S., Smith, B., & Demos, E. V. (Eds.). (1995). *Exploring affect: The selected writings of Silvan S. Tomkins: Studies in emotion and social interaction*. London: Cambridge University Press.
Traverso, A. (2010). Dictatorship memories: Working through trauma in Chilean post-dictatorship documentary. *Continuum: Journal of Media and Cultural Studies, 24*(1), 179–191.
Tumarkin, M. (2009). Disturbing the sound of silence: Towards the thick vision of the long Soviet silence. *Performance Paradigm, 5*(2). www.performanceparadigm.net. Accessed 25 June 2012.
Tumarkin, M. (2011). Beyond truth and justice. In J. Schultz (Ed.), *Griffith Review* (Vol. 33). (pp. 1–6).
Valenzuela, L (1977). *Como en la guerra*. Havana: Casa de las Américas.
Valenzuela, L. (1982). *Cambio de armas*. Buenos Aires: Grupo editorial Norma.
Verbitsky, H. (1995). *El Vuelo*. Barcelona: Seix Barral.
Vezzetti, H. (1996). Variaciones sobre la memoria social. *Punto De Vista, 19*(56), 1–6.
Vezzetti, H. (2002). *Pasado y Presente: Guerra, Dictadura y Sociedad en la Argentina*. Buenos Aires: Siglo Veintiuno Editores.
Vezzetti, H. (2009). *Sobre la violencia revolucionaria: memories y olvidos*. Buenos Aires: Siglo Veintiuno Editores.
Watkins, M. (2010). Desiring recognition, accumulating affect. In M. Gregg & G. J. Seigworth (Eds.), *The affect theory reader* (pp. 269–288). Durham: Duke University Press.
Wertsch, J. V. (2002). *Voices of collective remembering*. Cambridge: Cambridge University Press.
White, H. (1996). The modernist event. In V. Sobchack (Ed.), *The persistence of history: Cinema, television, and the modern event* (pp. 17–38). New York: Routledge.
Wieviorka, A. (2006). The witness in history. *Poetics Today, 27,* 385–397.
Wilde, O. (2007). *The picture of Dorian Gray*. London: Vintage.
Yaeger, P. (2006). Testimony without intimacy. *Poetics Today, 27*(2), 399–423.
Young, A. (1995). *The harmony of illusions: Inventing Post-Traumatic Stress Disorder*. Princeton: Princeton University Press.

Interviewees

Lita Boitano, Buenos Aires, 02.05.2009.
Nenina Boulliet, Buenos Aires, 24.06.2009.
Eliana Carreira, Buenos Aires, 08.06.2009.
Mercedes Castrofini, Buenos Aires, 12.07.2009.
Noemi Ciollaro, Buenos Aires, 26.06.2009.
Maria del Socorro Alonso, Buenos Aires, 04.05.2009.
Gladys Echegoyen, Buenos Aires, 22.07.2009.
Monica Escudero, Buenos Aires, 16.06.2009.
Lorenza Ferrari, Buenos Aires, 29.07.2009.
Silvia Ibarzábal, Buenos Aires, 28.07.2009.
Graciela Lois, Buenos Aires, 23.06.2009.
Raquel Marizcurrena, Buenos Aires, 17.06.2009.
Cristina Mendieta, Buenos Aires, 22.07.2009.
Cristina Muro, Buenos Aires, 14.06.2009.
Victoria Paz, Buenos Aires, 12.07.2009.
Buscarita Roa, Buenas Aires, 17.06.2009.
Barbara Tarquini, Buenos Aires, 17.07.2009.
Vittoria Villaruel, CELTYV, Buenos Aires, 29.06.2009.

Index

J. Stockwell, *Reframing the Transitional Justice Paradigm*,
Springer Series in Transitional Justice 10, DOI 10.1007/978-3-319-03853-7,

MIX
Papier aus verantwortungsvollen Quellen
Paper from responsible sources
FSC® C105338

Printed by Books on Demand, Germany